Contributions to Economics

The series *Contributions to Economics* provides an outlet for innovative research in all areas of economics. Books published in the series are primarily monographs and multiple author works that present new research results on a clearly defined topic, but contributed volumes and conference proceedings are also considered. All books are published in print and ebook and disseminated and promoted globally.

The series and the volumes published in it are indexed by Scopus and ISI (selected volumes).

Yoshitaka Hosoi · Tuvshintugs Batdelger ·
Khashchuluun Chuluundorj
Editors

# Economic Dependence of Mongolia on Minerals

## Consequences and Policies

Springer

*Editors*
Yoshitaka Hosoi
Japan International Cooperation Agency
Tokyo, Japan

Khashchuluun Chuluundorj
Department of Economics
National University of Mongolia
Ulaanbaatar, Mongolia

Tuvshintugs Batdelger
Economic Research Institute
National University of Mongolia
Ulaanbaatar, Mongolia

ISSN 1431-1933 ISSN 2197-7178 (electronic)
Contributions to Economics
ISBN 978-981-19-5514-3 ISBN 978-981-19-5515-0 (eBook)
https://doi.org/10.1007/978-981-19-5515-0



This Springer imprint is published by the registered company Springer Nature Singapore Pte Ltd.
The registered company address is: 152 Beach Road, #21-01/04 Gateway East, Singapore 189721, Singapore

# Acknowledgments

This book is a product of "The Project for Capacity Building on the Natural Resources and Mining Sector in Mongolia" implemented by the Economic Research Institute (Mongolia) in collaboration with the Ministry of Mining and Heavy Industry and generously supported by the Japan International Cooperation Agency (JICA).

The editors are grateful to JICA for their substantial support. Without it, this book and project would not have been possible. We are also grateful to all the contributors, advisors, project coordinators, and the staff of the ministry involved in the project.

The excellent Economic Research Institute's researchers and visiting researchers who were educated in overseas graduate schools in economics carried out core research studies that provided the backbone of the chapters. Without all the contributors' cooperation, we could not have completed this book.

The academic advisors from Japan and Mongolia gave us invaluable advice on each of the studies. Their reviews, comments, and suggestions greatly improved each study.

It should be noted that our contributors also greatly benefited from feedback during the annual conferences and meetings organized in Ulaanbaatar and Tokyo. We thank the participants of Ulaanbaatar conferences and Tokyo workshops for their comments, feedback, and suggestions.

This book was coedited by Yoshitaka Hosoi, a senior advisor at JICA; Tuvshintugs Batdelger, director of the Economic Research Institute (Mongolia) and an associate professor of economics at the National University of Mongolia; and Khashchuluun Chuluundorj, an associate professor of economics at the National University of Mongolia. Chapters of the book were authored by the many analysts/writers listed as introductory authors and on each chapter. We thank all of them for their efforts.

We hope this book will become a compass for resource-holding developing countries.

Tokyo, Japan — Yoshitaka Hosoi
Ulaanbaatar, Mongolia — Tuvshintugs Batdelger
Ulaanbaatar, Mongolia — Khashchuluun Chuluundorj
2022

# Contents

# Editors and Contributors

## About the Editors

**Dr. Yoshitaka Hosoi** has qualifications both in mining and in economics. He is currently a visiting professor/lecturer at Akita University, Hokkaido University, and Kyushu University, all of which are in Japan. He teaches courses in international relations, resources economics, and international cooperation. He has taught at the University of Tokyo, Osaka University, and others as well. He is also a senior advisor for natural resources of the Japan International Corporation Agency (JICA), which is a Japanese government organization for Official Development Assistance (ODA). His task is to advise JICA and developing countries in the mining field, formulate projects, supervise implementing projects, and conduct human resource development in Africa, Asia, the Pacific, and South America. Before joining JICA, he worked for the Deep Ocean Resources Development Co., Ltd. (DORD), which holds a manganese nodules concession in the Central Pacific, as general manager of the Exploration Department for planning and executing exploration. Before DORD, he worked for the Japan Oil, Gas, and Metals National Corporation (JOGMEC), which is a Japanese governmental organization, for 33 years. He has experience in mineral exploration, mine development, technology development, mine pollution surveys and prevention, and mineral economics in almost 100 countries. He has been a visiting lecturer at the University of the South Pacific in Fiji, and Adamson University in the Philippines. He has held positions in the SODIMIZA mining company in Zaire, Metal Mining Agency of Japan (MMAJ), Japan Mining Engineering Center for International Cooperation (JMEC), and South Pacific Applied Geosciences Commission (SOPAC) in Fiji. He has also published numerous papers and articles in areas of exploration, the mining industry, and economics. He has published the books *Mining and Development* (2009), *Mineral Resources Frontier* (2012), and *Mining in Africa* (2014). He holds a Bachelor of Mining Engineering degree from Akita University and has done postgraduate research in mining at the University of Tokyo, a master's in economics from the University of Santo Tomas in the Philippines, and a Ph.D. in economics from the University of Queensland in Australia.

**Dr. Tuvshintugs Batdelger** is the director of the Economic Research Institute (ERI) and an associate professor of economics at the National University of Mongolia. He has a bachelor's degree in economics from the National University of Mongolia; a master's degree in economics from the University of Manchester, UK; and a Ph.D. in economics from Boston University, USA. He has experience working at the Bank of Mongolia and was the head of the Economics Department of the National University of Mongolia from 2014 to 2017. He has been a member of the Economic Policy Council under the prime minister of Mongolia since 2012 and was a member of the Monetary Policy Committee from 2011 to 2016. He has been actively involved in policy discussions in the country through the establishment and operation of ERI since 2010, one of the longest-running think tanks in the country. Through ERI, he successfully contributed to policy discussions on wide-ranging economic and social issues by coordinating and implementing many projects by international organizations, such as the World Bank, Asian Development Bank, and JICA. In particular, he successfully led research teams conducting an economic assessment of big mining and industrial projects on the country's economy and society in general. He has successfully conducted and published policy research studies in international peer-reviewed journals and publications such as *Applied Economics, Resources Policy* and *East Asia Forum* and has authored chapters on the Mongolian economy in numerous books. His current research interests are the role of mining in the economy and society, the role of monetary policy in regulating the Mongolian economy, and the impact of economic development on income distribution and the country's middle class.

**Dr. Khashchuluun Chuluundorj** is an associate professor of economics at the National University of Mongolia. He has a bachelor's degree in economics from Moscow State University, Russia; a master's degree in economics from Yokohama City University, Japan; and a Ph.D. in economics from Keio University, Japan. He worked with the JICA project on national economic development policy in 1997–1999 and then served as the dean of the Economics School of the National University of Mongolia from 2004 to 2009. From 2009 to 2012, he served as the chairman of the National Development and Innovation Committee of Mongolia (NDIC), a government agency, where he oversaw the establishment of the national economic planning system in the market economy, introduced the public investment program (PIP), and supervised the establishment of the Development Bank of Mongolia, for which he served as an inaugural chairman of the Board of Directors. In addition, he supervised the creation of a legal system to support innovation in the country and oversaw the development of national public–private partnerships. Currently, he is a member of the Economic Policy Council under the prime minister of Mongolia as well as a member of the Monetary Policy Committee of the Central Bank of Mongolia. He is also working as an independent member on the boards of directors for numerous financial and mining companies in Mongolia and is a visiting professor at the Plekhanov Russian University of Economics, in addition to his teaching at the National University of Mongolia's Department of Economics. He has published in international peer-reviewed journals and publications such as *Resources Policy*, the *Journal of Applied Economic Sciences*, *Inner Asia*, and others.

## Contributors

**Batbayar Nyambaatar** Concordia University, Montreal, Canada

**Batdelger Tuvshintugs** The National University of Mongolia, Ulaanbaatar, Mongolia;
Economic Research Institute, Ulaanbaatar, Mongolia

**Batjargal Munkh-Ireedui** Concordia University, Montreal, Canada

**Bayartsogt Khorol-Erdene** Economic Research Institute, Ulaanbaatar, Mongolia

**Begz Delgermaa** Economic Research Institute, Ulaanbaatar, Mongolia

**Chuluundorj Khashchuluun** The National University of Mongolia, Ulaanbaatar, Mongolia

**Davaa Unurjargal** Economic Research Institute, Ulaanbaatar, Mongolia

**Davaakhuu Oyuntugs** Economic Research Institute, Ulaanbaatar, Mongolia

**Delgerchuluun Ankhbayar** Economic Research Institute, Ulaanbaatar, Mongolia

**Galindev Ragchaasuren** Economic Research Institute, Ulaanbaatar, Mongolia

**Hosoi Yoshitaka** Akita University, Akita, Japan;
Hokkaido University, Sapporo, Japan;
Kyushu University, Fukuoka, Japan

**Lkhanaajav Esmedekh** Economic Research Institute, Ulaanbaatar, Mongolia

**Munkh-Ireedui Bayarjargal** Concordia University, Montreal, Canada

**Narantuya Chuluunbat** The National University of Mongolia, Ulaanbaatar, Mongolia

**Tserendorj Oyunzul** Economic Research Institute, Ulaanbaatar, Mongolia

**Tuvshintugs Dulguun** Economic Research Institute, Ulaanbaatar, Mongolia

**Usny-Ekh Enkhsaikhan** Economic Research Institute, Ulaanbaatar, Mongolia

**Zagdbazar Manlaibaatar** Economic Research Institute, Ulaanbaatar, Mongolia

# Introduction

**Khashchuluun Chuluundorj, Tuvshintugs Batdelger, and Yoshitaka Hosoi**

## 1 General Background

In many resource-rich countries, the mining sector plays a critical role in economic growth and social development. The mining sector can significantly benefit the national economy and local communities in various ways.

Mongolia benefits greatly from the mining sector as the sector accounts for 88% of its exports and 22% of its GDP. In comparison, other transitioning Central Asian countries, such as Kazakhstan and Kyrgyzstan derive only 18% and 11% of their respective GDP and 12% and 45% of their exports from mining.[1] These indicators are much lower for Russia, Armenia, Tajikistan, Ukraine, and other transitioning countries. Mongolia's mining sector is comparable to resource reliant countries such

[1] European Bank for Reconstruction and Development (2017), *EBRD Extractive Mining Industries Strategy*, 2018–2022.

K. Chuluundorj (✉) · T. Batdelger
The National University of Mongolia, Ulaanbaatar, Mongolia
e-mail: khashchuluun@num.edu.mn

T. Batdelger
e-mail: tuvshintugs@eri.mn

T. Batdelger
Economic Research Institute, Ulaanbaatar, Mongolia

Y. Hosoi
Akita University, Akita, Japan

Hokkaido University, Sapporo, Japan

Kyushu University, Fukuoka, Japan

 
Y. Hosoi et al. (eds.), *Economic Dependence of Mongolia on Minerals*,
Contributions to Economics, https://doi.org/10.1007/978-981-19-5515-0_1

as Kuwait, where the mining sector accounts for 92%[2] of exports, and Saudi Arabia, where the mining sector makes up 15% of GDP.[3]

There are 2796 mining licenses for exploration (1126) and production (1670), covering 7.4 million square hectares of land (MRPAM, 2019). In 2019, Mongolia produced 57.1 million tonnes of coal, of which 36.8 million tonnes were exported, 6.8 million barrels of oil, of which 6.5 million barrels were exported, and 11 thousand tonnes of refined copper in addition to many other types of mineral commodities.

Mongolia increased its financing of geological surveys from MNT 11 billion in 2015 to MNT 24 billion in 2019 to open new areas for exploration. The latest data show that private exploration financing reached MNT 170 billion as of 2016. Market capital valuation of listed mining companies operating in Mongolia approached USD 5 billion, excluding Rio Tinto. Overall, mining makes up the vast majority of investment in Mongolia, with MNT 5.2 trillion (43%) of the MNT 12.5 trillion in total investment going into the mining sector in 2018. These numbers underline the significance of mining in the Mongolian economy.

The transformation of Mongolia's agriculture-based economy into a mining-based economy occurred gradually. The mining sector's strong manifestation in the Mongolian economy through external and internal factors can be shown by the following major milestones:

- Milestone 1 is the amendment to the Minerals Laws, the creation of state-owned mining companies, and strategic planning based on mining revenue in 2006. This step accentuated the government's involvement in the mining sector and underlined the growing importance of mining for the national economy.
- Milestone 2 is the Oyu Tolgoi Investment Agreement, which greatly expanded Mongolia's economy and created many institutional changes. The agreement also broadened Mongolia's access to international financial markets, helped it connect to transnational corporations, and resulted in a much more complex and fast-developing financial system. There were also improvements in the quality of human resources, training, and investment systems.
- Milestone 3 is the adoption of the United Nations Sustainable Development Goals (SDG) in the "Long-Term Sustainable Development Vision of Mongolia 2030" policy document and the explicit inclusion of long-term development planning in the Constitution of Mongolia with the goal of economic diversification. This created an incentive to align mining with sustainable development and ultimately promoted inclusiveness (see Box 1).

---

[2] https://www.azomining.com/Article.aspx?ArticleID=118.

[3] https://www.statista.com/statistics/996012/saudi-arabia-mining-sector-contribution-to-gdp-by-type/.

**Box 1** Mining and the United Nation's Sustainable Development Goals (SDG).[4]

As the world continues to pursue sustainable development, mining is either directly or indirectly related to all SDG goals. According to the United Nations, the mining sector most impacts SDG 15 (Ecosystem), 13 (Climate action), 9 (infrastructure, innovation and industrialization), 8 (Employment and economic growth), 7 (Energy access) and 6 (Clean water and sanitation) (Fig. 1).

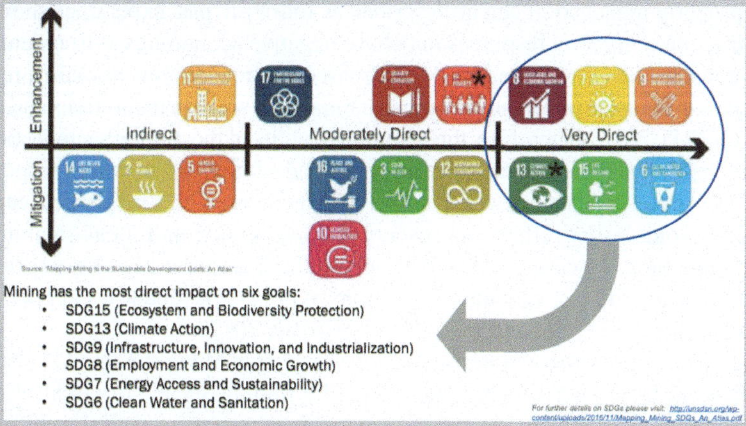


**Fig. 1** Mapping of mining impact to SDG

As stated in a report by the UNDP,

> the mining industry has the opportunity and potential to positively contribute to all 17 SDGs. The mining industry can impact positively and negatively across the SDGs. Mining can foster economic development by providing opportunities for decent employment, business development, increased fiscal revenues, and infrastructure linkages. Many of the minerals produced by mining are also essential building blocks to technologies, infrastructure, energy and agriculture. Historically, however, mining has contributed to many of the challenges that the SDGs are trying to address – environmental degradation, displacement of populations, worsening economic and social inequality, armed conflicts, gender-based violence, tax evasion and corruption, increased risk for many health problems, and the violation of human rights. In recent decades, the industry has made significant advances in mitigating and managing such impacts and risks by improving how companies manage their environmental and social impacts, protect the health of their workers, achieve energy efficiencies, report on financial flows, and respect and support human right.

[4] Mapping Mining to the Sustainable Development Goals: An Atlas, a report, prepared jointly by the United Nations Development Programme, the World Economic Forum, the Columbia Center on Sustainable Investments and the Sustainable Development Solutions Network, 2016.

However, the development of the mining sector is principally different from the development of other sectors such as the agriculture sector. Mining is dependent on the locations of the mines, is strongly impacted by world market commodity prices, and is heavily reliant on international financial markets for financing. Moreover, local infrastructure development is vital, and sectoral growth rates are highly volatile. Mining is also a highly competitive sector as it produces generally available raw materials that are priced based on world demand and supply.

The development of the mining sector also has adverse effects. In particular, it can have a strong negative environmental impact if its usage of water and surrounding area is not properly managed. It can be described as follows: "past experience shows that the extraction of mineral resources may have negative economic, environmental and social consequences, as it can result in increased macroeconomic volatility, reduced incentives to invest in physical and human capital, and weaken institutions and governance (EBRD, 2012). Therefore, the potential benefits of the mining sector depend on whether mining and the associated revenues are developed and managed responsibly over time. "Poor environmental and social management of mining projects can have significant long-lasting effects on resources, biodiversity, and local communities. At the same time, however, endowment with natural resources can represent major opportunities to improve economic conditions of the COOs [countries of operations] and to contribute to regional development" (EBRD, 2012).

The desired policy to promote mining development in Mongolia should be directed at mitigating the negative consequences of the mining sector. It would also help amplify the positive outcomes, work toward making the sector a critical contributor to economic activity at the local, regional, and national levels and establish downstream value-chain linkages in the economy.

The specific features of mining create significant policy challenges for Mongolia. However, the following issues could be solved by creating a mining development strategy:

- Link the mining sector to sustainable development,
- Present solutions for better taxation and budget revenue management,
- Improve transparency and reporting,
- Improve contracting in the sector,
- Derive more national value through better trading of export products.

These issues are crucial for enhancing the benefits of the mining sector to the national government and for making mining a platform for further sustainable growth. However, these benefits cannot be achieved by a single policy document; these benefits depend on the legal environment of the country and its enforcement.

When implementing any mining development policy, it is important to remember that its successful implementation is difficult to achieve in the absence of a strong legal and policy framework. According to the International Institute for Sustainable Development (IISD), "such a framework must promote the economic and social development benefits of mining while upholding strong environmental and social standards. In the absence of such a framework, mining activities can threaten to pollute and degrade the environment, endanger workers, lead to non-inclusive growth and promote corruption, among other things".[5]

Within the framework of sustainable development, the 52 member countries of the United Nations decided to create a joint framework for mining policy (IGF) in 2005. The IGF is a voluntary initiative that allows national governments with an interest in mining to work collectively to advance sustainable development priorities. It is a global policy forum for the mining and metals sector with the objective of enhancing capacities for good governance. In 2012, the IGF recommended the following best practices in mining policy, divided into six key pillars:

1. The legal and policy framework;
2. Financial benefit optimization;
3. Socioeconomic benefit optimization;
4. Environmental management;
5. Mine closure and the post-mining transition;
6. Artisanal and small-scale mining (ASM).

These policies were elaborated to address "activities [the IGF member countries] have identified as best practice for exercising good governance of the mining sector and promoting the generation and equitable sharing of benefits in a manner that will contribute to sustainable development".[6] Studies in developing countries, such as Madagascar, Uganda, and the Dominican Republic (IGF Study), as well as in other developing countries, show that many countries have unique circumstances, but also share some general weaknesses.

As with any developing country, Mongolia has its own unique set of circumstances, which on the one hand, promotes the use of mining for economic growth, and on the other hand, tackles barriers for investment, trading, and contracting to enhance the "benefits" from mining.

Under the "Capacity Building on the Natural Resource and Mining in Mongolia" project implemented by the Japan International Cooperation Agency (JICA), the Ministry of Mining and Heavy Industry (MMHI), and the Economic Research Institute (ERI), the research team covered numerous mining-related topics to obtain a better understanding of Mongolia's mining sector and its future development. In the studies, the research team tackled the following issues in the mining sector and offered unified policy recommendations.

---

[5] The Mining Policy Framework: Assessing the implementation readiness of member states of the Intergovernmental Forum on Mining, Minerals, Metals and Sustainable Development, SYNTHESIS REPORT, International Institute for Sustainable Development, Canada, 2015.

[6] Intergovernmental Forum on Mining, Minerals, Metals and Sustainable Development (2013). "*A Mining Policy Framework*".

## 2 Mining Sector Contracting in Mongolia

Projects in the mining sector have several key impacts on the host country. First, due to the sheer size of large mining projects, the socio-economic impacts pertaining to social responsibility, management of displacement, issues of water and land usage, and provisions of local employment opportunities are significant. Second, mining projects spill over into other sectors such as the energy, infrastructure, and transportation sectors as mining projects usually require additional investments. Third, due to the complex nature of financing mining projects, the repercussions on the country's finances can be sizable. Therefore, it is crucial for the host country to enter into a well-developed contract that considers all direct and indirect effects.

In this study, the authors provide a framework of a model contract between the Government of Mongolia (GoM) and mining companies based on international best practices.

Mining contracts should be built upon and work in conjunction with the country's investment environment created by the combination of domestic laws, investment treaties, and investment contracts. Currently, Mongolia has 35 contracts related to mineral resources. However, a large majority of these are local level agreements (LLAs), a formal agreement between mineral resource companies and subnational or local level stakeholders affected by company projects. LLAs became mandatory in 2006 with Article 42.1 of the Mineral Law of Mongolia. Among the 35 contracts, Mongolia does have a couple of model agreements available, such as the "Model Agreement on Protecting the Environment, Developing Infrastructure related to Mine Operation and Plant Construction, and Creating Jobs" for LLAs and a production or profit-sharing model agreement for crude oil. However, none of them provide guidance for negotiating, drafting, and concluding a production, profit sharing, or investment agreement about mineral products such as iron ore, gold, silver, coal, and so on. It should be noted that the only publicly available investment agreement is the investment agreement between the GoM and Ivanhoe Mines and Rio Tinto for the Oyu Tolgoi Project.

The Natural Resource Governance Institute's (NRGI) 2013 Resource Governance Index (RGI) found that of 58 countries studied, 20 countries publish all or some of their extractive contracts. Mongolia is on the list; however, the level of transparency is not high as in countries such as Liberia and Australia. This study compares Mongolia's agreements with those of other nations as well as examines the International Institute for Sustainable Development's (IISD) Model Mining Development Agreement (MMDA) and identifies the gaps and duplications within the existing agreements of Mongolia.

The assessment of the current agreements between the GoM or LLA with mining companies as well as Mongolia's legal and institutional environment is required to gain a better understanding of the current state of investment contracts. The study assesses the current agreements and compares them with best practices to highlight the shortcomings of these agreements. By addressing these shortcomings, Mongolia can follow the examples of best practices in negotiating future contracts.

One key aspect of the model contract should be its flexibility to be tailored to specific projects while the outline and necessary articles remain. The contract's purpose is to build upon the domestic laws, the paramount provisions and clauses for each project, and outline the key terms and conditions of the project, such as duration, royalties, and taxation. The study's main outcomes are it clarifies what clauses need to be included in the contract, the role of stakeholders during the negotiation process, and the type of model contract to be used by mining projects for future contracts. Moreover, the study proposes improvements in the legal and policy framework for entering into agreements with mining companies and offers enhancements in Mongolia's practice of negotiating contracts.

## 3 Foreign Direct Investment in Mongolia: Impact and Determinants

Mineral commodity prices continue to be the primary determinant of FDI inflows into Mongolia. As a price taker, the Mongolian economy is susceptible to drastic fluctuations. As such, to attract more investment, the country should improve the investment climate through legal reforms, increased transparency, and combating corruption.

FDI inflows fluctuate considerably due to the country's resource dependence and uncertain investment climate. In this study, the authors review the effect of FDI on the economy, local development, and financial and labor markets. In doing so, the authors assess how the FDI environment is reflected in the national development strategy documents and the government's strategy toward creating an enabling environment for FDI in the mining sector. In analyzing the impact of FDI on the Mongolian economy, the authors estimated the investment multiplier of additional FDI using the input–output table of 2010 and 2015.

Moreover, the authors performed a comparative analysis of the business and institutional framework and investment climate. They chose Chile, Kazakhstan, Peru, and Zambia for comparison as FDI inflows into these countries heavily depend on respective mining sectors. Investment policies and institutions of the country exacerbated the FDI fluctuations. These countries' mining sector only recently contributed to GDP and exports immensely. Additionally, these countries are categorized as middle-income, similar to Mongolia. In addition to updating the various indices related to the local business environment for selected countries, their regulatory and institutional frameworks were studied to determine what gave some of these countries an edge over the others in attracting investment. In particular, the policies and trends of each country's promotion and facilitation of FDI into the extractive industries were analyzed.

As determined by other studies, disputes with foreign investors are the endogenous factor that constrains FDI in Mongolia, similar to many other developing countries. Thus, the authors also covered the international settlement of disputes, especially arbitration, and aimed to identify ways and mechanisms for avoiding possible future conflicts ex-ante and resolving disputes efficiently ex-post, and generally, for improving contract enforcement institutions in the mining sector.

## 4 Mining Development Strategy in Mongolia

There are many national strategic and policy documents on resource management, such as "Vision 2050", "Sustainable development goals until 2030", "Policies to be conducted in the minerals sector", "Concept of socio-economic development in the medium term", and "Annual agenda of the socio-economic development".

One of the primary goals of this study is to assess what gaps if any exist in these documents. The authors will identify issues that are not addressed in these documents and issues that are not. Additionally, the study identified and analyzed issues that should be addressed in the national strategy.

Analytically, the study followed the guidelines developed and advocated by the Natural Resource Governance Institute. Since commodity prices are volatile, the national strategy is prone to changes in response. The national strategy should be cognizant of various scenarios of commodity prices.

In this study, the authors assessed the national strategy documents along the following two pillars of the benchmarking in detail: long-term view and gaps and duplications in the strategy.

The country should not be overly reliant on commodity exports in the long term. The national strategy should promote economic diversification and related policies regulating the mineral sector.

Moreover, it should be noted that generations of citizens should benefit from the extractive sector. This means that the strategy should take a long-term view of the mining sector's impact on the environment, society, and economy. Thus, the strategy should address the long-term impact of the mineral sector.

Additionally, long-term management of the resources sector requires a legal and institutional framework. Therefore, the assessment focused on whether the current legal and institutional framework adequately addresses the sector's need for proper long-term management.

The national strategy should also give guidance on the implementation of the strategy. NRGI stresses the importance of the pace of licensing, the fiscal impact of the sector, revenue management, and the role of private and public companies in the sector.

Moreover, the national strategy should reflect how the country sees itself developing in the future. In particular, strategy documents should expose tradeoffs the country faces regarding what strategic sectors the country prioritizes. The country's strategic documents tend to be general, but the government should have a clearer picture of what priorities are in place in the long and medium term.

Since the national strategy covers a wide range of issues such as planning, taxation, environmental management, financing, labor, and education, the authors focused on gaps or conflicts in policies that require more clarity and regulations or areas where it can be further streamlined so that the sector's performance is improved.

## 5 Budget Revenue Management

The Parliament of Mongolia passed the Fiscal Stability Law (FSL) in 2011. Implementing the FSL could curb the excessive economic fluctuations caused by changes in mineral commodity prices. However, its constraints on budget revenue, expenditure, and debt must work in unison and be strictly enforced to benefit from this revenue management framework.

In light of the FSL, the Fiscal Stability Fund (FSF) was established in 2011. The purpose of the stabilization fund was to prevent the economy from the fluctuations related to mineral commodity prices and encourage economic growth. In addition, the government established the Future Heritage Fund (FHF) in 2016. The money that is being and will be put into the Fund will not be spent until 2030 and assets will be invested in a way that will maximize returns. The majority of the revenue into the FHF is expected from mining royalty taxes while the remaining revenue will be from dividends of state-owned enterprises and the net income of the fund itself.

In this study, the research team assessed this budget revenue management framework by utilizing an in-house Computable General Equilibrium Model (CGE). First, the authors analyzed the current state of revenue management in Mongolia using comprehensive information from the Ministry of Finance, Mongolbank, and other organizations. Then they used CGE simulation analysis to assess whether the FSL framework could counteract and lessen the de-industrialization effect of mining in the long run. The authors also estimated the sensitivity of economic performance to changes in some of the key requirements of the FSL. In particular, two key benchmark parameters of the FSL were relaxed: ceiling on the growth of budget expenditure and restriction on the budget revenue.

Finally, the authors assessed the impact of the FSF and FHF. First, international practices of similar stabilization funds or sovereign wealth funds were reviewed and compared with Mongolia's funds. Then, they estimated the impact of FSF and FHF by running simulations with and without those funds to highlight the role these funds play in dampening economic volatility.

## 6 Social License to Operate

The social license to operate (SLO), in a broad sense, refers to the ongoing acceptance of a company or industry's standard business practices and operating procedures by its employees, stakeholders, and the general public. It does not refer to a formal agreement or document but the actual or current credibility, reliability, and acceptance of organizations and projects. The SLO is created and maintained slowly over time as the actions of a company build trust with the community in which it operates and other stakeholders. The concept has evolved relatively recently from the broader and more established notions of "corporate social responsibility" and "social acceptability" and is also closely tied to the concept of sustainability. In particular, there has been increasing attention to this subject during the last two decades.

In Mongolia's case, SLO is most relevant to the mining sector. In addition to obtaining legally required licenses to operate from the government and other regulatory agencies. There have been several instances where mining developments have been delayed, interrupted, or even shut down due to opposition from the public and/or local communities. Thus, mining companies need to obtain and maintain a SLO from local communities to avoid these costly conflicts.

In this study, the authors assessed the relationship between the Mongolian mining sector and the local community. In doing so, they determined the key challenges the companies and communities are facing. The analysis covered international and domestic case studies, which reflect either successful or unsuccessful developments of SLO. Based on the literature review and case study findings, the authors prepared a baseline document to develop guidelines for the SLO and developed a social licensing evaluation methodology to promote sustainable mining development. Then, they assessed the level of SLO of a particular project by applying the evaluation methodology proposed by Moffat and Zhang (2013).[7] Using a structural equation model for survey data, the authors estimated the effect of maintaining a civil and respectful relationship with the public, such as the impact of social infrastructure, ongoing communication with stakeholders, transparent disclosure of information, and participation in decision-making.

**Khashchuluun Chuluundorj** is an associate professor of economics at the National University of Mongolia. He has a bachelor's degree in economics from Moscow State University, Russia; a master's degree in economics from Yokohama City University, Japan; and a Ph.D. in economics from Keio University, Japan. He worked with the JICA project on national economic development policy in 1997–1999 and then served as the dean of the Economics School of the National University of Mongolia from 2004 to 2009. From 2009 to 2012, he served as the chairman of the National Development and Innovation Committee of Mongolia (NDIC), a government agency, where he oversaw the establishment of the national economic planning system in the market economy, introduced the public investment program (PIP), and supervised the establishment of the Development Bank of Mongolia, for which he served as an inaugural chairman of the Board of Directors. In addition, he supervised the creation of a legal system to support innovation in the country

[7] Kieren Moffat, ба Airong Zhang. "The paths to social license to operate: An integrative model explaining community acceptance of mining." *Resource Policy 39*, 2013: 61–70.

and oversaw the development of national public–private partnerships. Currently, he is a member of the Economic Policy Council under the prime minister of Mongolia as well as a member of the Monetary Policy Committee of the Central Bank of Mongolia. Khashchuluun Chuluundorj is also working as an independent member on the boards of directors for numerous financial and mining companies in Mongolia and is a visiting professor at the Plekhanov Russian University of Economics, in addition to his teaching at the National University of Mongolia's Department of Economics. He has published in international peer-reviewed journals and publications such as *Resources Policy*, the *Journal of Applied Economic Sciences*, *Inner Asia*, and others.

**Tuvshintugs Batdelger** is the director of the Economic Research Institute (ERI) and an associate professor of economics at the National University of Mongolia. He has a bachelor's degree in economics from the National University of Mongolia; a master's degree in economics from the University of Manchester, UK; and a Ph.D. in economics from Boston University, USA. He has experience working at the Bank of Mongolia and was the head of the Economics Department of the National University of Mongolia from 2014 to 2017. He has been a member of the Economic Policy Council under the prime minister of Mongolia since 2012 and was a member of the Monetary Policy Committee from 2011 to 2016. He has been actively involved in policy discussions in the country through the establishment and operation of ERI since 2010, one of the longest-running think tanks in the country. Through ERI, he successfully contributed to policy discussions on wide-ranging economic and social issues by coordinating and implementing many projects by international organizations, such as the World Bank, Asian Development Bank, and JICA. In particular, he successfully led research teams conducting an economic assessment of big mining and industrial projects on the country's economy and society in general. He has successfully conducted and published policy research studies in international peer-reviewed journals and publications such as *Applied Economics*, *Resources Policy*, and *East Asia Forum* and has authored chapters on the Mongolian economy in numerous books. His current research interests are the role of mining in the economy and society, the role of monetary policy in regulating the Mongolian economy, and the impact of economic development on income distribution and the country's middle class.

**Dr. Yoshitaka Hosoi** has qualifications both in mining and in economics. He is currently a visiting professor/lecturer at Akita University, Hokkaido University, and Kyushu University, all of which are in Japan. He teaches courses in international relations, resources economics, and international cooperation. He has taught at the University of Tokyo, Osaka University, and others as well. He is also senior advisor for natural resources of the Japan International Corporation Agency (JICA), which is a Japanese government organization for Official Development Assistance (ODA). His task is to advise JICA and developing countries in the mining field, formulate projects, supervise implementing projects, and conduct human resource development in Africa, Asia, the Pacific, and South America. Before joining JICA, he worked for the Deep Ocean Resources Development Co., Ltd. (DORD), which holds a manganese nodules concession in the Central Pacific, as general manager of the Exploration Department for planning and executing exploration. Before DORD, he worked for the Japan Oil, Gas, and Metals National Corporation (JOGMEC), which is a Japanese governmental organization, for 33 years. He has experience in mineral exploration, mine development, technology development, mine pollution surveys and prevention, and mineral economics in almost 100 countries. He has been a visiting lecturer at the University of the South Pacific in Fiji, and Adamson University in the Philippines. He has held positions in the SODIMIZA mining company in Zaire, Metal Mining Agency of Japan (MMAJ), Japan Mining Engineering Centre for International Cooperation (JMEC), and SOPAC South Pacific Applied Geosciences Commission (SOPAC) in Fiji. He has also published numerous papers and articles in areas of exploration, the mining industry, and economics. He has published the books *Mining and Development* (2009), *Mineral Resources Frontier* (2012), and *Mining in Africa* (2014). He holds a Bachelor of Mining Engineering degree from Akita University, has done postgraduate research in mining at the University of Tokyo, a master's in economics from the University of Santo Tomas in the Philippines, and a Ph.D. in economics from the University of Queensland in Australia.

# Mining Sector Contracting in Mongolia

**Khashchuluun Chuluundorj, Dulguun Tuvshintugs, Manlaibaatar Zagdbazar, and Unurjargal Davaa**

## 1 Introduction

In many regions, foreign direct investment (FDI) plays a crucial role in the economic growth of resource-rich, developing host countries, providing necessary financing, know-how and technology to develop mining resources. In Mongolia's case, most inflows of FDI are directed into the mining sector,[1] as investors find natural resources an attractive investment due to geographical proximity to major East Asian markets.

As with many investment projects, the business environment, the rule of law, contracts, and their implementation are necessary conditions to ensure a stable inflow of FDI into sectors such as services, agriculture, or textiles.

In Mongolia, investments in these sectors are generally governed by generic investment contracts without any sector-specific clauses and are subject to the Company Law. As of 2018, approximately 7 billion USD of FDI was made in those industries, particularly construction, trade, and services, being primary recipients. However,

[1] Source: National Statistics Office of Mongolia. As of 2018, based on the latest available data on FDI, out of total stock of FDI of 20.2 billion USD, 14.56 billion USD or approximately 77% of all foreign direct investment were invested in mining in the country.

K. Chuluundorj (✉)
The National University of Mongolia, Ulaanbaatar, Mongolia
e-mail: khashchuluun@num.edu.mn

D. Tuvshintugs · M. Zagdbazar · U. Davaa
Economic Research Institute, Ulaanbaatar, Mongolia
e-mail: dulguun@eri.mn

M. Zagdbazar
e-mail: manlaibaatar@eri.mn

U. Davaa
e-mail: unurjargal@eri.mn

 
Y. Hosoi et al. (eds.), *Economic Dependence of Mongolia on Minerals*,
Contributions to Economics, https://doi.org/10.1007/978-981-19-5515-0_2

mining investment is more complicated than investing in those sectors, and thus, the business environment is even more critical for FDI in the industry.

FDI inflows into the mining sector are governed by the Company Law and other legislation, such as the Minerals Law, which can make the contracts in mining much more complex, as investors have more requirements to fulfill in the case of investment in mineral resources.

There are the following specific features of contracting in mining compared to investment in services or construction. Due to the sheer size and volume of the mining resources, most investments in the sector are invested in large mining projects, which can have several consequences.

First, due to the large scale of investment projects, the socioeconomic impact of social responsibility, management of displacement, water, and land usage issues, and provisions of local employment opportunities are significant. In many cases, those issues are regulated by related laws, which adds to the overall complexity.

Second, mining projects create spillovers related to other sectors of the economy, which require significant additional investment in energy, infrastructure, and transportation. As the Minerals Law does not regulate these types of investments, other investment provisions are necessary for the contracts, thus increasing the project cost substantially.

Third, due to the complex nature of the mining project's financing and the magnitude of its revenues and capital expenditures, the repercussions on the country's finances may be sizable, especially if the economy is relatively small. At the initial stages, investment may contribute more to rising sovereign debt due to features of international accounting standards, especially during the early stages of mine development, rather than functioning as an engine of economic growth. Therefore, a host country must enter into a well-prepared contract that considers all the abovementioned effects. Within the agreement, the additional issues related to FDI should be addressed and managed. In Mongolia's case, as the country has borders only with two giant neighboring countries of the Russian Federation and the People's Republic of China, a specific issue, which sometimes may arise for a landlocked country, is the careful consideration of sensitive national economic security issues of the host country, which usually do not rise in contracts elsewhere but may create a barrier if not addressed.

In addition, a large mine may require signing a special agreement on local development. Under Article 42.1 of the Minerals Law of Mongolia, local-level local-level agreements between mineral resource companies and subnational or local-level stakeholders became mandatory in 2006. As of December 2021, out of the 884 contracts available on the "Resource Contract Database",[2] 368 can be classified as local-level agreements. The Open Society Forum established the database in Mongolia in cooperation with the Extractive Industry Transparency Initiative and the Ministry of Mining and Heavy Industry of Mongolia. The primary purpose of the collaboration was to enhance the transparency of contracts in Mongolia's extractive sector. Contracts made between mining companies and the Government of Mongolia

[2] https://iltodgeree.mn/.

or agencies within the Ministry of Mining and Heavy Industry were not considered. However, agreements made with the governors of provinces or districts were considered and analyzed. Of the 368 local-level agreements, 18 were social responsibility contracts that contractually obligated the mining companies to develop infrastructures related to mine operation and plant construction, protect the environment, and create jobs.

Since 2006, Mongolia has designated 15 mineral deposits as strategically important, which means a deposit may potentially impact national security, economic and social development, or is producing or has the potential to make more than 5% of Mongolia's total GDP in a year. The State may own up to 34% of a mineral deposit of strategic importance, which is determined by an agreement where financing, management, and equity share is negotiated. It should be noted that in Mongolia's case, every time Mongolia enters a negotiation for the strategic type of investment (a mining investment project is viewed as a strategic one if it exceeds 5% of GDP), a parliament resolution is adopted, which creates a mandate for the agreement and defines the framework for negotiations.

Generally, in this case, the mandate and resolutions guide the process of negotiations with an investor and prescribe a list of desired outcomes. The mandate is mainly based on the Mineral Law; however, it may include items not covered in the law and are subject to negotiation with the investor. According to the Mongolian Constitution, the government must comply with the mandate outlined in the adopted parliament resolution, as Mongolia is a parliamentary republic. However, the resolution may be amended to reflect the prevailing conditions at the time of the negotiations if the original set of income is unrealistic and unsupported by analysis and/or government. For investment in smaller deposits (with revenue less than 5% of GDP), the procedure is much more straightforward, as investors may choose to invest in exploration or directly in the mine just based on procedures regulated by the Mineral Law, which is more prevalent.

Currently, the only strategic investment agreement the Government of Mongolia (GoM) has made thus far regarding the 15 strategic deposits is a one signed with Ivanhoe Mines and Rio Tinto for the Oyu Tolgoi Project (copper) in 2009. In addition to the Oyu Tolgoi deposit, a copper deposit in Tsagaan Suvarga was strategically important, and the development rights belonged to a Mongolian company, MAK. However, the Parliament rejected a 34% equity stake, worth 350 million USD, in MAK's Tsagaan Suvarga copper project with the adoption of Parliament resolution No. 54 on 1 July 2014. The rejection of ownership in the Tsagaan Suvarga deposit came after the government paid roughly twice the cost of equity for Rio Tinto's Oyu Tolgoi Project in an attempt to avoid another complex negotiation of financing.

This research aims to study the case of Mongolia's legal and policy framework and its agreements with mining companies to compare with international practices of mining investment agreements. Mining projects may be an essential source of FDI and drive economic growth in a host country; they should be built upon and work in conjunction with the investment environment of the host country, created by the combination of domestic laws, investment treaties, and investment contracts.

The chapter contains a case assessment of the Oyu Tolgoi agreement, as it is currently the only publicly available strategic investment agreement for Mongolia. In the international literature, the Oyu Tolgoi agreement is deemed a good contract due to its transparency (EITI, 2014). The Oyu Tolgoi project is one of the world's largest copper mines operated by one of the largest companies. The agreement considers several issues, making it a good starting point in constructing a model contract. Analyzing the advantages and disadvantages of the contract will assist in identifying the clauses needed for subsequent agreements and the changes required to be made in Mongolia's mining sector and institutional environment.

In the case of Mongolia, studying an optimal contract for the four primary exported mineral commodities—coal, copper, gold, and iron ore—is vital, as these commodities account for a majority of the tax revenue from mining. For a developing country, having a template for large investments or a model agreement, which calculates the optimal returns for the host country (and the investor) based on the features of the project, can be advantageous, as it can significantly reduce the time and preparations necessary to launch a mega-project in mining. However, one should remember from the very outset that mining deposits can be diverse—ranging from natural gas to rare earth metals—so developing a one-size-fits-all template may be difficult. Some of the challenges in writing one-size-fits-all guidance are also several factors mentioned above, such as the assortment of mining resources, size of deposits, constant changes in the country's rating, varying financing availability, fluctuating borrowing costs, negotiation of equity, and royalties.

Research regarding contracts in mining may promote an inflow of future investments into the country. All these factors make it difficult to pinpoint the best model contract, resulting in creating an investment agreement on a case-by-case basis. Nevertheless, the distillment of a set of the most basic and important features of a mining contract will assist in making the negotiation process clearer and more efficient.

## 2 Mongolia's Mining Contracts: Specific Features

The inflow of FDI into Mongolia depends on the legal and institutional environment. However, this environment is generally determined by its path dependence. In other words, past decisions determine the trajectory of strategic planning and current decision-making. To understand Mongolia's history of foreign investment, a review of its industrialization policies is needed. As a planned economy, a member of COMECON (CMEA) or Council for Mutual Economic Assitance, the country has been receiving foreign direct investment during its industrialization in 1950-the 1980s from Eastern Europe and the Soviet Union.

## 2.1 *Mongolia's Contracts with Foreign Enterprises for Investment: Before the Transition to a Market Economy and Early Transition Years 1990–2000*

Mongolia entered an intensive development stage between 1940 and 1950. The main sector was animal husbandry, but starting from the 1940s, the country began to develop more advanced industries, such as light industry, communications, energy, transport, road infrastructure, and public utilities. Since 1948, social and economic development has followed the set-out plans similar to economic plans adopted in other socialist countries. The first 5-year plan was introduced in 1948, and the following plan was a 3-year mid-term plan from 1957 to 1960. The subsequent six plans after 1960 were 5-year plans until 1990 (1961–1965, 1966–1970, 1971–1975, 1976–1980, 1981–1985, 1986–1990). To develop a national development policy strategy, the central government collaborated with local and foreign research institutes to develop appropriate economic strategies and made necessary changes to organizations and institutions. Each 5-year strategic planning plan had a specific objective it aimed to fulfill. For instance, the first plan included objectives such as shifting the economy from purely animal husbandry to a mixture of the agricultural and industrial sectors. Some of the goals for these plans were (ADB, 1992):

- To intensively develop the industrial sector (1960),
- To establish the industrial city of Darkhan (1961),
- To improve productivity, industrialize the agricultural sector, provide energy to rural areas, and establish a new city of Choibalsan (1966),
- To develop the carpet and leather industry, lay the foundations for biotechnology, and establish the meat and food industry (1971),
- To improve the quality of products of all sectors, develop the mining and heavy industry (1976),
- To develop the dairy industry, modern agricultural farms should be established and developed, and a new export sector should be established to develop the cashmere industry (1986).

However, the Mongolian economy faced several challenges related to investment and financing due to the small population size and the fact that most people's wealth at that time consisted of livestock. Until 1962, when the country became a member of the CMEA, the main sources of investment were assistance from the two neighboring countries of the Soviet Union and the People's Republic of China, directed to light industry, mining, road, and housing projects (Mongolia also assisted the Soviet Union during World War II). As Mongolia became a member of the Council for Mutual Economic Assistance (CMEA) in 1962, it allowed the other CMEA members to invest in the country, provide loans, and establish joint ventures with Mongolia in other sectors. The largest joint venture projects established under the CMEA umbrella were the Erdenet Mining Corporation between the Soviet Union and Mongolia (a copper mine and ore enrichment plant) and a joint mining company Mongolrostsvetmet LLC, a geological exploration and mining enterprise. In addition to various joint enterprises with countries of Eastern Europe, some other projects were mainly financed and supported through loans with ownerships that remained 100% Mongolian. To coordinate these major projects, special decisions and resolutions were issued by the government, and intergovernmental cooperation was crucial for the initial agreements of these projects. In addition, the CMEA countries had to use transferable rouble as a special currency and use multiple exchange rate coefficients for financial transactions.

These joint ventures were some of Mongolia's first "megaprojects", financed and implemented under joint agreements, such as CMEA rules. These projects were not purely commercial but rather more developmental projects with joint management teams, experts, and advisers from Eastern Europe working and residing in Mongolia. After transitioning to a market economy, those enterprises and joint ventures had to be restructured according to new market economy regulations. As a result, the Erdenet and Mongolrostsvetmet projects' legal framework was renewed in 1990. The joint ventures became LLCs with joint equity, while the Ulaanbaatar railway still adheres to its 1946 agreement and is not a joint-stock company.

Attempts to bring in foreign capital for development intensified after the collapse of the CMEA by the end of 1990. CMEA and its member countries, mainly the USSR, funded the majority of big infrastructure and industrial projects in Mongolia and contributed in various ways; however, after the dissolution of CMEA, Mongolia found itself without primary investment sources. As a result, Mongolia's new Foreign Investment Law (FI law) was approved in 1993. It created the legislative basis for foreign investment and specified which government agencies should manage and promote FDI. In addition, this law led to the creation of the Foreign Investment Agency or FIFTA, which exists today under a different name (Investment Mongolia Agency in 2016). It is a part of the National Development Agency and deals with foreign investment and concession treaties.

However, even after the approval of the FDI law, most financing to Mongolia in early transition years came through not commercial investment but multilateral agreements and donor assistance. The most important sources of funding for infrastructure projects in the country became ADB, EBRD, World Bank, Japan, and other donors and international organizations; however, this sort of financing, while crucial for saving the country's economy, was not aimed at the industry and did not result in a much higher inflow of foreign investment.

In the 1990s, based on the experience of the previous mining (copper) megaproject in Erdenet, mining was thought of as a possible primary source of FDI; however, the general market outlook, lack of infrastructure, and Asian crisis resulted in a lack of FDI projects in mining at that time. Therefore, the leading destination for FDI in Mongolia in the 1990s surprisingly turned out to be the garment sector.

Thus, in the 1990s, the first major wave of private FDI into Mongolia occurred in the garment sector, not in mining (Table 1), and it was led by SME investors, who were using Mongolia as an outlet for the export of garments to the USA. The new FDI law at that time did not have a stability agreement clause; nevertheless, it was instrumental in supporting FDI in textiles in the country, which utilized the existing trained Mongolian labor force and industrial base to export garments to large US retail chains. The largest investor, by far, was China, followed by Hong Kong and Taiwan. Exports of sewed goods increased rapidly from 1993 to 1999, growing by 1800%, while exports of knitted goods grew almost tenfold between 1993 and 1999. Textile in 2002 made up as much as 27.7% of total exports in 2002, before the expiration of the MFA (Multi-Fiber Agreement) in 2004. Orders were received from large US retailers such as Walmart, QVC shopping, J. C. Penney and Target and included several brands, such as Ann Taylor, Sears, Liz Claiborne Inc., Express LLC, Pacific Trail Inc., and Lollytogs LTD.

The textile industry emerged as the third-largest recipient of FDI in the country after mining and trade/services; for some time, foreign investment in light industry exceeded that of mining in 2000, reaching USD 26 million compared to USD 18 million in mining. By the end of 2000, the number of companies with FDI in the sewing sector reached 49. There were 20 companies from China, 15 from South Korea, 4 from Hong Kong, 3 from Taiwan, 2 from Germany, one from the USA, and one from Great Britain and Kazakhstan. By 2004, the number of foreign companies increased further, reaching approximately 100 business entities in the textile industry, 38.3% or 36 of which were established with 100% foreign direct investment, 46.8% or 44 were joint companies, and 14.9% or 14 were domestically owned companies. These garment companies employed as much labor as the whole textile and clothing industry before the transition to the market economy started. By the end of the MFA agreement in 2004 in Mongolia, "the textile industry alone employed more than 20 thousand workers, which is approximately 17.5% of the total employment in the industrial sector and produced 5% of industrial goods, and 10% of exports goods. The expiration of the MFA agreement in 2004 and China's entry into the WTO, however, dealt a heavy blow to the development of the export-oriented garment industry in Mongolia. The US market quota system was abolished, and Mongolia no longer enjoyed a guaranteed export niche, which has been overtaken by cheaper producers. As a result, a large number of foreign investors began to leave the country and shift production to other more competitive countries. This led to the closure of many plants and mass dismissals of workers. The total output of the industry in the first 10 months of 2005 fell by 26%.

## 2.2 *Modification of the 1993 Law on FDI and Its Implications for Contracts in Mining*

The 1993 FDI legislation contained an important feature: it established the possibility of appealing disputes related to investment contracts in Mongolian and foreign courts. Article 25 stated that "disputes between foreign investors and Mongolian investors

**Table 1** FDI inflow by sector from 1994 to 2005, million USD

| | Total | 1994 | 1995 | 1996 | 1997 | 1998 | 1999 | 2000 | 2001 | 2002 | 2003 | 2004 | 2005 |
|---|---|---|---|---|---|---|---|---|---|---|---|---|---|
| Mining and exploration | 571.8 | 1.0 | 8.3 | 4.2 | 17.6 | 19.4 | 25.1 | 18.1 | 59.9 | 37.1 | 158.3 | 106.8 | 116.1 |
| Trade, services | 221.3 | 1.0 | 0.9 | 1.4 | 7.3 | 3.6 | 5.2 | 5.5 | 5.9 | 89.5 | 6.3 | 38.8 | 53.9 |
| Light industry | 86.8 | 2.8 | 2.0 | 12.0 | 1.5 | 4.8 | 19.2 | 26.5 | 4.9 | 2.9 | 4.4 | 2.7 | 1.8 |

*Source* FIFTA, Government of Mongolia, 2006

as well as between foreign investors and Mongolian legal or natural persons on the matters relating to foreign investment and the operations of the business entities with foreign investment and a branch of a foreign legal entity, shall be resolved in the Courts of Mongolia unless provided otherwise by international treaties to which Mongolia is a party or by any contract between the parties to the dispute (this paragraph was amended by the Law of January 3, 2002)".

This article will later be crucial for promoting large projects in mining, which are legally protected not only in Mongolia but also in foreign courts specified by an investor. As usual, due to geographical proximity and the prevalence of commercial codes, London, Hong Kong, and Singapore are selected as foreign courts; however, the investor can specify any other court as well.

From 2002 onward, the FDI law includes an added article on an **investment agreement**. In the article of 2002, the "Investment Agreement" is described as "an agreement and/or a contract on concession, product sharing, marketing, management, financial leasing and franchise investment concluded by foreign investors for implementation of the concrete project without having to establish a legal entity". Furthermore, it was noted that a foreign investor should "follow commitments stated in the Agreement and Statute of the business entity with foreign investment, branch of a foreign legal entity and Investment agreement; (this subparagraph was re-edited by the Law of January 3, 2002)". This clause opened doors to equity sharing projects such as the Oyu Tolgoi and its management contract.

The stability agreement concept was introduced first in the Minerals Law adopted in 1997. It contained a clause that if the project in the first 5 years results in at least 2 million USD investment, the investor is eligible to apply for a stability agreement with the Ministry of Finance. For a USD 2 million investment, the tax regime stability duration would be 10 years; for investment exceeding USD 20 million, it would be 15 years. As most mining contracts, perhaps except exploration, would exceed USD 20 million thresholds, it was a welcome addition for promoting investment in the mining sector.

Moreover, in 2002, the Stability Agreement Article 20 was added to the Foreign Investment Law, which described the **stability agreement** with an investor in all sectors, not just mining. The "Article 20 Conclusion of a Stability Agreement" states that "an investor willing to conclude a Stability Agreement shall submit its application and draft a Stability Agreement to the State central administrative body in charge of tax policy issues," which indirectly points to the essence of stability agreement concerning mainly taxes. This clause will be crucial for the Stability agreement with Rio Tinto on the Oyu Tolgoi project. In 2008, the clause was amended to raise the threshold to USD 20 million investment to stabilize the legal environment. Furthermore, for the USD 20 million investment, the stability agreement duration was 10 years, and for investment equal to or exceeding USD 50 million, the agreement duration was stipulated to be 15 years. It can be speculated that the previous stability clause influenced the "stability" clause in the Minerals Law, instead of expanding the concept to all sectors, not just mining. More significant investments are related to the risk issue of taxation changes, which may negatively affect the project; therefore, the necessary clauses were added in 2002.

The Foreign Investment Law of Mongolia, adopted in 1993, was replaced in 2013 by a broader Investment Law. The new Investment Law contained the previous stability clauses, concentrating in four tax areas and expanding its eligibility to domestic companies, thus supporting mining investment and replacing USD investment with MNT equivalents of MNT 10 and 50 billion. In addition, the stability agreement had to be signed with the economy, finance, and taxation authorities.

The 2002 amendments and additions to the Foreign Investment law were instrumental for starting large investment projects—one can see that by 2002, the law already contained all major parts necessary to bring large investment projects in the country, such as the following:

- The investment agency in charge
- Definition of the investment agreement
- The concept of stability agreement and the agency in charge
- Possibilities for equity participation and the possibility to protect investment in foreign courts.

These parts are important for any contract in mining.

While the FI law did not result in the very active growth of FI in the 1990s, it laid the groundwork for the successful large FDI projects in later decades, and it contained all major features necessary to describe in the contract relevant to all sectors. However, it was a specific sector and its law, which further shaped the investment contracts in Mongolia, as we see in the current form. However, it was not Foreign Investment law that promoted most foreign investments—it was the Minerals Law.

The Minerals Law of Mongolia was adopted in 1997. It ultimately resulted in a massive increase in FDI in Mongolia after the 1990s to create the main new projects of the national economy, which currently defines the Mongolian economy. It invited foreign exploration companies to Mongolia, one of which, called Ivanhoe Mines, resulting in a USD 12 billion Oyu Tolgoi project.

The 1997 Minerals Law introduced several potential contract negotiation issues, such as refunding of costs incurred to agricultural or cultural value property during mining exploitation and incurring expenses related to replacing cultural value artifacts. It also stipulated that an investor may hold public hearings if deemed necessary by the investor. The 33rd clause of the law also called for the creation of a local investment council with regional authorities concerning an increase in regional employment, infrastructure development, and environmental protection. Later, these articles would be included or reflected in the large mining contract, especially in the case of Oyu Tolgoi.

The 1997 Minerals Law included a clause on the environmental impact assessment and the investor's environmental protection plan. However, in general, the law did not have any articles that would necessitate a broad strategic type contract. Instead, it viewed mining in a way similar to garments and other sectors, which did not need any special investment agreement and were coordinated by the umbrella Foreign Investment Law. The law opened Mongolia to mining companies; changes in the commodities markets after 2001 made Mongolian deposits attractive to investors, marking the start of mining-based economic growth in the country. The World Bank

(2003) stated that "there has been a rapid rise in mineral exploration in Mongolia. This is partly due to the 1997 Minerals Law, which has played a pivotal role in attracting foreign exploration companies. Other important factors were the government's abolition of a 10% gold tax and the widely publicized discovery of the Oyu Tolgoi copper/gold deposit in 2001. Since this discovery, the number of exploration licenses held and the amount of land held by licensees has increased fivefold. There are now 2595 exploration licenses in Mongolia covering 40 million hectares, 26% of its territory". Mining quickly overtook garment sectors to become a leading FDI recipient industry in subsequent years.

## *2.3 Contract Spillovers from Mining to Finance*

In a decade after 2000, commodity prices, particularly minerals, rose significantly; exploration in Mongolia rapidly discovered new promising deposits; after a decade, the 1997 Minerals Law was replaced by the 2006 Minerals Law, which had significant implications for contracting in mining.

First, the new Minerals Law of 2006 included clause 4.1.12 on the **strategic** mining deposits, broadly defining them as very significant or output exceeding 5% of GDP in the given year. This clause required special treatment and, therefore, special contracting only for large strategic projects.

Furthermore, Article 5.4 on **strategic** deposits discovered with state exploration stated that the government may own up to 50% of equity on such deposits if the deposit is to be developed by a private entity. The rights are to be defined by a deposit usage contract. Furthermore, Article 5.4 states that once a state share is defined in the contract, it can be substituted by royalties. Article 5.5 states that in the strategic deposits discovered by private exploration, the equity's state ownership may be up to 34%; similarly, the precise share is to be defined by the contract. Again, the share may be substituted by royalties. Clauses 5.4 and 5.5, therefore, were a major step ahead for regulating and signing the contract on the deposit utilization.

The Minerals Law gave the government the right to find and decide on financing issues regarding the state equity share by Article 9.6. Potentially, it resulted in an issue where the investor and government may together cooperate in raising the necessary financing, which will result in an additional contract issue, with its ways of negotiation and dispute resolution, because the financial issues are not directly related to the main mining activities and, therefore, are viewed as a credit/loan or equity investment relations, each regulated by either Law on Banks in Mongolia or Company Law.

This article also had significant implications in broadening the impact of a mining contract, spilling outside to finance, credit, and sovereign borrowing issues. For example, if a government would need to borrow finances necessary for the equity share of a major project, the equity financing for GOM would itself increase sovereign debt, which is regulated by either Law on Government Debt Management (2014) and is reflected in the annual Budget Laws.[3]

The Minerals Law's new clauses 5.4 and 5.5 directly led to the necessity to regulate financing and general mining issues if the government chooses to own equity ownership, not exercise its royalties rights.

In 2014, the Mineral's Law had an additional clause on possible compensation issues if the government may decide to revoke the special rights for mining granted earlier. This procedure will include by law the negotiation with the investor regarding the compensation by the newly added Article 9.1.13.

However, the investment treaty is no longer contained in the Mineral's Law, and all its related articles are governed by the Investment Law adopted in 2013. The possibility to have a Stability agreement is still there, however.

Another important regulation, which was added later, concerns regional development. Mining companies are now obliged to contribute to regional development based on the specific law on Local Level Agreements (LLA).[4] Local cooperation is now required by Article 42.1 to proceed based on the contract with local authorities regarding regional cooperation. The local cooperation agreement contract involves the following issues:

- Environmental protection
- Mine usage
- Mine-related infrastructure development
- Employment increase issue.

Article 43.1 now requires more Mongolian workforce for both the miner and its suppliers.

Article 47 specifies royalties on each kind of mineral. In Articles 47.1–47.3, the investor and government may negotiate how the owner may be substituted by royalties, which may not exceed 5% for the strategic deposit.

Based on the issues above, the investment contract in mining in current Mongolian legislation is now generally a broad document that may involve at least 10 major items (especially in the case of a large deposit):

- Equity ownership share
- Equity financing issues such as the interest rate, repayment schedule, other loans/credit/equity management issues
- Management contract
- Royalty issue if royalties are used for substitution for equity

[3] By definition, the sovereign debt issue will also be related to the general macroeconomic situation, debt ratings, and the possibility to raise additional funding not only for mining but also for general development or financing needs. The large equity share, however advantageous it may seem for the Government, may increase sovereign borrowing, which will increase sovereign debt. That may lead to lower ratings and potentially borrowing cost increase for all future debt. This may cripple the financial sovereign ability to mobilize funds necessary for general economic development by raising the sovereign bond interest rate on international markets.

[4] https://resourcegovernance.org/blog/it-takes-village-local-level-agreements-mongolia-mining-sector.

- Labor force and its structure
- Regional cooperation
- Environmental protection
- Mine usage issues
- Mine-related infrastructure development
- Employment increase issue
- 4 major taxation stability duration and others.

It is clear that with the rise of world commodity prices in the mid-2000s, the Mineral's Law was amended to reflect the new realities and have more benefits from mining. However, it turned out later that the law could not fully capture the national needs for large project management. Moreover, it omitted several crucial issues, which later became clear when a real large megaproject contract was concluded with Rio Tinto.

It can be viewed not as a weakness of the Mining law but rather an issue of the overall management of a large project, not necessarily a mining one. However, in Mongolia, there is a high probability that any large project will be based on mining. Therefore, it is an issue that has to be somehow settled from a legal point of view.

The mining contracts in Mongolia have thus grown from very simple contracts in the 1990s to broad agreements, which encompass various sectors, address various macroeconomic and national economic needs, relate to public finance and local development, contain labor market-related articles and significantly contribute to economic growth.

## 3 Ensuring a Positive Outcome on the Host Country: Crucial Issues, International Practices, and the Oyu Tolgoi Agreement Example

Major mining projects have an enormous impact not only on the economy but also on society and the environment. Additionally, as their operations can last for many years and the impacts mentioned above have lasting consequences, the concept of sustainable development should be reflected in project development planning and implementation. In other words, when the government and company start negotiations of a mining development project, both parties must establish the main objectives of the agreement, such as the growth of national and local economies, the reduction of poverty, and the minimization of the project's adverse effects on local communities and the environment.

Both the government and company are interested in a fair distribution of the project's benefits and enter into the negotiation stage with their calculations of possible benefits. A negotiation can be described as deciding how to divide the calculated benefits. The project carries benefits but may also significantly impact the host economy. These may include socioeconomic impacts at the macroeconomic

of product sales to support the local mining sector, accounting for a small portion of the economy. In contrast, in the agreement for the Qara-Zaghan gold mine in Afghanistan (2011), the royalty rate is significantly higher in the case of gold. The agreement states that the mining company will pay 26% of gross revenue to the Ministry of Mining every month since the start of production, and the reference price will be the price set at the London Metal Exchange the day the gold is sold.

In many resource-rich countries, such as Chile and Peru, a royalty based on profit, not sales value, is used to attract foreign direct investment. In Chile, the royalty rate is between 5 and 14%, depending on profit, while it is between 1 and 6.28% in Peru (Miyatake, 2018). The royalty is based on gross revenue in Laos and ranges from 1 to 7%, depending on the commodity type. The royalty rate declines in Australia as the processing level increases to support the refinery industry. For instance, in Western Australia, the royalty rates are 7.5% for crude ore sales, 5.0% for concentrate sales, and 2.5% for metals.

Another benefit from the mining project includes taxable income from corporate income tax (CIT) and other mining-specific taxes. Like other businesses, mining companies must also pay CIT. However, the CIT rate on mining projects has declined worldwide in recent years, currently standing between 25 and 35%. In Chile, for instance, the highest rate of CIT is 18.5%, while it is 20% in Kazakhstan and 25% in China and Indonesia. The federal tax rate is 15% in Canada, and the state tax ranges from 10 to 16%. The CIT rate is 28% in South Africa, 30% in Australia, Peru, Tanzania, 34% in Brazil, etc. (PwC, 2012). However, some countries offer a CIT rate reduction for companies until they fully cover their investment costs to stimulate the mining sector. In contrast, some countries impose a higher tax rate on windfall profit.

The taxable income of mining companies is the total net income of the business, less operating costs, royalties, import duties, prepaid costs, etc. To recover its initial investment in the project, the depreciation cost is deducted incrementally over several years. The calculation methods utilized when defining the depreciation rate, the number of years of the asset's useful life, and reducing the tax burden on mining companies in the earlier years of the project depend on the government's objective.

All businesses must use a constant depreciation rate for all assets in Australia. Nevertheless, an accelerated depreciation method (150%) is used for special promoting purposes for oil exploration and mining rehabilitation activities (Australian Tax Office, 2014). In Canada, an accelerated depreciation method (100%) is used for equipment, machinery, and buildings purchased before mine production or during significant expansion.

Another critical concern is the issue of loss carryforward. Mining projects usually have large losses in their initial years of production due to more investments and higher operating expenditures than income. Therefore, to allow the mining company to recover its current loss in the following years, tax laws will enable it to carry the current year's loss forward into the next year and deduct it from the following year's revenue. In Indonesia, for instance, the period limit is 5 years, while it goes up to 10 years in Kazakhstan, Mexico, and Russia (PwC, 2012). In addition, there is an unlimited carryforward period in some cases until the loss is fully offset (EITI, 2014).

A necessary type of tax relevant to mining projects is withholding tax. Withholding tax is a tax on the following costs of a mining company: interest payments to creditors, dividends to owners, service payments to service providers, and expenses to subcontractors. However, withholding taxes are limited by double tax treaties. The withholding tax rate is usually between 5 and 10% in most countries. For instance, in an agreement between the government of Liberia and China Union Ltd., the withholding tax rate is 0% for dividends, 5% for interest payments, and 5% for service payments (Government of Liberia, 2009).

In addition, the mining company pays taxes such as VAT, import duties, commodity export taxes, local taxes, land or license payments, and other fees. The negotiation process between the two parties determines whether those taxes are stabilized at the current rate, negotiated to different rates, or special tax exemptions are provided either fully or partially.

Finally, another common type of tax in oil and gas extraction contracts is resource rent tax and production sharing agreements. A company is responsible for all mining costs and risks in a production sharing agreement. The company is permitted to use the oil revenues in a given month to recover its investment and operating costs. The remaining money, dubbed "profit oil," is split between the government and the company as negotiated in the agreement. In contrast, a resource rent tax is imposed on "economic profit," far exceeding normal profit levels when resource prices soar. It is easy for tax agencies to collect taxes under production-sharing agreements, while it is difficult to collect taxes and resolve disputes when resource rent taxes are used (Guj, 2012). Mongolia uses the production sharing agreement for its oil.

In the investment agreement between the Government of Mongolia and the Oyu Tolgoi Investor (Rio Tinto), the following taxes were stabilized as they were in the tax codes and the mineral code at the time of signing the agreement:

- Royalty. The royalty rate is 5% of gross revenue, and the royalty will be deducted from taxable income (Article 3.13).
- Corporate income tax. If annual taxable income is up to MNT 3 billion, the tax rate will be 10%. When it is above MNT 3 billion, the investor shall be taxed MNT 300 million plus 25% of taxable income exceeding the threshold. If there is a loss, it will be carried forward in the following 8 years. For all assets with a useful life of more than one year, asset depreciation shall be calculated by the straight-line method and deducted from taxable income by the Law of Corporate Income Tax (Article 2.5, 2.12–2.14).
- VAT. Imported, manufactured, or sold goods, performed works, and rendered services shall be taxed at the rate of 10%. It will be deducted from the taxable income (Article 2.18).
- Customs duties. Imported goods shall be taxed at the rate of 5% of their value (Article 2.19).
- Withholding tax. The following income of nonresident taxpayers earned in Mongolia shall be taxed when transferred to the nonresident taxpayer from the investor at the rate of 20%: loan interest and payment for issuing a guarantee, income from royalty, income from interest on financial leases, payments

for administrative expenses or management services fee, rent payments, lease payments income from the use of tangible and nontangible assets (Article 2.8–2.9).
- Other taxes. Revenue from dividends, royalties, and interest shall be taxed at the rate of 10%, revenue from the disposal of immovable property shall be taxed at the rate of 2%, and revenue from the sale of rights shall be taxed at the rate of 30% (Article 2.7).

Between 2010 and 2020, the Oyu Tolgoi project paid $2760 million for state and local taxes. Table 2 shows paid taxes as stated in annual reports of Rio Tinto, a majority shareholder of the project. Before 2013, VAT and customs duties contributed more due to intensive investment of the first phase of the mine development. After that, CIT and royalty contributed more due to starting the open-pit mine production.

The royalty payment amount fluctuated due to commodity price changes, as discussed above. For instance, in 2014 and 2015, when the copper price was relatively high (~$6000 per ton), the royalty increased, but in 2016, when the price was lower than $5000, royalty decreased sharply. Finally, since 2017, when the price was recovered, the amount of royalty increased.

The tax rates stabilized in the investment agreement are basically in the range of the rates in other investment agreements and tax codes in resource-rich countries. However, most importantly, those tax rates were stabilized at the rate in tax codes that were effective at that time.

However, the double tax treaties to which Mongolia is a party have been questionable. In the agreement, it was agreed that loan interest and payment for issuing a guarantee, income from interest on financial leases, management service payments, and rent payments that a nonresident taxpayer in Mongolia earns should be taxed at 20% when transferred to the nonresident taxpayer. However, according to Article 2.2 of the General Taxation Law, if a tax rate in the double tax treaty Mongolia has entered is different from the rate in the investment agreement (2009), the rate in the double tax treaties will be applied. Consequently, the agreed tax rates could be lowered, and government revenue from the project could decrease. The government of Mongolia lost much revenue from the withholding tax due to its double tax treaty with the Netherlands, according to an article posted on the website of the Ministry of Finance (MoF, 2012). When the project makes a profit, Oyu Tolgoi LLC will transfer dividends to its affiliate, Oyu Tolgoi Netherland B.V. registered company at Netherland. The government of Mongolia will tax the transfer at 20%. However, according to the double tax agreement, the government of Mongolia will receive 0 tax from the dividend transfer. The rate of tax on the transfer of loan interest payments also has to be reduced from 20 to 10% due to the treaty. Thus, the government will receive only half of the expected withholding tax on interest payment transfer of the loan due to the treaty. Consequently, as estimated in a SOMO report, the government lost USD 232 million withholding tax revenue between 2011 and 2015 (Kiezebrink et al., 2018).

Provision related to the management service payment (IA (2009) Article 2.9, 2.25 and ARSHA (2011) 7.4) is another questionable issue. As stated in the agreement, the payment shall be paid quarterly. The payment rate shall be 3% of the total cost,

**Table 2** Taxes paid by Oyu Tolgoi, USD million

| Year | CIT | Royalty | Other tax, payment | Total national | Local fees and taxes | Employer payroll taxes | Other payments | Total local | Total |
|---|---|---|---|---|---|---|---|---|---|
| 2010 | 0 | 0 | 95 | 95 | 0 | 0 | 0 | 0 | 95 |
| 2011 | 0 | 0 | 366 | 366 | 0 | 6 | 10 | 16 | 382 |
| 2012 | 0 | 0 | 244 | 244 | 0 | 18 | 4 | 22 | 266 |
| 2013 | 0 | 4 | 175 | 179 | 0 | 20 | 21 | 41 | 220 |
| 2014 | 16 | 46 | 95 | 157 | 0 | 16 | 12 | 28 | 185 |
| 2015 | 66 | 111 | 74 | 251 | 9 | 13 | 5 | 27 | 278 |
| 2016 | 67 | 39 | 43 | 149 | 9 | 14 | 43 | 66 | 215 |
| 2017 | 0 | 54 | 76 | 130 | 8 | 16 | 74 | 98 | 228 |
| 2018 | 0 | 66 | 83 | 149 | 13 | 18 | 129 | 159 | 309 |
| 2019 | 1 | 71 | 80 | 152 | 14 | 21 | 119 | 153 | 305 |
| 2020 | 0 | 69 | 70 | 140 | 13 | 23 | 101 | 137 | 277 |
| Total | 150 | 460 | 1401 | 2012 | 66 | 165 | 518 | 747 | 2760 |

*Source* Rio Tinto—Taxes paid reports, 2010–2020

including investment and operation costs, until starting production; since then, it shall be 6% of the total cost. However, in the underground mine development and financing plan, the management service payments for underground mine development were separated.[6] As stated in the plan, the payment rate shall be 3% of the investment cost of an underground mine, and since the production of underground mines starts, the rate shall be 6% of the total cost. Although this change reduces the total project cost to some extent, the provision of management service payments is inherently a wrong incentive for managers to increase their earnings by rising project costs. Therefore, the provision that management service payments shall be 6% of the total cost, including sustaining capital costs, could lead to future disputes (Shafaie, 2015). The issue is currently being renegotiated.

## 3.2 *Equity and Financing Arrangements*

Another long-term benefit the government can receive is its ownership of a share in a project. In this case, the government can participate in the project's management, be represented on the board, and earn additional revenue via dividends. The public tends to expect more from ownership as they think that, in the case of shared ownership, the benefits from the project will notably increase while negative social and environmental impacts will be limited.

The practice of governments owning a share in mining projects has become more common, but the percentage of shares owned varies widely. For example, in 1953, Liberia agreed on the LAMCO iron ore mine, where in exchange for a 50% share in the project, the company does not pay any taxes. However, this agreement did not provide the government with the desired benefits and thus is no longer practiced in Liberia. In the Democratic Republic of Congo, since 2002, it became legal for the government to own a 5% stake in any mining project, while in Kenya, since 2012, the requirement has been a 35% stake in projects.

In the case of being a shareholder via free carry shares, the government must be responsible for a part of the investment costs proportional to its equity share. In most cases, the government does not have access to a readily available fund for the investment. In such cases, the shares and their financing responsibility can be transferred to the Development Bank, or the government can obtain a commercial loan from the company in exchange for future dividends.

However, equity ownership by the government leads to issues related to reaping the benefits from the project. In most cases, both sides have no right to sell their shares. In this case, the government cannot obtain capital gains by selling its shares. Most importantly, government participation in equity sharing usually leads to a disadvantageous situation.

[6] Oyu Tolgoi Underground Mine Development and Financing Plan (2015), Article 4.8.

Investors can use the government's share and future dividends as leverage against government actions. Especially in developing countries with unstable policy environments, the investment risk of the majority shareholder company is reduced significantly by letting the government own a minority share ranging from 21 to 40%. The government's measures on the environment, public health, wages, or social benefits can increase the project's costs and lower dividends received by the government. The government must then make a difficult choice between its revenue stream in the form of dividends and implementing vital measurements for the future sustainability of the economy. If, on the other hand, the government is not a shareholder in the project, making beneficial decisions for the overall society would be more straightforward and more accessible.

Even if the government were to become a shareholder, it has no real influence on board decisions that affect dividend payments due to its status as a minority shareholder. In terms of detailed project information and voting rights, the government will always be lacking compared to the majority shareholder company. If the investor decides not to distribute dividends this year, the board will invariably choose in favor of that decision. There is also a risk of reduced profits due to increasing costs caused by various measures, such as the company taking loans with a higher interest rate from its affiliated companies, providing loans with a lower interest rate to its affiliated companies, or selling its product to them at a lower price. Even when commodity prices increase, the right to cease or lessen distribution belongs to the company. In reality, not receiving or postponing dividends means that the government invested in the other side and reduced its benefits.

In general, an assessment of whether it is more beneficial for the government to take part in the ownership of the project should be based on a realistic cost–benefit analysis using a comprehensive financial model.

The Oyu Tolgoi is such a large project that needs USD 11 billion for Development Phase 1 and 2 and approximately USD 800 million for annual operations (and the cost is continuing to increase due to various problems, which has been a subject of negotiations as well). Therefore, several agreements among shareholders were made to arrange the project funding.

According to the agreement, the state owns 34% of Oyu Tolgoi LLC for the initial 30 years of the agreement, and the government may increase its share up to 50% after the extension of 20 years. This arrangement reflects the Minerals Law (2006), which gave the state a right up to 34% of strategically important deposits discovered by a private fund. Parliament Resolution #27 dated 6 February 2007 lists Oyu Tolgoi as one of 15 strategically important deposits. The state participation arrangement was also approved by Parliament Resolution #40 during the negotiation of the agreement in December 2008.

The government was provided a loan to invest its 34% mine share by the investor. However, as per the agreement, if the prices of gold and copper remain low for a more extended period, the government may not even receive any dividend before the project closure. The reason is that only after the principal and interest of the loan for its contribution in the funding period are entirely withheld from project profit by the investor will the dividend be distributed to the government. According to the

Amended and Restated Shareholders' Agreement (ARSHA), the annual interest rate of the government loan shall be calculated at the rate of 9.9% + US CPI for the loan before January 31, 2011. After that, the annual rate of interest shall be 6.5% plus LIBOR.

These equity and financing arrangements have significant impacts on the benefit to the government and are the most controversial issues of the agreement, which makes the financial calculation more complicated (IA 2009, Article 1.6; ARSHA 2011, Article 10–13).

This was partially related to a declining trend of interest rate international markets during that period. On the other hand, the interest rate agreed upon in the agreement was still higher than Rio Tinto's average corporate-level cost of borrowing (Open Oil, 2016). When the agreement was signed at the end of 2009, Rio Tinto's total net debt was USD 18.9 billion, finance cost was USD 1.1 billion, and the financial cost-to-debt ratio was 5.6%. Around that time, the annual interest rate of Rio Tinto's long-term bonds ranged from 5.75 to 7.25% (Rio Tinto, 2009). At the end of 2011, its debt was USD 8.5 billion, its finance cost was USD 0.7 billion, and the finance cost to debt ratio was 8.7%. Around that time, the annual interest rate of a corporation's long-term bonds ranged from 3.5 to 7.25% (Rio Tinto, 2011). The higher interest rate bearing by the Government of Mongolia could be related to the additional payment for the insurance of political risks (by Multilateral Investment Guarantee Agency of the World Bank) and other risks that were not covered by the guarantee. However, in late 2021, Rio Tinto offered to cancel the debt.

### *3.3 Local Purchases of Goods and Services*

Governments typically focus on taxes and dividends in mining contracts. However, mining companies' local purchasing of goods and services has a decisive impact on the economy and the country's sustainable development. As mining companies spend approximately 50% of their total spending on goods and services, a dynamic negotiation needs to be held between the host country and the investor (IISD, 2015). In particular, as mining companies purchase local goods and services, the quality and capacity of goods and services of the local companies will be boosted, which promotes the technical, marketing skills, and competitiveness of businesses. Additionally, the government tax income, employment, and livelihood of citizens can improve. Reducing dependence on mining is an important aspect of developing countries that tend to be highly dependent on mining. Developing countries can use local purchasing to reduce dependence on mining by expanding domestic production and services and improving competitiveness.

However, domestic companies need to become more skilled in supplying products and services to multinational companies to fulfill conditions for becoming a supplier. On the other hand, multinational companies sometimes provide preferential treatment to the host country's companies. For example, in Liberia, when purchasing goods and services related to the operation, the mining company and its principal contractor have to provide Liberian citizens, foreign citizens who live in Liberia, and Liberian companies an advantage that evenses the playing field for producing goods and services of the same quality, price, delivery conditions and quantity as that of imports.[7] In Guinea, the contract on the purchase of goods and services such as transportation, insurance, construction, and procurement contracts should provide advantages to local producers when domestic producers' price, quantity, and quality of delivery are in line with foreign producers' price, quantity, and quality of delivery.[8] In Afghanistan, if the domestic producers' price, quality, and delivery terms align with foreign producers', the mining company and its contractors should provide an advantage to the domestic producers.[9]

The Oyu Tolgoi Investment Agreement does not contain detailed provisions for purchasing goods and services for local sources. However, the agreement includes two articles that implicitly aim to boost the local purchase of goods and services. It also includes measures to support numerous programs aimed at assisting local enterprises that supply goods and provide services to the Oyu Tolgoi project (Article 2.23, 4.12). In addition, the investor must pay the relevant taxes as defined by Mongolian law on both the domestic and imported goods it purchases. As a result, imported products no longer have a price advantage over domestic goods, and there is a positive impact on domestic purchases.

Although local goods and services were not explicitly mentioned in the Oyu Tolgoi Investment Agreement, company reports show that 80–85% of total purchases[10] were bought from domestic suppliers, including national suppliers that owned Mongolian citizens and foreign suppliers that registered in Mongolia. For instance, in the first three quarters of 2021, 87% of all purchased services and goods were supplied domestically, such as 75% from national suppliers and 13% from foreign suppliers, registered in Mongolia and pay taxes (Table 3). In addition, in the first three quarters of 2021, while fuel, construction, and production consumables work was fully supplied by domestic suppliers, 99, 90, and 74% of transportation, production supplies, and

[7] Mineral Development Agreement between the Government of the Republic of Liberia, China-Union (Hong Kong) Mining Co., Ltd. and China-Union Investment (Liberia) Bong Mines Co., Ltd, 2009; Iron Ore Appraisal and Exploration Agreement for the Putu Range between the Republic of Liberia and Mano River Iron Ore Ltd, 2005; Mineral Development Agreement the Government of the Republic Liberia, Putu Iron Ore Mining, Inc, and Mano River Iron Ore Ltd, 2010; Mineral Development Agreement between the Government of Liberia and Western Cluster Limited, Sesa Goa Limited, Bloom Fountain Limited, Elenilto Minerals & Mining LLC, 2011; Amended Mineral Development Agreement between the Government of the Republic of Liberia and Mittal Steel Holding A.G and Mittal Steel Holdings Ltd, 2006; Exploration Agreement between the Government of the Republic of Liberia and African Aura Resources Limited, 2004.

[8] Convention de Base Entre La Republique de Guinee et BSG Resources, 2009; Convention de Base Entre La Republique de Guinee at Alliance Mining Commodities, 2010; Convention de Base Entre La Republique de Guinee et Simfer SA La Societe Pour L'Exploitation des Gisements de fer de Simandou, 2002.

[9] Qara Zaghan Gold Project Contract between Krystal Natural Resources Company and the Ministry of Mines of the Islamic Republic of Afghanistan (2011).

[10] Procurement of underground mining is not included.

**Table 3** Domestic procurement in the first three quarters of 2021, the share of total spending and million USD

| | National supplier | | Foreign supplier[12] | |
|---|---|---|---|---|
| | Spend (%) | Spend mln.$ | Spend (%) | Spend mln.$ |
| Construction | 100 | 6.8 | 0 | 0 |
| Fuel and lubricants | 100 | 41.7 | 0 | 0 |
| Fixed plants and equipment | 74 | 26.7 | 26 | 14.5 |
| Logistics | 99 | 14.8 | 1 | 0.3 |
| Mobile equipment | 77 | 62.2 | 23 | 19.3 |
| Repairs and consumables | 90 | 35.4 | 10 | 4.7 |
| Production consumables | 100 | 27.7 | 0 | 0 |
| Services | 89 | 100.5 | 11 | 14.7 |
| Total | 87 | 315.8 | 13 | 53.5 |

*Source* Purchase data of Oyu Tolgoi (www.ot.mn)

production equipment purchases, respectively, were given domestically.[11] Generally, the Oyu Tolgoi project has been instrumental in raising the standards of Mongolian suppliers and providing them with a large market for their goods and services.

## 3.4 *Infrastructure Development*

Mining operations require infrastructures such as water, electricity, information, communication, and transport. Therefore, the cost of infrastructure accounts for approximately 40–80% of the cost of mining development (EITI, 2014). Mining infrastructure bolsters economic activity and promotes the development of the country. The infrastructure of a developing country is limited in quality and capacity. When a new mine is being built and infrastructure is being constructed, it provides beneficial opportunities for the country. Thus, if the government manages the issues and plans, the economy can greatly benefit from these infrastructures. In establishing an investment agreement, the government needs to consider the following issues and answer the following questions (IISD, 2015):

- Identify what infrastructures are needed: roads, ports, railroads, energy, telecommunication, and water management.
- Who will be responsible for setting up the infrastructure?
- Who will pay for the infrastructure?
- Who will use the infrastructure?
- An environmental and social impact assessment must be completed.

[11] http://ot.mn/procurement/procurement-in-numbers/.

[12] Organizations, registered in Mongolia and pay taxes.

One of the most important considerations is the user of the mining infrastructure. The shared usage of infrastructure creates profitable conditions in an economy. Therefore, the government needs to carefully make an agreement. There are two types of shared usage of infrastructure (EITI, 2014):

- Several mining companies use common infrastructure objects.
- Mining companies share the infrastructure with the government and third parties.

If the government can make an investment agreement precisely based on research, all types of shared usage are profitable in the domestic economy provided that the relevant parties have open access rights. In most cases, the investor prefers nonshared infrastructure usage if they are the sole financier of the mining infrastructure. In that case, the shared use of infrastructure has significant costs caused by the overspill of capacity and cost of coordination. On the other hand, if the government and/or a third party owns the infrastructure, the usage of infrastructure on mining companies will be limited. As a result, the efficiency of the mining project will be limited. However, agreeing on shared use is relatively easy (EITI, 2014).

In the investment agreement, extensive planning and research are needed to make decisions about the shared use of infrastructure. For each mining project, the required infrastructure is different. The necessary infrastructure depends on the size of the project, the type of commodity, demand for infrastructure, nonmining demand for infrastructure, and the regulatory capacity available to ensure open access to mining-related infrastructure (EITI, 2014).

The standard agreement regarding the use of government and third-party infrastructure is Liberia-Putu (Government of Liberia, 2010). Within the agreement, the shared usage of every infrastructure is clearly outlined. The power plant built by investors supplies the necessary power to the mining project. If there is excess capacity in electricity, investors may supply electricity to third-party users located within a 10 km radius. If the company uses the surrounding communities' water sources, the company is obliged to set up other sources of drinking water for the population affected. The government and third parties may use the port and the railway within a certain parameter of conditions. If additional capacity is needed, the government and third parties must finance the infrastructure needed.

The most common examples of shared usage of mining infrastructure are observed in Australia. There are two polar cases of shared use of infrastructure. One case was in the Pilbara region of Western Australia. Several iron ore bulk mining companies constructed their rails and ports due to an inability to negotiate shared usage of mining infrastructure. The other case was in the Queensland state of Australia, which was coordinated by Aurizon, the largest Australian rail freight operator. Unlike the first, the second case is an example of efficient shared usage of mining infrastructure, which was challenging and costly.

While the subject of infrastructure was reflected in a relatively flexible manner in the Oyu Tolgoi Investment Agreement, many of the issues surrounding infrastructure were incorporated in an unclear and broad manner in the agreement. Mongolia's Long-term National Comprehensive Development Strategy (2008), approved in Parliament before the agreement, called for regional infrastructure to be funded by investors in strategic deposits. Accordingly, in the 2009 Oyu Tolgoi Investment Agreement, the investor is expected to utilize its own capital to construct any necessary infrastructure that is not readily available. The investor also has the option to couse the infrastructure with either the public, the government, or any third party for a fee so long as it does not negatively impact the project's activities.

The investor has the duty to work and confer with the government when making decisions involving roads, railways, and power infrastructure projects so that any decisions will be in line with the government's long-term development plans. The investor has an obligation to obtain any necessary licenses and pay any relevant taxes when implementing infrastructure projects. If the investor chooses to utilize domestically available infrastructure, under the principle of nondiscrimination, the investor is expected to pay market prices for any goods or services it receives. Compared to international model contracts, the Oyu Tolgoi Investment Agreement does not detail specific obligations concerning cousing infrastructure, simply mentioning it as a possible alternative. As the shared use of infrastructure is not clearly defined, the possibilities to reap the benefits of better infrastructure are limited (IA chapter 7).

The investor may provide the public, government, and third parties access to certain infrastructure and services, such as roads, power, water/heating systems, water drawing facilities, etc., as long as it does not interfere with the project's operations. The agreement may also transfer these infrastructures and services ownership and/or governance to the local communities and authorities. For roads constructed between the mining site and the Gashuunsukhait border, the government will be responsible for the timely maintenance of the road and charging and collecting road user fees from all users except the investors, its affiliates, and respective contractors and subcontractors (IA chapter 7).

In terms of implementation, while the water supply network and construction of the airport have been realized, issues surrounding roads, electrical power, and railways have yet to be resolved. This is partly due to Mongolia's political instability and weaknesses in policy continuity.

The Oyu Tolgoi project utilizes water from aquifers, and to shift away from using groundwater, a water purification plant was constructed. In 2020, this plant purified 87.7% of all water used for the project, which was then reused for further production. While the water purification plant is used exclusively by Oyu Tolgoi, to supply drinking water to the local population, the investors established a clean water complex in Khanbogd district. This complex has the capacity to supply clean water to 13,000 people (Turquoise Hill, 2018).

According to the agreement, the investor can use domestic and foreign electrical power sources within 4 years. However, after 4 years of beginning production, the investor has an obligation to use domestic energy sources for power production. In 2012, a 96 km 220 kW electricity transmission line from Oyu Tolgoi to the Chinese border was constructed to be the main power line.[13] Ownership of this transmission line was then transferred to the GoM along with related maintenance responsibilities.

[13] http://ot.mn/news-20151019-en/.

As a result, residents of the southern region of Mongolia have the opportunity to be connected to a stable electricity provider.

The GoM and Oyu Tolgoi investors signed the "Southern Region Power Sector Cooperation Agreement" in 2014. According to this agreement, the GoM would establish the Tavan Tolgoi power plant, which would then be used as a domestic power source by Oyu Tolgoi. Had the Tavan Tolgoi power plant been constructed according to plan, Oyu Tolgoi would have entirely shifted to a domestic power source by 2017. However, as the agreement was not implemented, Oyu Tolgoi has yet to find a domestic power provider.

Investors also develop local infrastructure based on the LLA with the regional government. It includes various local projects and is implemented according to the local agreement with Umnugobi province and neighboring soums under the umbrella of a specialized local development fund, set up by Rio Tinto according to law.

Therefore, the approach to developing regional infrastructure is based on the concept outlined in the Comprehensive National Development Strategy 2008. The main infrastructure objects, such as roads, power stations, and other related projects, are financed mainly by investors or built on private–public partnerships.

## *3.5 Maximization of Employment Opportunities*

Mining can also be used to increase the employment and livelihood of citizens. Of the total operational cost of an average mining company, 16% is related to employment. The government receives a number of benefits in the form of mining taxes, royalties, and dividends, which in turn can have a positive influence on the economy. High rates of employment of locals in the mining company can increase the benefits received by the economy from the mining projects.

The requirement of the mining company is significantly greater than the availability and capacity of skilled laborers in the host country. With the development and acquisition of the necessary skillsets, the domestic labor market will experience an influx of skilled workers. The increase in the labor market's skills and productivity will positively contribute to their wages, which translates to an improvement in the income and livelihood of the host country's citizens. For these reasons, the government should take the necessary measures to improve citizens' knowledge of advanced technologies and professional skills desired in the mining sector.

Within the investment agreement about employment, the government should be mindful of the following aspects:

- How big the mine will be in the future and during operations.
- For every operational position, how many and what types of roles are needs/unskilled, skilled, management, professional/.
- Whether the country's capabilities of workers are in line with the requirement of investors.

- What types of skill development can be done by the mining company and government?

Using these points as guides, the government should clearly define the level of employment of citizens in the company, the employment conditions and training that will be implemented, and investment in the host country's education system in the investment agreement.

For example, in Liberia, the company and any other contractor do not have to hire individuals who are not citizens of Liberia for unskilled labor positions. Furthermore, the country's citizens must work in financial, accounting, technical, administrative, supervisory, managerial, executive, and other skilled positions. If workers' skill is not enough to perform these positions, the company should train citizens to work in these positions. In addition, in the first five years of operation, at least 30% of the management position and in the next 10 years, 70% of the management position must be staffed by domestic citizens. Furthermore, until the award of mining license, the company shall provide USD 100,000–200,000 of education funding to students who study mining engineering in foreign and local universities. After the grant of the mining license, the company has to increase the total annual contribution to USD 250,000–500,000. Furthermore, the company shall contribute a scientific research fund of USD 100,000 USD.

In Guinea, the mining company must compose 90–95% of the total workforce from domestic workers within the five years since mining production. Therefore, the company does not have to hire individuals who are not citizens of Guinea for unskilled labor positions. However, if citizens' skill is enough to work in a skilled position, the company must hire these citizens for a skilled position. Additionally, the company should organize training for citizens of Guinea to work in skilled jobs.

Compared to international model contracts, the Oyu Tolgoi Investment Agreement contains relatively detailed articles on maximizing employment opportunities. Significant articles/provisions of the agreement compared to international model contracts:

- The investor must ensure that at least 90% of the project's workforce comprises Mongolian citizens. The investing company is also encouraged to work with its partners to ensure that at least 60% of its partner construction company and 75% of its partner mining company's workforce are Mongolian. The agreement included provisions on employment for partner companies in addition to the investor company. However, the agreement is unclear about how to evaluate the efforts of the investor company to encourage employment requirements among its partner companies.
- If the share of foreign workers is above the prescribed threshold of 10%, for every position, the investor company is obligated to pay a fine equivalent to 10 times the minimum wage every month. Additionally, the investor must also pay a monthly fee amounting to two times the minimum wage for each foreign employee. This fee is added to the Employment Support Fund, which is then used to train and

increase the working capacity of Mongolian citizens. This article acts as a strong incentive to look toward the domestic market for employment prospects.

- The investor is also required to do everything in its power to ensure that after 5 years of production, at least 50% of the engineers and technical workers employed are Mongolian. This share then increases to 70% within 10 years of beginning production. However, this provision has the disadvantage of disregarding other job positions such as finance, governance, quality control, and other management-level positions. Additionally, no concrete method to measure and evaluate the investor's efforts in fulfilling employment requirements is reflected in the agreement.
- Within 90 days of the agreement coming into effect, the investor must provide and introduce a detailed 5-year training strategy and plan for its Mongolian employees to the Government of Mongolia. While many international contracts include general articles on training the domestic workforce, the Oyu Tolgoi Investment Agreement has the benefit of requiring a detailed plan and training the workforce according to the outlined plan.
- Over 6 years, the investor must provide 120 scholarships to university students pursuing mining engineering and technical studies. They must also offer scholarships to 30 Mongolian students studying at universities abroad. Relative to international contracts, in which investors usually have to provide scholarships during the entirety of the project's lifespan, a timeline of 6 years is short in comparison.

In the case of the Oyu Tolgoi Investment Agreement, as of 2020, 95.4% of Oyu Tolgoi's employees are Mongolian citizens. According to the agreement, Oyu Tolgoi has also provided domestic and international scholarships from 2010–2015. From 2016 onward, the company decided to continue the scholarship program out of its own volition. Since beginning in 2010, the company has provided scholarships to 432 university students. In general, the agreement has been vital in modernizing technical education and providing stable, permanent employment for many Mongolian citizens. It has also been crucial in transferring modern mining technology and know-how to Mongolian universities.

### *3.6 Community Engagement*

Community engagement plays a crucial role in the long-term success of mining projects. A major part of a successful project and engagement with the community is ensuring that interests are clearly communicated before and during the negotiations. Poor community relations may promote distrust and averseness, which may result in resistance or cause conflicts to arise.

There were many obstacles when consultants from Adastra Minerals initiated public engagement in relation to the Kolwezi Tailings Project in the Democratic Republic of Congo. In addition to the local officials, most of the potentially affected community members did not speak the national language of French, and literary rates

visual aids, and translating to ensure that everyone could participate in the negotiation. In return, the traditional owners provided the company with information about their customs and even performed ceremonies to ensure that the mining operation would be conducted safely and free from interruption from ancestral spirits.[17]

One way to encourage gender equality in mining is to ensure that women are heard during community consultations. However, in most instances, the only way the women's opinions in the community are listened to is through women-only sessions. Thus, unless a company takes special measures to include women in the conversation, they are usually left on the sidelines. In 2012, the Chilean government issued a national standard on "Gender equality and reconciliation of professional, family, and personal life," which Codelco adopted to guide its approach to promoting gender equality and an inclusive workplace.[18] As a result, Codelco's commitment to promoting gender equality has steadily increased female representation in its workforce over the past few years.

There are no mentions of a formal or special program designed specifically for women within the Oyu Tolgoi investment agreement. First, a Community Advisory Group was established to open communication channels between the investor, Rio Tinto, and the community; only men were elected as members. Then, Rio Tinto began a formal program of consultation to gather feedback from the women in the community. The engagement of the community's women greatly expanded the dialog to address topics not discussed by the men. For example, while the men talked more about the significant spiritual areas and the grass, the women voiced concerns about vegetation, seasonal migrations, and shelters in greater detail than the men. Community mapping was significantly improved with the information gathered from both men and women. In Oyu Tolgoi's annual report-2019, it was mentioned that the workforce—including contractors and employees—stood at over 93% Mongolian and 35% female, including the underground development workforce.

Especially in developing countries, mining-induced displacement and resettlement pose a major risk to societal sustainability.[19] There is a wide range of good practice policies, standards, and guidance for land access and resettlement by reputable institutions, such as the International Finance Corporation (IFC)'s Sustainability Framework, the European Bank for Reconstruction and Development's Environmental and Social policy, and the World Bank policy in relation to projects not in the private sector pertaining to involuntary resettlement.

Glencore company followed the IFC's Performance Standard 5 during the resettlement of three communities near its Calenturitas coal mine in Colombia.[20] They

[17] The Manthe ceremony is regularly conducted on the employees, contractors, and visitors to welcome them and to ensure they are safe while on the Argyle site.

[18] ICMM's promoting gender diversity in Chile.

[19] One of the commonly used models for organizing the risk patterns of MIDR is the Impoverishment Risk and Rehabilitation Model developed by Michael Cernea and his team at the World Bank. These risks include joblessness, homelessness, marginalization, food insecurity, loss of common lands and resources, increased health risks, social disarticulation, loss of civil and human rights and the disruption of formal educational activities and loss of access to basic public services.

[20] Case study excerpt from ICMM's Land Acquisition and Resettlement.

implemented three different planning processes in which communities were actively engaged. This participative approach included a comprehensive census, socioeconomic surveys, and asset inventories. In addition, Glencore continued to provide training in agricultural skills to enable the communities to support themselves following the resettlement. This was in response to the communities' request and open communication between the two parties.

In the Oyu Tolgoi Investment Agreement, Chapters 5 and 6 address land affairs. Under the agreements, land use for the Oyu Tolgoi projects shall be obtained through relevant permits under the laws and regulations on land. The government may take land that is in the investor's possession if the land is for special needs or public purposes that cannot be reasonably satisfied by land, not in the contract area. However, in exchange, the government must cooperate with the investor to minimize the impact on the Oyu Tolgoi project and provide compensation based on the laws and regulations of Mongolia, international laws and principles, and international treaties.

Article 10 of Chapter 4 states that the investor must consult with local administrative organizations to provide appropriate compensation for resettlement to the herder families located in the contract area who are directly impacted by the Oyu Tolgoi project. Before privatizing land, the soum would track which herder families used which areas for pasture by season and authorized those families to use those areas. The Oyu Tolgoi contract area is 10 km × 10 km, which overlays traditional pasture and water sources of a group of 11 herder families who were involuntarily resettled in 2004. One aspect of the relocation and site selection that is often overlooked is that the herders, prior to 2004, were using the best sites that the region had to offer so that any alternative location would be inferior.

According to a 2011 Oyu Tolgoi site visit report filed by USAID, several herder families have moved back to their original sites as their livestock either went back to their original pasture on their own or herder took them back because of better pastures, housing, and water conditions. Out of the families that were initially resettled, four or five have continued herding, while the remaining have stopped.

Some of the actions numerous companies take include minimizing water losses during processing while maximizing water recycling, reducing evaporative losses in hot and dry areas, reducing water usage across mining operations in areas of water stress,[21] and investing in the treatment of contaminated water supplies.

BHP Billiton's Olympic Dam in South Australia is the world's fourth-largest copper and gold resource. All the water used at the Olympic Dam is sourced from the Great Artesian Basin (GAB).[22] BHP Billiton operates a water savings project to reduce the volume of water used at the Olympic Dam site. The project was developed to reduce the consumption of GAB water by optimizing water recovery and recycling and substituting poor-quality local groundwater in some areas. Teams at BHP Billiton, Olympic Dam, and the Australian government continue to identify

[21] Water stress occurs when the water demand exceeds the available amount during a certain n period or when poor quality restricts its use.

[22] Case study excerpt from ICCM's Water Management in Mining.

opportunities to minimize water use to contribute to the sustainability of the GAB and future generations.

According to the Oyu Tolgoi Investment Agreement, the company shall apply modern technology and procedures to minimize the volume of water used by the Oyu Tolgoi project, maximize the efficiency of water usage, and recycle used water where it is reasonably practicable to do so. During the third quarter of 2021, the average water recycling rate was 87%. However, the annual water use of Oyu Tolgoi will likely increase as the project ramps up, and underground production commences. According to a 2014 ADB report, Oyu Tolgoi's projected annual water use is estimated to be 9.5 million cubic meters in 2015 and 25.5 million cubic meters in 2025.

If Oyu Tolgoi chooses to access and use self-discovered water resources, it has the right to be within the approved volume and is in line with its Water Approval. Excess water resources may be available for other economic entities or household purposes, herder families, and agricultural activities of the local soum communities. Oyu Tolgoi must also pay fees to the state budget for surface and underground water removed and consumed for mine development and mining of minerals at the rate specified in the Law on Fees for the Use of Water and Mineral Water.

According to the Water Law, a separate contract with Oyu Tolgoi on water utilization is for a period of 30 years, as the Oyu Tolgoi Deposit is classified as a mineral deposit of strategic importance and may be extended by 20 years each time. The obligations that must be followed in regard to water utilization are as follows:

- Abide all conditions and requirements outlined in Article 24 of the Water Law, the contract on water utilization, and the EIA Reports and compliance
- Not reduce from the current level the quality and quantity of the existing potable and livestock water supplies used by existing users at the date of agreement within the water resource areas defined in the EIA reports.

Generally, Oyu Tolgoi's case shows the importance of managing environmental issues with local and national governments. While projects of such a large scale rarely proceed without any environmental issues, in this case, the most discussed issues were not those of the environment and were mostly related to equity financing, taxes, and payments.

## 4 Recommendations for a Sample Mining Developing Contract for Mongolia

### *4.1 General Issues*

The issue of successfully contracting large projects has recently been well covered in studies (Scott & Levitt, 2017). In addition, IFIs and other organizations have tried to help developing countries develop the most beneficial contracts and have published guidebooks and other materials, which may be helpful to negotiators. However, developing countries often lack adequate legal and human resources to estimate and conclude such contracts, so developing countries must utilize international best practices.

The international experience of such large projects calls for many specific items in the contract as a prerequisite for a successful mega project.

The first item is the issue of the area of the project and the size. The megaproject is defined as a project of USD 0.5–1 billion, which requires substantial sectoral coordination (or spills to different sectors), requires 3–5 years of construction, and involves 30–50 years of exploitation. It may also have several stakeholders with varying and sometimes conflicting interests. These projects were led by international IFIs such as the World Bank in 1950–2000, which led to the successful management and implementation of several large projects in developing countries. However, due to financial limitations, the rise of public–private partnerships, and a shift in thinking toward the Washington consensus, international financial organizations rarely directly participate in such massive public projects. In that case, Mongolia's mining sector and the Oyu Tolgoi project are good examples of the new approach, where the investors are private, and the project itself is essentially a public–private partnership with fixed equity participation.

A mega project involves many stakeholders, including the local and regional economies. It is essentially also an ecosystem of main project drivers and suppliers.

The ecosystem may benefit the local economy well, but the process should be coordinated and have a solid foundation. A possible approach is to have an Integrated Project Delivery (IPD) draft contract. All stakeholders, including local suppliers, develop an integrated form of agreement (IFOA) before the project commences to agree on significant project features. Early project stakeholders' participation in the planning stages is welcomed, and sides may also make nonbinding promises not necessarily included in the final contract.

## *4.2 Mongolia's Case*

In Mongolia's case, it is apparent that the country was less prepared to face the issue of contracting large strategic mines. A 2004 study by the World Bank, "Mongolia's Mining Sector: Managing the Future," recommended options for government actions to improve the mining industry's management and investment climate. However, the recommendations did not provide insight into how to conclude an investment or stability agreement with investors or address the issues arising from contracts of large projects.

Consequently, until 2006, there was little need to deal with the issue of equity financing of large megaprojects because there were no such megaprojects or proposals. However, the National Comprehensive Development Strategy, ratified in 2008, called for large mining deposits as economic growth engines. It was developed parallel with the 2007 Parliament resolution on designating 15 large mining deposits as strategic mines. Therefore, by 2009, there was an actual contract (with Rio Tinto) to sign and to lead the first contemporary national megaproject in mining to development. Therefore, in a way, the National Comprehensive Development Strategy[23] 2008 successfully prepared foundations for launching the Oyu Tolgoi agreement as a first mover in leading economic development. It shows the importance of a national development strategy, which, if approved, creates foundations and public consensus for particular investments and deals.

As described in the NCDS, large mining projects have also been designated to become national growth drivers and finance significant investments in infrastructure—roads, energy, water usage, housing, urban development, and transportation. This is, in particular, valid for Mongolia because in its development strategies beginning from the 2008 National Comprehensive Development Strategy, the country designates large mining deposits as an engine of economic growth and hubs for local and regional development, including infrastructure and urban development. Oyu Tolgoi and later Tavan Tolgoi (another giant coal mine) contributed significantly to local infrastructure development.

The infrastructure projects accompanying the primary mine become independent projects, even though they are linked to the mining project's main driver. These investments are not mining projects and, therefore, may be subject to less favorable tax treatment, and their mounting costs can ultimately make the main project itself uncompetitive. This leads to confusion regarding such large projects' ecosystem building. In some cases, large projects designed to accompany the major mine, such as the Tavan Tolgoi power plant project, stalled because of uncertainty regarding the major mine project.

Many infrastructure projects, connected to the main Oyu Tolgoi and Tavan Tolgoi projects, led to the necessity of developing better legal infrastructure regarding big projects in general, not necessarily only mining projects. Thus, by 2010 Mongolia had to approve a new law on Concessions (or Public–Private Partnership) and by 2013 to approve Investment Law (to regulate heavy industry taxation). Furthermore, by 2011, Mongolia approved the Development Bank law to finance the development of large projects and to raise necessary financing. By 2011, to manage the increasing revenue flow to the budget from mining, the country adopted the Fiscal Stability Law and created its first stabilization fund. By 2015, a unified law managing the national sovereign borrowing system was also developed. To coordinate the various megaprojects, by 2015, Mongolia adopted the law on development planning. By 2016, financing from the Development Bank and concession projects were included in the unified national budget, allowing for better management of sovereign resources.

Therefore, one can conclude that contracting the first megaproject spurred the related development of large infrastructure projects and led to further development of the necessary legal infrastructure and new laws on PPP and foreign borrowing,

[23] Developed by the Government of Mongolia in 2006–2008, the National Comprehensive Development Strategy for Millennium Development Goals was ratified by the Parliament in 2008. Its first stage was 2008–2015 in accordance with the UN's Millennium Development Goals which were planned for 2000–2015 period. The NCDS was replaced in 2015 by the Long-Term Sustainable Development Policy 2030, ratified by the Parliament in 2015.

developed national planning, and further improved the national financial system, making it more suited to financing economic development.

The increasing complexity of investment agreements shows the sheer size of legal changes and the necessity to reflect various new requirements in contracts. The more complex projects become, the higher the need to regulate the ever-growing number of related issues.

As the country plans to undertake new megaprojects, the complexity of related investment agreements may require improvements to the current national planning, coordination, and financing of such projects. For example, to undertake large complex projects, Mongolia may need some case of umbrella project law, which will allow having unified business and taxation treatment to various parts of a single megaproject. In Mongolia's case, there may be a need to look at the megaprojects and their surrounding projects as a whole and apply the favorable treatment to the whole group, rather than taking each one independently, which itself will fall under the jurisdiction of completely different laws such as Concession Law or Investment law and in each case, require additional bureaucratic procedures, prolonging the main project's completion time and increasing costs. In any way, the coordination of such megaprojects became so urgent that in January 2022, the country created the Economic Development Ministry to manage these megaprojects.

This unified approach, however, will require substantial changes in existing laws. Meanwhile, under the current legal regime, Mongolia still has few large deposits of mineral resources to develop. The 2007 Parliament resolution designated 15 large projects as of strategic importance and prepared a list of 40 projects as reserves. To date, only one, the Oyu Tolgoi project, has been contracted. In contrast, Tsagaan Suvarga has avoided contracting.

Moreover, the Parliament did not review a contract draft of The Tavan Tolgoi coking coal project and rejected it at the draft contract analysis stage. From that point of view, Oyu Tolgoi is also the only agreement that both the government and investors successfully ratified. Thus, it is valuable as an example of a megaproject implemented, making it a possible template for future contracts.

The Oyu Tolgoi project, despite all its shortcomings, created a blooming supplier ecosystem and thus far significantly contributed to local development and macroeconomic growth. Based on the Oyu Tolgoi agreement, the country is continuing to learn best international practices for contracting large multinational companies in domestic mines while also learning to define its own development goals to be put in the legal, contractual obligations, such as the development of local suppliers, required number of jobs and coordination of related infrastructure projects.

Based on these issues, one can say that a mining contract, which addresses well the major problems in mining contracting mentioned and regulates the financing issues well based on well-managed local cooperation, environmental protection, and a growing number of local suppliers, may be most beneficial for both sides. For Mongolia, in just 30 years, starting from a minuscule number of foreign companies operating in its garments industry in the 1990s, the country is now hosting an FDI project with capital expenditures, equal to its annual GDP and learning to cooperate with multinationals, work with world's largest banks and trade on a global scale, while also developing and modernizing its legal environment, human resources, and infrastructure—which is remarkable progress for a relatively short time, during which the country's GDP grew from about1 billion USD in 2003 to nearly 14 billion USD dollars in 2020.

## References


ADB. (1992). *Mongolia: A centrally planned economy in transition*. Asian Development.

Australian Tax Office. (2014). *Guide to depreciating assets*. Australian Tax Office.

EITI. (2014). *Mining contracts: How to read and understand them*. Extractive Industry's Transparency Initiative.

EITI Mongolia. (2020, November 15). *EITI Mongolia E-reporting system—Report*. EITI Mongolia E-reporting system: http://ereporting.eitimongolia.mn/-ээсГаргасан

Government of Liberia. (2009). *Mineral Development Agreement between the Government of the Republic of Liberia*, China-Union (Hong Kong) Mining Co., Ltd. China-Union Investment (Liberia) Bong Mines Co., Ltd. www.resourcecontracts.org

Government of Liberia. (2010). *Mineral Development Agreement the Government of the Republic Liberia*. Putu Iron Ore Mining, Inc., Mano River Iron Ore Ltd. www.resourcecontracts.org

Guj, P. (2012). *Mineral royalties and other mining-specific taxes*. I. M. Centre-Д, Mining for Development: Guide to Australian Practice. International Mining for Development Centre.

ICCM. (2017). *Indigenous peoples and mining and Rio Tinto's Argyle diamond mine sustainable development report*. ICCM.

IISD. (2015). *IISD handbook on mining contract negotiations for developing countries: Volume 1 prepare for success*. International Institute for Sustainable Development.

Kiezebrink, V., Ahlers, R., & Dugersuren, S. (2018). *Mining taxes: The case of Oyu Tolgoi and profitable tax avoidance by Rio Tinto in Mongolia*. SOMO and OT Watch.

Miyatake, S. (2018, April). *Review of the legal/fiscal framework of resource countries*. Presentation at workshop. JOGMEG.

MoF. (2012, May 31). *Rationale, comment and explanation on canceling double tax treaties* (in Mongolian). Ministry of Finance. www.iltod.gov.mn

MoM Afghanistan. (2011). *Qara Zaghan gold project contract between Afghan Krystal Natural Resources Company and Ministry of Mines of the Islamic Republic of Afghanistan*. www.resourcecontracts.org

Open Oil. (2016). Oyu Tolgoi Financial Model: Narrative Report. Open Oil.

PwC. (2012). *Corporate income taxes, mining royalties and other mining taxes*. PwC.

Rio Tinto. (2009). *Annual report*. Rio Tinto.

Rio Tinto. (2011). *Annual report*. Rio Tinto.

Scott, W. R., & Levitt, R. E. (2017). *Institutional challenges and solutions for global megaprojects*. E. B. Flyvbjerg-Д, The Oxford Handbook of Megaproject Management. Oxford University Press.

Shafaie, A. (2015, July 30). *Rio Tinto, Mongolia, and the art of negotiating Amidst Price Volatility*. Resource Governance. www.resourcegovernance.org/blog/rio-tinto-mongolia-and-art-negotiating-amidst-price-volatility

Turquoise Hill. (2016). *2016 Oyu Tolgoi technical report*. Ore Win.

Turquoise Hill. (2018). *Made by Mongolia, annual report 2017*. Turquoise Hill Resources Ltd.

World Bank. (2003). *Mongolia mining sector: Managing the future*. World Bank.

**Khashchuluun Chuluundorj** is an associate professor of economics at the National University of Mongolia. He has a bachelor's degree in economics from Moscow State University, Russia; a master's degree in economics from Yokohama City University, Japan; and a Ph.D. in economics from Keio University, Japan. He worked with the JICA project on national economic development policy in 1997–1999 and then served as the dean of the Economics School of the National University of Mongolia from 2004 to 2009. From 2009 to 2012, he served as the chairman of the National Development and Innovation Committee of Mongolia (NDIC), a government agency, where he oversaw the establishment of the national economic planning system in the market economy, introduced the public investment program (PIP), and supervised the establishment of the Development Bank of Mongolia, for which he served as an inaugural chairman of the Board of Directors. In addition, he supervised the creation of a legal system to support innovation in the country and oversaw the development of national public–private partnerships. Currently, he is a member of the Economic Policy Council under the prime minister of Mongolia as well as a member of the Monetary Policy Committee of the Central Bank of Mongolia. Khashchuluun Chuluundorj is also working as an independent member on the boards of directors for numerous financial and mining companies in Mongolia and is a visiting professor at the Plekhanov Russian University of Economics, in addition to his teaching at the National University of Mongolia's Department of Economics. He has published in international peer-reviewed journals and publications such as *Resources Policy*, the *Journal of Applied Economic Sciences Inner Asia* and others.

**Dulguun Tuvshintugs** is a researcher at the Economic Research Institute (ERI). She received her bachelor's degree from Bentley University in the United States, where she majored in finance with a concentration in corporate finance and a minor in law. Her research interests include monetary policy, capital markets, and financial modeling.

**Manlaibaatar Zagdbazar** is a project manager and senior researcher at the Economic Research Institute (ERI) of Mongolia. He has a bachelor's degree in applied mathematics from the Khan-Uul Institute, Mongolia; a master's degree in economic policy from the Central European University, Hungary; and is currently a Ph.D. candidate in economics at the National University of Mongolia. He has abundant teaching and research experience, working as a lecturer at Khan-Uul Institute, Mongolia, and the National University of Mongolia. Previously, he worked as a researcher at the Development Strategy and System Research Centre in Mongolia; an assistant researcher at the Research Department of the Central Bank of Hungary; and a consultant at the Independent Research Institute of Mongolia. He has published in international and domestic peer-reviewed journals such as *Resources Policy* and *Sociology* and coauthored several economic textbooks in Mongolian.

**Unurjargal Davaa** is a researcher at the Economic Research Institute (ERI). She received her bachelor's degree in economics from the National University of Mongolia and is currently pursuing her master's from the same institution. Her research area of focus includes CGE modeling and institutional economics.

# Foreign Direct Investment in Mongolia: Impact and Determinants

**Chuluunbat Narantuya, Manlaibaatar Zagdbazar, Khorol-Erdene Bayartsogt, Dulguun Tuvshintugs, Bayarjargal Munkh-Ireedui, and Delgermaa Begz**

## 1 Introduction

FDI is considered to be an important source of capital, especially for developing and emerging economies. According to the recent World Investment Reports, it has remained the largest source of external financial funds to developing countries, far surpassing official aid and remittances (with the exception of the least-developed countries). Most importantly, it remains a more stable source of financing, as opposed to highly volatile portfolio investment and bank loans. FDI is also believed to foster high-quality jobs and promote the adoption of modern production, know-how and management practices in these economies, which plays a substantial role in their social development (OECD, 2008). The latter aspect has been studied to a limited degree, as most research focuses on FDI's impact on economic growth (Hansen & Rand, 2006).

C. Narantuya (✉)
The National University of Mongolia, Ulaanbaatar, Mongolia
e-mail: cnarantuya@num.edu.mn

M. Zagdbazar · K.-E. Bayartsogt · D. Tuvshintugs · D. Begz
Economic Research Institute, Ulaanbaatar, Mongolia
e-mail: manlaibaatar@eri.mn

K.-E. Bayartsogt
e-mail: khorol-erdene@eri.mn

D. Tuvshintugs
e-mail: dulguun@eri.mn

D. Begz
e-mail: delgermaa@eri.mn

B. Munkh-Ireedui
Concordia University, Montreal, Canada



Y. Hosoi et al. (eds.), *Economic Dependence of Mongolia on Minerals*, Contributions to Economics, https://doi.org/10.1007/978-981-19-5515-0_3

Global FDI inflows have fluctuated around $1.4 trillion over the recent decade, reaching an all-time high of USD 2.06 trillion in 2016 (UNCTAD, 2021). In 2019, global FDI inflow stood at USD 1.5 trillion before falling drastically to below USD 1 trillion in 2020 owing to the COVID-19 pandemic (UNCTAD, 2021a). The share of developing countries has been steadily increasing both in terms of FDI inflow and outflow. Developing Asia, most notably Singapore, Hong Kong (China), China and, more recently, India, is becoming the most notable global recipient of FDI.

In terms of sectoral distribution, the services industry—trade, finance, business activities, telecommunications—is a major recipient of FDI inflow, accounting for approximately two-thirds of global FDI in 2015 (UNCTAD, 2017). The primary sector's share, including extractive industries, is low (6% of global FDI in 2015) and has been shrinking in recent years. FDI in the mining sector is significant in Africa, Latin America and West Asia but plays a minor role in other parts of the world.

Numerous studies have examined the impact of FDI on economic growth. Tiwari and Mutascu found a correlation between FDI, exports and economic growth using panel data from 1986 to 2008 on 23 Asian countries (Tiwari & Mutascu, 2011). Similarly, Yao found that FDI had a strong positive effect on economic growth when analyzing panel data of 28 Chinese provinces from 1978 to 2000 (Yao, 2006). These findings were also in line with results found in other regions of the world. Obwona studied the linkages between FDI and GDP using Ugandan data from 1981 to 1995, concluding that FDI had a positive impact on GDP (Obwona, 2001). Popescu also looked at the relationship between FDI and the economic growth of central and eastern European countries, finding that FDI was positively correlated with economic growth based on panel data from 1993 to 2013 (Popescu, 2014). Iqbal and Shaikh (2010) concluded that the two factors accelerating growth in Pakistan were FDI and trade—albeit FDI encourages trade. Almfraji et al. (2014) found that there was a correlation between FDI and economic growth in Qatar—growth tends to attract FDI, while at the same time, FDI supports growth (Almfraji et al., 2014).

While the positive association between FDI and economic growth has been well studied, several studies have also focused on determining the causality between the two. Looking at the data from 31 developing countries over a period from 1970 to 2000, Hansen and Rand found that FDI had a significant long-term impact on GDP regardless of the country's development level. Additionally, there were no significant differences in the impact on economic growth based on the country region (Hansen & Rand, 2005). Chowdhury and Mavrotas also looked at the direction of causality between FDI and growth in Chile, Malaysia, and Thailand using data from 1969 to 2000. They found that GDP supported FDI in Chile and that they mutually supported each other in Malaysia and Thailand (Chowdhury & Mavrotas, 2006).

Countries, both developed and developing alike, strive to attract more investment from abroad, which leads to heightened global competition. There are several factors that motivate multinational corporations and other global investors to invest across the border. Traditionally, the economic determinants of FDI were the availability of natural resources, national market factors such as market size and population income and location-specific determinants such as the availability of low-cost unskilled labor

(UNCTAD, 1998). More recently, according to the Global Investment Competitiveness survey commissioned by the World Bank in 2019, the determinants of FDI vary greatly depending on the type of investor. For instance, multinational corporations in the mining sector value access to land and resources, while market-seeking FDI values the size and purchasing power of the domestic market, while efficiency-seeking FDI[1] values policies that facilitate the import and export of goods and lower production costs (World Banks, 2020). In the 2017 survey, investors named political stability and security, the legal and regulatory environment and a large domestic market size critically important factors that affected investment decisions. Investors also stated that transparency and predictability in the conduct of public agencies, investment protection guarantees and the ease of obtaining government approvals were of critical importance when considering the investment climate of the host country (World Bank, 2018a, 2018b, 2018c).

The "commodity supercycle" that emerged in the late 1990s and early 2000s, which pushed oil and metal prices steadily to historically high levels, boosted the Mongolian economy to unprecedented levels. Since then, the Mongolian economy has gone through a number of boom-and-bust cycles. The supercycle was interrupted in 2008 by the global financial crisis. After the global financial crisis, the economy recovered quickly and grew at an unprecedented 17.3% in 2011, followed by a mere 1.0% in 2016. Thus, the supercycle, which gained some strength following the crisis, entered its downward phase and remained moderate since 2016.

According to recent studies, FDI is one of the major driving factors behind economic growth in Mongolia. In turn, FDI is conditioned by a multiplicity of economic and policy determinants. Since 2011, FDI into Mongolia has steadily declined before recovering somewhat in 2017. Unfortunately, the few studies conducted have not been successful in identifying the cause. Although a comprehensive study does not yet exist, many economists attribute the flux in FDI to mineral commodity prices and the investment climate.

Anand (2011), using the 'OLS regressions with fixed effect' method, concluded that FDI supported economic growth directly and indirectly through its interaction with labor. To disaggregate the effect of FDI inflow by sector, the researcher then ran the regression with dummy variables for each major sector in Mongolia (agriculture, mining, construction, energy, finance, transportation). Interestingly, while FDI inflow into the energy and agriculture sectors supported sectoral growth, FDI inflow into the mining and transportation sectors had a negative effect on growth. Despite this, approximately half of all FDI into Mongolia between 2000 and 2004 and more than 70% of FDI between 2005 and 2009 was concentrated in the mining sector.

Munkhtsetseg and Gantumur (2015) estimated the impact of FDI on 20 sectors using Leontief's inverse matrices based on the input–output tables for 2010–2013. They estimated how a hypothetical increase of 1% in the mining sector's FDI would influence the whole economy. It was found that the additional FDI stimulation would induce the economy to grow by 1.5, 2.45, 1.43, and 0.63% in 2010, 2011, 2012, and

[1] This term refers to FDI that "enters the country to save costs in international production networks" (World Banks, 2020).

2013, respectively. The hypothetical additional FDI stimulus strongly supported the mining and trade sectors. However, as the two sectors are highly correlated, it is probable that the shock promoted the mining sector, which in turn fostered trade. Thus, the authors argue that the trade sector is likely to be boosted by expansion in the mining sector rather than FDI inflow (Munkhtsetseg & Gantumur, 2015).

A couple of studies have also looked at the determinants of FDI in Mongolia. For instance, Javzandorj and Dehong (2012) found that most FDI into Mongolia was market seeking and export oriented. Mongolian FDI is largely determined by market size, political and economic stability, bilateral trade agreements and a favorable climate. However, FDI into Mongolia is hindered by political instability, crime and insecurity, and institutional factors (Javzandorj & Dehong, 2012). Och et al. (2017) used several econometric methods to analyze the determinants of FDI in Mongolia. They found that market size and human capital had a positive short-term impact on FDI and a negative long-term impact. Macroeconomic instability had a long-term negative impact on FDI; imports had a complementary effect on FDI, while exports and FDI were substituted. Financial development also had a substitute relationship with FDI, negatively affecting it in both the short and long term. Interestingly, infrastructure had no significant impact on FDI (Och et al., 2017).

This chapter will aim to identify the main causes of FDI fluctuations, estimate the impact of FDI on the Mongolian economy, and determine ways to attract more FDI based on the best practices of other countries.

The chapter will proceed as follows. In the next section, we depict the dynamics of FDI in Mongolia in the past decade or so. FDI has been closely correlated with economic growth and fluctuates greatly. Additionally, the main countries of origin and the sectors where the FDI flowed were identified. Then, in the following section, we turn to the economic effect of FDI in the mining sector on the entire economy. We use the input–output tables (IOT) for 2010 and 2015 to estimate the growth induced in these years by a hypothetical increase in the FDI equal to 1% of total mining output. The Leontief's inverse matrix technique is commonly used in similar studies. We find that FDI has a positive but varying effect on all sectors, with the trade and services sector being the greatest beneficiaries. We then estimate the mining FDI multiplier on the economy as a whole.

In the third section, we turn to the determinants of FDI. In the mining sector, these comprise the natural resource potential (including global commodity prices) and the policy and institutional environment. The former is exogenous to Mongolia, while the latter can be changed by adequate policy measures. Using several indicators, we find that the investment climate is not favorable in Mongolia. The last section addresses economic diversification issues. Developing countries have had divergent outcomes in their diversification efforts. Some turned into industrial powerhouses, while many are still struggling to diversify the sources of their growth and export earnings. This is especially challenging for resource-dependent developing countries such as Mongolia. Some countries, e.g., Chile, provide a good example to follow. We wrap up the chapter with concluding remarks.

## 2 Dynamics of FDI in Mongolia

The Mongolian economy has grown rapidly in the past few decades. However, the growth rate fluctuated greatly, with GDP growth ramping up since the early 2000s and reaching double digits from 2011 to 2013 before slowing down again. While there are many factors that contribute to economic growth, FDI inflow is regularly cited as a key indicator of growth, with several studies exploring the strong correlation between FDI and economic growth. As a result, the Mongolian government has focused on attracting FDI to encourage economic stability and growth.

FDI inflow into Mongolia began with the implementation of the Foreign Direct Investment Policy to encourage FDI in 1993. The implementation of this policy also led to the ratification of the Foreign Investment Law in the same year. This was later replaced by the more general Investment Law in 2013, which reduced the legal distinctions between foreign and domestic investment. The 2013 Investment Law provides guarantees for investors against illegal confiscation, citing that private property can only be expropriated by due process and with full compensation according to prevailing market rates. Additionally, the 44 bilateral investment treaties signed by Mongolia with other countries provide extensive investment protections, stating that foreign investments will be treated equally and fairly, without discrimination relative to domestic investment. These treaties also provide guarantees against arbitrary expropriation, requiring such actions to be compensated according to international law. Moreover, in August 2016, Mongolia established a cabinet-level investor protection council that was designed to receive investor feedback concerning difficulties in undertaking investments and settling investment disputes through negotiations.

While FDI inflow into Mongolia remained fairly low for a number of years, it began to increase considerably in 2008, with the mining sector accounting for the majority of overall investment from abroad. The spike in FDI in 2008 was followed by a decrease in 2009 owing to the global financial crisis before experiencing dramatic growth in 2010 and 2011. This boom was mainly due to growth in the mining sector and suggested that Mongolia could increase its FDI in the short run by boosting its mineral commodity production. For reference, in 2009, Mongolia produced 0.8% and 0.2%, respectively, of the world production of copper and coal (British Geological Survey, 2011), before coal production ramped up to 0.7% of total world production in 2010. Currently, Mongolia supplies approximately 20–30% of Chinese coking coal imports, the world's largest consumer of coal (Economic Research Institute, 2017a) (Table 1).

FDI inflows to Mongolia have illustrated a boom-to-bust trend during the last decade. FDI inflows increased drastically following the expansion of the mining sector and, in particular, the development of the Oyu Tolgoi open pit mine. After 2011, however, weak commodity prices along with deteriorating investor sentiment in Mongolia led to the ultimate drop in FDI inflows. The continuous decline in FDI since 2011 was reversed in 2017, when it reached USD 1.4 billion. This improvement was due to higher commodity prices, a clear indication that commodity prices heavily influence investment into Mongolia.

**Table 1** Economic growth and FDI inflow in Mongolia, 2006–2020, billion USD

| | 2006 | 2007 | 2008 | 2009 | 2010 | 2011 | 2012 | 2013 | 2014 | 2015 | 2016 | 2017 | 2018 | 2019 | 2020 |
|---|---|---|---|---|---|---|---|---|---|---|---|---|---|---|---|
| GDP growth (%) | 8.6 | 10.2 | 8.9 | −1.3 | 6.4 | 17.3 | 12.3 | 11.6 | 7.9 | 2.4 | 1.2 | 5.3 | 7.2 | 5.2 | −5.3 |
| FDI (billion USD) | 0.2 | 0.4 | 0.8 | 0.6 | 1.6 | 4.5 | 4.2 | 2.0 | 0.2 | 0.1 | −4.2 | 1.4 | 2.1 | 2.3 | 1.7 |
| Growth (%) | 3 | 88 | 133 | −32 | 186 | 175 | −6 | −52 | −89 | −64 | −5131 | −135 | 48 | 8 | −27 |

*Source* Bank of Mongolia, and NSO

The annual FDI inflow exceeded USD 1 billion in 2010, peaking at USD 4.6 billion in 2011. This was due to the inception of the Oyu Tolgoi project.

**Box 1. FDI in the Oyu Tolgoi Copper and Gold Mine**

Oyu Tolgoi is a large copper–gold deposit located in the South Gobi region of Mongolia. The Oyu Tolgoi project was developed as a joint venture between the Turquoise Hill Resources, a subsidiary of Rio Tinto, and the Government of Mongolia. The start of this project saw Mongolia's share of world copper production increasing to 1.8% in 2015, ranking 15th overall production (Economic Research Institute, 2017b). Future production is also expected to continue to rise as the Oyu Tolgoi project develops its underground mine, with a peak production expected to more than double by 2027 (Rio Tinto, 2016). Overall, the Oyu Tolgoi project is expected to be the fourth largest copper mine in the world by 2030 (Reuters, 2021).

The beginning of the Oyu Tolgoi project and its related FDI brought considerable economic prosperity. For instance, investments into the Oyu Tolgoi project peaked between 2011 and 2012 where a reported USD 2.5 and USD 2.1 billion were invested. During this time, the Mongolian GDP experienced unprecedented growth rates of 17.3 and 12.3%, respectively. Investments into the Oyu Tolgoi project fell following this initial capital investment into the open pit mine before ramping up again following the decision to begin investing into Oyu Tolgoi's underground mine development (Fig. 1).

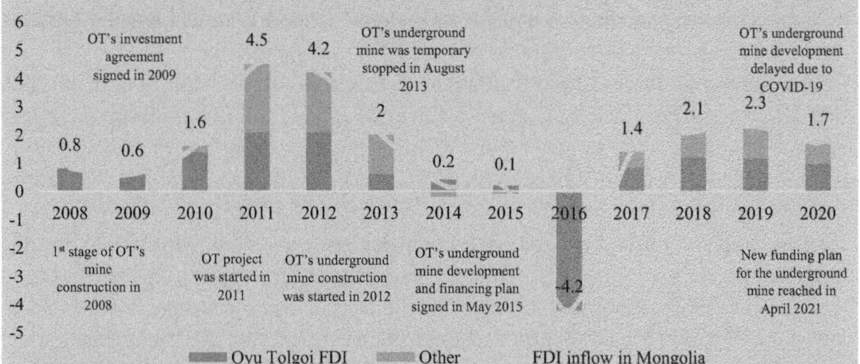


**Fig. 1** Oyu Tolgoi FDI inflow, 2008–2020, billion USD. *Source* Bank of Mongolia, and the research team's calculation

While the Government of Mongolia and Turquoise Hill came to an agreement on Oyu Tolgoi's underground mine development financing plan in May 2015, this decision later faced opposition from the Government of Mongolia.

The negative FDI inflow in 2016 of USD 4.2 billion was mainly due to reclassification of USD 3.8 billion of investment into Oyu Tolgoi. The GoM's 34% stake in the Oyu Tolgoi project was registered as FDI on the balance of payment at the time of initial agreement in 2009. However, in 2016, the 34% stake was reclassified as a foreign loan as the stake is financed by the profits the GoM receives in the future. A new funding plan was finally reached in April 2021. Between 2017 and 2020, FDI inflows into the Oyu Tolgoi remained relatively high as continued progress was made on the underground mine development. However, it is important to note that the project continues to face delays due to poor ground conditions in addition to the delays related to COVID-19 restrictions.

The majority of FDI into Mongolia is concentrated in the mining sector. The Mongolian mining sector accounted for 23.3% of Mongolia's total GDP as of 2020. It plays a vital part in exports, with mineral commodity exports of coal, gold, copper concentrate and iron ore making up 28.1, 23.6, 23.5 and 8.4%, respectively, of Mongolia's total exports, valued at USD 7.5 billion. Table 2 shows FDI inflow by sector and highlights the importance of the mining sector in bolstering FDI inflow into Mongolia.

In addition to the mining sector, the wholesale and retail trade sector as well as the financial and insurance services sector are key recipients of FDI. This is plausible, as the trade sector is highly reliant on the mining sector and provides secondary services to mining projects. The negative changes in FDI inflow into most sectors in 2020 can largely be attributed to the overall global economic slowdown and growing uncertainty caused by the outbreak of the COVID-19 pandemic.

The following Table 3 breaks down total FDI inflow into Mongolia from 2010 to 2020 by country of origin. Canada, China, Singapore and Luxembourg are major investors. Canada is the largest source of investment, accounting for over one-third of total FDI, followed by China, with 20%. The combined share of the two largest investor countries accounted for 59% of total FDI as of 2020 and is likely to rise.

Compared to similar resource-rich countries such as Chile, Mongolia's mining sector is still relatively new. In Chile, investment in the copper industry started to boom in the 1900s (Schmitz, 1986). Chile, a high-income country, is regarded as one of the few countries that attracted foreign investment into the mining sector and managed the associated revenue wisely by following far-sighted macroeconomic policies, including prudent fiscal rules and diversification policies. Chile sets a good example of a successful mining economy that Mongolia should strive to become in the long term. This will be discussed in more detail later in the chapter.

In the short term, Mongolia's mining sector can readily be compared to similar countries, such as Kazakhstan, Peru, and Zambia. As Mongolia, these countries are all considered middle-income countries, their economies are strongly dependent upon the mining and extractive industries, and the emergence and development of their mining sectors began within the past two to three decades. Kazakhstan and Peru

**Table 2** FDI inflow by sector, 2019 and 2020, million USD

| No. | Sector | 2019 | 2020 | Changes in inflow |
|---|---|---|---|---|
| 1 | Construction | 52.7 | 32.4 | −20.3 |
| 2 | Education | 2.0 | 0.2 | −1.8 |
| 3 | Manufacturing | 26.5 | 9.3 | −17.2 |
| 4 | Wholesale and retail trade services | 261.1 | 223.8 | −37.3 |
| 5 | Accommodation and food services | 13.5 | 0.2 | −13.3 |
| 6 | Telecommunication | 6.2 | 6.0 | −0.2 |
| 7 | Professional, scientific and technical, other business | 16.8 | 81.7 | 64.9 |
| 8 | Financial and insurance services | 192.2 | 110.4 | −81.8 |
| 9 | Transport service | 29.3 | 38.0 | 8.7 |
| 10 | Administrative and support service activities | 67.2 | 54.7 | −12.5 |
| 11 | Mining | 2374.5 | 1678.8 | −695.7 |
| 12 | Other service activities | 67.8 | 301.0 | 233.2 |
| 13 | Real estate services | 16.0 | 11.9 | −4.1 |
| 14 | Agriculture, forestry and fishing | 3.2 | 1.4 | −1.8 |
| 15 | Electricity, gas steam and its distribution | 0.9 | 9.9 | 9.0 |
| 16 | Other | 1.10 | 0.70 | −0.4 |
| | Total | 3130.8 | 2560.3 | −570.5 |

*Source* Bank of Mongolia

**Table 3** Top 10 investors by country, 2010–2020 (billion USD, accumulated)

| Country | 2010 | 2011 | 2012 | 2013 | 2014 | 2015 | 2016 | 2017 | 2018 | 2019 | 2020e |
|---|---|---|---|---|---|---|---|---|---|---|---|
| Total FDI | 8.44 | 13.33 | 17.67 | 19.58 | 20.25 | 20.70 | 16.28 | 18.02 | 20.22 | 22.56 | 24.21 |
| Netherlands | 0.64 | 0.66 | 0.67 | 0.66 | 0.64 | 0.66 | 0.64 | 0.72 | 0.69 | 0.68 | 0.69 |
| China | 2.45 | 2.90 | 3.24 | 3.59 | 4.00 | 4.39 | 4.38 | 4.69 | 4.92 | 5.07 | 5.24 |
| Singapore | 0.80 | 1.32 | 1.54 | 1.52 | 1.69 | 1.69 | 1.65 | 1.65 | 1.67 | 1.48 | 1.53 |
| United Kingdom | 0.43 | 0.52 | 0.53 | 0.50 | 0.47 | 0.44 | 0.37 | 0.40 | 0.44 | 0.50 | 0.48 |
| United States | 0.26 | 0.40 | 0.62 | 0.63 | 0.56 | 0.53 | 0.54 | 0.67 | 0.67 | 0.75 | 0.65 |
| Australia | 0.03 | 0.10 | 0.26 | 0.44 | 0.38 | 0.39 | 0.34 | 0.37 | 0.53 | 0.54 | 0.83 |
| Japan | 0.18 | 0.21 | 0.35 | 0.42 | 0.53 | 0.54 | 0.59 | 0.66 | 0.84 | 0.92 | 0.98 |
| Canada | 1.27 | 3.97 | 6.23 | 7.78 | 7.78 | 7.73 | 3.85 | 4.63 | 5.99 | 7.80 | 9.02 |
| Luxembourg | 0.76 | 1.10 | 1.68 | 1.45 | 1.55 | 1.39 | 1.26 | 1.38 | 1.41 | 1.48 | 1.51 |

*Source* Bank of Mongolia

tend to be well regarded for investments, as noted by their rankings on international indices such as Doing Business, Corruption Perception and Investment Attractiveness. Analyzing how these countries were able to overcome challenges and boost their respective investment environments can provide available insight for Mongolia, which can then be applied to improve the institutional and investment environment of the country. A look into this topic will be included further in this chapter.

## 3 Economic Impact of FDI in the Mining Sector

Most FDI inflow in Mongolia is concentrated in the mining sector, and any changes in FDI inflow into the mining sector greatly affect the overall Mongolian economy. Significant changes in FDI inflow may also cause structural economic shifts. In light of this, this section will analyze the impact of additional FDI inflow into the mining sector on the overall economy.

To estimate the impact of mining FDI on the whole economy, the research team utilized an input–output table (IOT) that showcases the relationships between actors in an economy by defining the flow of final and intermediate goods and services (OECD, 2021). This methodology was utilized in a study conducted by Munkhtsetseg and Gantumur in 2015 that calculated the FDI impact for 20 sectors using Leontief's inverse matrices, estimated from the 2010 to 2013 IOTs. In this study, the researchers looked at how a hypothetical increase of 1% in the mining sector's FDI would influence the whole economy. The impact of the additional FDI stimulation on the entire economy was estimated to be 1.5, 2.45, 1.43, and 0.63% in 2010, 2011, 2012, and 2013, respectively.

The hypothetical additional FDI stimulus strongly supported the mining and trade sectors. However, as the two sectors are highly correlated, it is probable that the "shock" considerably encouraged the mining sector, which, in turn, caused an increase in the trade sector. The researchers found that it is likely that the trade sector was more influenced by increases in the mining sector than the increase in FDI inflow per se (Munkhtsetseg & Gantumur, 2015).

Using the same methodology, the research team chose to use the 2010 and 2015 IOTs published by the National Statistics Office (NSO) of Mongolia, as the 2015 IOT is the most recent IOT available and the economic structures between the two periods are relatively different owing to differing economic circumstances.

The outputs of the sectors included in the 2010 and 2015 IOTs as a share of GDP are shown below. It is worth noting that in terms of economic structure, the mining sector's output as a share of GDP fell 4.5% points in 2015 compared to 2010, mostly due to the decline in FDI inflow and mineral commodity prices (Table 4).

Using the 2010 and 2015 IOTs, the research team calculated the impact of the addition FDI inflow, equal to 1% of the mining sector's total output, invested into the mining sector on the overall economy (see Estimate-1 below). This calculation was performed to highlight the potential repercussions of additional FDI on the

**Table 4** Sectors' output as a share of GDP (percent), 2010 and 2015

| | 2010 (%) | 2015 (%) | Changes (% points) | |
|---|---|---|---|---|
| Agriculture | 11.73 | 13.36 | 1.62 | ▲ |
| Mining and quarrying | 21.55 | 17.09 | −4.46 | ▼ |
| Manufacturing | 6.81 | 7.64 | 0.82 | ▲ |
| Electricity, gas, steam and air conditioning supply | 1.95 | 1.64 | −0.31 | ▼ |
| Water supply; sewerage, and waste management | 0.32 | 0.45 | 0.13 | ▲ |
| Construction | 2.56 | 4.22 | 1.66 | ▲ |
| Wholesale and retail trade; repair of motor vehicles and motorcycles | 12.29 | 11.53 | −0.75 | ▼ |
| Transportation and storage | 6.95 | 5.23 | −1.72 | ▼ |
| Accommodation and food service activities | 0.54 | 0.93 | 0.39 | ▲ |
| Information and communication | 2.62 | 2.15 | −0.48 | ▼ |
| Financial and insurance activities | 2.46 | 5.35 | 2.90 | ▲ |
| Real estate activities | 7.05 | 6.85 | −0.20 | ▼ |
| Professional, scientific and technical activities | 1.36 | 2.19 | 0.84 | ▲ |
| Administrative and support service activities | 0.83 | 0.94 | 0.11 | ▲ |
| Public administration and defense; compulsory social security | 4.36 | 4.58 | 0.22 | ▲ |
| Education | 3.89 | 4.38 | 0.49 | ▲ |
| Human health and social work activities | 1.71 | 2.04 | 0.33 | ▲ |
| Arts, entertainment and recreation | 0.33 | 0.46 | 0.13 | ▲ |
| Other service activities | 0.46 | 0.81 | 0.36 | ▲ |
| Net product taxes | 10.23 | 8.15 | −2.09 | ▼ |

*Source* GDP by sectors, NSO

entire economy. Overall, the additional FDI inflow into the mining sector will instigate spending across all other sectors in the form of intermediate and intersectoral spending. This increase in economic activity will be termed the "aftershocks" of the initial increase in FDI inflow into the mining sector.

To estimate the impact of the additional FDI on the whole economy, the following linear system can be used:

$$Ay + Bx = 0,$$

where $y$ is the vector of endogenous variables and $x$ is the vector of exogenous variables. $A$ and $B$ are coefficient matrices: each row corresponds to one equation; each column corresponds to one variable. The following shows how $y$ can be found as a function of $x$:

$$y = -A^{-1}Bx,$$

where $A^{-1}$ is the inverse matrix of A, also known as Leontief's inverse matrix.

We calculated the aftershocks allocated to each sector, both in terms of percent change and value added. Understandably, the impact of FDI on the economy will depend on the share of intermediate consumption that is absorbed domestically.

To see the impact of structural changes in the economy, the research team calculated the effect on the economy in a hypothetical situation where all of the FDI and its aftershocks were absorbed completely into the domestic market (reported as Estimate-2 below).

Using the linear system, the research system found that an additional FDI inflow equal to 1% of the mining sector's output in 2010 and 2015 would lead to an economic growth of 0.188% and 0.207%, respectively. These aftershocks for each sector are shown in Table 5.

Understandably, the additional FDI had a positive impact on all sectors. However, the magnitude of impact varies across different sectors. A significant positive influence is estimated to be on the utilities and services sectors, including accommodation and food service activities, water supply, electricity, gas, steam and air conditioning supply, transportation and storage, financial services and the construction sector.

The values created by these sectoral aftershocks are shown in Table 6. In 2015, the transportation and storage (MNT 8.79 billion), wholesale and retail trade (MNT 7.25 billion), and construction sectors (MNT 6.23 billion) were the most affected sectors. Although the additional FDI inflow was MNT 39.5 billion, its overall economic impact was MNT 41.17 billion. Its investment multiplier,[2] therefore, was approximately 1.04 units. In 2010, the additional FDI and economic impact were MNT 21

[2] An investment multiplier refers to "the concept that an increase in public or private investment spending has a more than proportionate positive impact on aggregate income and the general economy." It is an estimate of the additional benefits of investment spending beyond the initial investment. A higher investment multiplier indicates a larger positive effect on the economy (Fernando, 2020).

**Table 5** Growth by sectors (Estimate-1)

| Sectors | 2010 (%) | | 2015 (%) | |
|---|---|---|---|---|
| Agriculture | 0.05 | ▲ | 0.08 | ▲ |
| Mining and quarrying | 0.04 | ▲ | 0.05 | ▲ |
| Manufacturing | 0.24 | ▲ | 0.20 | ▲ |
| Electricity, gas, steam and air conditioning supply | 0.71 | ▲ | 0.48 | ▲ |
| Water supply; sewerage, and waste management | 0.88 | ▲ | 0.38 | ▲ |
| Construction | 0.57 | ▲ | 0.64 | ▲ |
| Wholesale and retail trade; repair of motor vehicles and motorcycles | 0.27 | ▲ | 0.27 | ▲ |
| Transportation and storage | 0.68 | ▲ | 0.73 | ▲ |
| Accommodation and food service activities | 0.91 | ▲ | 0.44 | ▲ |
| Information and communication | 0.21 | ▲ | 0.19 | ▲ |
| Financial and insurance activities | 0.58 | ▲ | 0.25 | ▲ |
| Real estate activities | 0.05 | ▲ | 0.05 | ▲ |
| Professional, scientific and technical activities | 0.43 | ▲ | 0.24 | ▲ |
| Administrative and support service activities | 0.56 | ▲ | 0.47 | ▲ |
| Public administration and defense; compulsory social security | 0.08 | ▲ | 0.05 | ▲ |
| Education | 0.03 | ▲ | 0.02 | ▲ |
| Human health and social work activities | 0.05 | ▲ | 0.03 | ▲ |
| Arts, entertainment and recreation | 0.07 | ▲ | 0.04 | ▲ |
| Other service activities | 0.11 | ▲ | 0.06 | ▲ |
| Total | 0.188 | ▲ | 0.207 | ▲ |

*Source* the research team's calculation

billion and MNT 18.4 billion, respectively. As a result, its investment multiplier was 0.87 units.

A factor that is key in determining the aftershocks of the increase in FDI inflow into the mining sector is the mining sector's ratio of intermediate consumption from the domestic market and foreign markets. For example, in the 2010 IOT, the Mongolian mining sector consumed 59% of its intermediate consumption from the domestic market, while it consumed 70% from the domestic market in the 2015 IOT. This means that the additional FDI inflow in 2015 will have a greater effect on the Mongolian economy, relative to 2010, as more of the investment is absorbed into the domestic market (Fig. 2).

This difference in investment multipliers can be attributed to the domestic market's share of intermediate consumption. The more investment that is absorbed by the domestic market, the greater the economic impact. Structural economic shifts can

**Table 6** Value added by sector, billion MNT (Estimate-1)

| Sectors | 2010 (billion MNT) | 2015 (billion MNT) |
|---|---|---|
| Agriculture | 0.59 | 2.55 |
| Mining and quarrying | 0.83 | 1.78 |
| Manufacturing | 1.61 | 3.47 |
| Electricity, gas, steam and air conditioning supply | 1.34 | 1.82 |
| Water supply; sewerage, and waste management | 0.27 | 0.40 |
| Construction | 1.42 | 6.23 |
| Wholesale and retail trade; repair of motor vehicles and motorcycles | 3.28 | 7.25 |
| Transportation and storage | 4.63 | 8.79 |
| Accommodation and food service activities | 0.48 | 0.94 |
| Information and communication | 0.55 | 0.95 |
| Financial and insurance activities | 1.39 | 3.08 |
| Real estate activities | 0.37 | 0.76 |
| Professional, scientific and technical activities | 0.57 | 1.20 |
| Administrative and support service activities | 0.45 | 1.02 |
| Public administration and defense; compulsory social security | 0.33 | 0.48 |
| Education | 0.11 | 0.16 |
| Human health and social work activities | 0.08 | 0.15 |
| Arts, entertainment and recreation | 0.02 | 0.04 |
| Other service activities | 0.05 | 0.11 |
| The total amount of additional GDP | 18.38 | 41.17 |
| The amount of the additional investment | 21.0 | 39.5 |

*Source* the research team's calculation

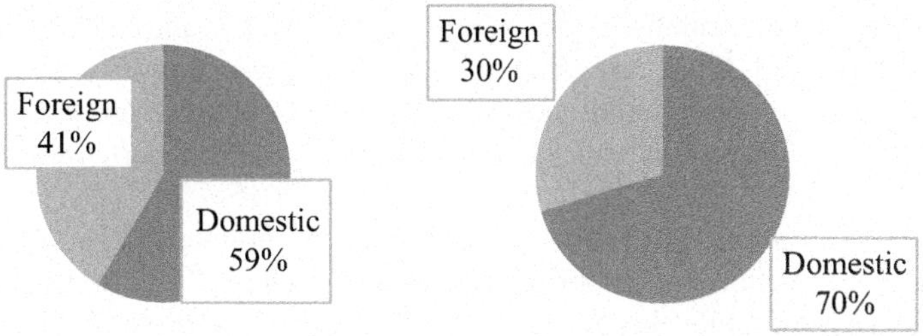


**Fig. 2** Intermediate consumption in 2010 (left) and 2015 (right), by sources. *Source* IOT table 2010 and 2015, NSO, and the research team's calculation

also affect the multipliers, and in recent years, shifts have occurred due to a boom in the mining sector.

The following Table 7 shows how much each sector grows if the aftershocks are entirely absorbed in the domestic market. In this estimation, the differences between the investment multipliers are only caused by structural economic shifts.

**Table 7** Growth by sectors, percent (Estimate-2)

| Sectors | 2010 (%) | 2015 (%) |
|---|---|---|
| Agriculture | 0.09 | 0.12 |
| Mining and quarrying | 0.07 | 0.06 |
| Manufacturing | 0.41 | 0.28 |
| Electricity, gas, steam, and air conditioning supply | 1.20 | 0.68 |
| Water supply; sewerage, and waste management | 1.50 | 0.54 |
| Construction | 0.97 | 0.91 |
| Wholesale and retail trade; repair of motor vehicles and motorcycles | 0.47 | 0.39 |
| Transportation and storage | 1.16 | 1.03 |
| Accommodation and food service activities | 1.56 | 0.62 |
| Information and communication | 0.37 | 0.27 |
| Financial and insurance activities | 0.99 | 0.35 |
| Real estate activities | 0.09 | 0.07 |
| Professional, scientific, and technical activities | 0.73 | 0.34 |
| Administrative and support service activities | 0.95 | 0.66 |
| Public administration and defense; compulsory social security | 0.13 | 0.06 |
| Education | 0.05 | 0.02 |
| Human health and social work activities | 0.08 | 0.04 |
| Arts, entertainment, and recreation | 0.12 | 0.06 |
| Other service activities | 0.18 | 0.08 |
| Economic growth (%) | 0.321 | 0.253 |

*Source* the research team's calculation

According to the calculations, the aftershocks created 0.32 and 0.25% of economic growth in 2010 and 2015, respectively. Sectors such as electricity, water supply, transportation and storage, and accommodation and food service activities were positively boosted by the aftershocks in 2010, whereas the transportation and storage sector was the only sector with a significant boost in 2015.

In 2010, the transportation and storage (MNT 7.90 billion), wholesale and retail trade (MNT 5.6 billion), and construction sectors (MNT 2.75 billion) experienced significant growth, while the transportation and storage and wholesale and retail trade sectors were greatly boosted in 2015. In both 2010 and 2015, the investment aftershocks benefited the transportation and storage and wholesale and retail trade sectors considerably (Table 8).

Figure 3 shows how the investment multipliers changed from Estimate-1 to Estimate-2 when the aftershocks were entirely absorbed into the domestic market.

**Table 8** Value added by sectors, MNT billion (Estimate-2)

| Sectors | 2010 (billion MNT) | 2015 (billion MNT) |
|---|---|---|
| Agriculture | 1.02 | 3.63 |
| Mining and quarrying | 1.41 | 2.54 |
| Manufacturing | 2.75 | 4.94 |
| Electricity, gas, steam, and air conditioning supply | 2.29 | 2.59 |
| Water supply; sewerage, and waste management | 0.47 | 0.56 |
| Construction | 2.42 | 8.86 |
| Wholesale and retail trade; repair of motor vehicles and motorcycles | 5.60 | 10.32 |
| Transportation and storage | 7.90 | 12.51 |
| Accommodation and food service activities | 0.82 | 1.34 |
| Information and communication | 0.94 | 1.35 |
| Financial and insurance activities | 2.38 | 4.38 |
| Real estate activities | 0.63 | 1.08 |
| Professional, scientific, and technical activities | 0.97 | 1.71 |
| Administrative and support service activities | 0.77 | 1.45 |
| Public administration and defense; compulsory social security | 0.57 | 0.68 |
| Education | 0.19 | 0.22 |
| Human health and social work activities | 0.14 | 0.21 |
| Arts, entertainment, and recreation | 0.04 | 0.06 |
| Other service activities | 0.08 | 0.15 |
| The total amount of additional GDP | 31.37 | 58.58 |
| The amount of the additional investment | 21.02 | 39.56 |

*Source* the research team's calculation

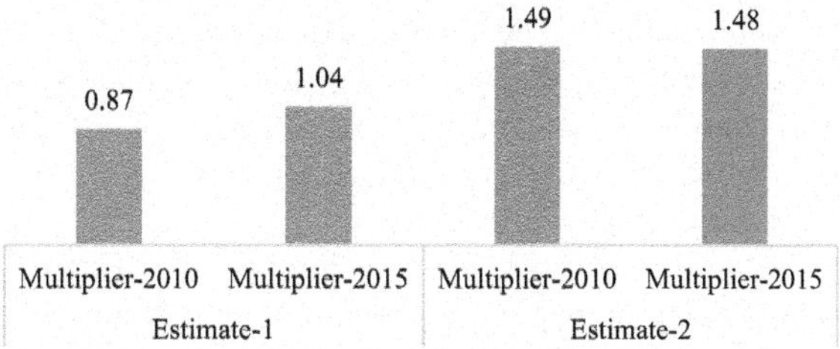


**Fig. 3** The investment multiplier by years and estimates. *Source* the research team's calculation

The investment multipliers were relatively higher in Estimate-2 than in Estimate-1 owing to how much of the aftershock was absorbed in the domestic market. In Estimate-2, the investment multiplier was 1.49 in 2010 and 1.48 in 2015. This negligible difference was caused by structural economic shifts. Conversely, the relatively large difference in multipliers in Estimate-1 was caused by both structural economic shifts and differences in the absorption amount of the aftershocks in the domestic market.

Overall, the direct impact of additional FDI inflow on the sectors depends on how the aftershocks are allocated and what percent of it is absorbed by the domestic market. According to the simulations, the more aftershocks that are absorbed by the domestic market, the higher the impact of the additional FDI inflow. As the mining sector is capital intensive, the aftershocks in the mining sector encourage increases in imports, as the domestic manufacturing sector cannot provide the equipment needed. As a result, the development of the manufacturing sector continues to be relatively weak. Thus, developing the Mongolian manufacturing sector that can benefit from increased FDI into the mining sector will improve investment multipliers.

## 4 The Determinants of FDI

Researchers have found that one of the key influencers on FDI is the regulatory and institutional environment. For instance, FDI encourages growth in high-income developing countries but not in low-income ones (Blomstrom et al., 1992), as their environments differ. The regulatory and institutional environment is also known as the investment climate. A study on Latin America reached the same conclusion and demonstrated that there exists a strong correlation between investment climate and FDI (Quazi & View, 2007). Similarly, Nnadozie argued that a country with little to no mineral resources may be able to increase its chances of attracting FDI if it instituted business regulation reforms. The reforms would promote a business-friendly environment, making the investment climate more favorable for investors. However, high trade barriers, repressive taxation and other restrictive policy changes can have a negative impact on FDI (Nnadozie, 2011).

In resource-rich developing countries, the main determinants of FDI inflows are the availability of minerals for exploitation and the investment climate. The investment climate is determined by regulatory and institutional factors such as strategies, programs and legislations pertaining to foreign direct investment, competitiveness, trade barriers, corruption, etc.

However, something to keep in mind is that each respective country's history has a significant impact on the country's attitude toward foreign investors, exploitation of natural resources and development of the country's regulatory framework. The foundation of the legal system and regulations are strongly influenced by past forms of government (monarchy, communism, dictatorship, etc.).

In Mongolia, the NRGI determined three main factors that may explain the recent fall in FDI inflow into Mongolia. They concluded that lower commodity prices, disputes with foreign investors, and ill-conceived policy decisions were the main causes. While the first factor was dependent on many variables and Mongolia had no way to influence world commodity prices, the latter two factors are highly dependent on Mongolia's investment environment (NRGI, 2015).

## 4.1 Global Commodity Prices and FDI in the Mining Sector

The global prices of mineral commodities are largely determined by supply and demand factors and fluctuate due to common shocks. For instance, the prices of select mineral commodities increased steadily from 2000 to 2008 before falling sharply in 2009 due to the global recession (World Bank, 2021). Mineral commodity prices recovered and normalized shortly after the crisis, with significant economic growth in developing countries such as China. However, China's shift away from industrial growth led to a decrease in mineral commodity prices from 2015 (World Bank, 2015). Supply constraints in 2017 led to commodity price surges, and commodity price changes have been mixed with the outbreak of the COVID-19 pandemic. In short, the world has observed tremendous volatility in commodity prices since the turn of the century (Fig. 4).

These fluctuations had considerable effects on Mongolia's terms of trade. Terms of trade (ToT) indicates the ratio between the export prices of a country and the import prices (Investopedia, 2018). While there are various ways of calculating a country's ToT, a simple ratio of a country's export price index to its import price index is suggested by the IMF. More significantly, changes in the terms of trade of an economy affect the real income of the economy. An increase in the terms of trade means that the value of exports is increasing relative to the value of imports. The country can afford to buy more imports with the revenue from its exports. For example, an increase in the price of oil improves the terms of trade for oil-exporting countries and lowers it for other countries. One study found that the world price of three or fewer exported commodities accounted for more than 50% of the annual change in the ToT of a developing country (Bidarkota & Crucini, 2000).

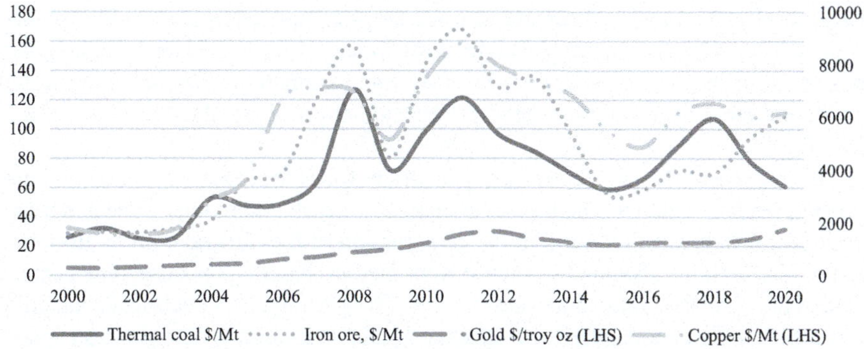


**Fig. 4** Select mineral commodity prices, 2000–2020. *Sources* World Bank

Noticeably, Mongolia's mineral and mineral products constitute over 70% of exports. Thus, changes in mineral commodity prices are especially important for Mongolia's ToT. To further understand Mongolia's terms of trade, the research team used the simple method put forth by the IMF to calculate its ToT relative to the base year (2000 = 100). The following Fig. 5 illustrates Mongolia's and Chile's ToT from 2000 to 2020. Chile's ToT was included as a comparison role model. While still heavily reliant on mineral commodity exports, Chile successfully transitioned from the mining sector, contributing approximately 84% of exports in 1970, to approximately only 50% in 2016. They also went from exporting raw mineral products to processing and refining them over the years. Conversely, Mongolia is reliant on raw mineral commodity exports, with refined copper only making up approximately 1% of exports in 2017. The similarities between the countries further showcase how both are affected by mineral commodity prices, particularly copper prices.

As Mongolia cannot influence world mineral commodity prices, they are an exogenous variable that impacts FDI inflow. To compare mineral commodity prices and

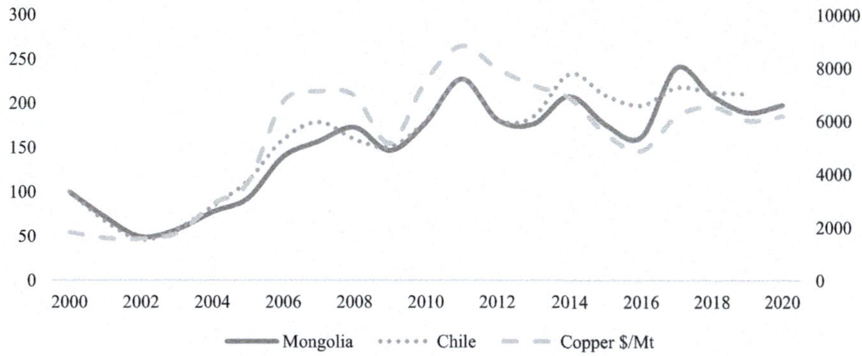


**Fig. 5** Terms of trade for Mongolia and Chile. *Source* TheGlobalEconomy.com, NSO and ERI estimates

FDI inflow in Mongolia, we created a price index comprised of coal, gold, iron and copper. The index is created by weighting the prices of coal, gold, iron, and copper. Historical prices are derived from the IMF and World Bank, while the projected prices are an average of forecasted prices by analysts from the World Bank and Bloomberg.

All prices are relative to 2009 base-year prices for each respective commodity and reflect price movements. The base year analysis of each commodity price generated an index, which was then used in the construction of the mineral commodity price index. The weights allocated to each commodity are based upon Mongolia's export data of the corresponding commodity (NSO, 2016). Mongolia's historical coal, gold, iron, and copper exports were aggregated and then measured to determine an appropriate weight. The weights of the commodities fluctuated from year to year to reflect a more realistic representation of price movements.

The following Fig. 6 depicts a comparison of the mineral commodity price index and Mongolian FDI inflow. As seen below, the trends between FDI inflow and commodity prices are closely related—as prices decline, FDI inflow also experiences a decline.

This trend is not unique to Mongolia. It is also detected in other commodity exporters. The FDI net inflows into Kazakhstan and Zambia are shown in Figs. 7 and 8, along with the prices of their main export mineral commodity, crude oil and copper, respectively.

The data in the figures above show that FDI inflows into Kazakhstan and Zambia are generally in line with fluctuations in their respective mineral commodity. Various studies have also found support for the link between commodity prices and FDI inflow movements (Céspedes & Velasco, 2012; Fornero et al., 2016; Kose, 2002).

Commodity prices are crucial for foreign investment but unfortunately an exogenous factor for Mongolia, as for many other countries. Thus, to ensure economic stability and reduce uncertainty, Mongolia should try to drive its own FDI inflow through efforts independent of global prices. To achieve that, Mongolia needs to

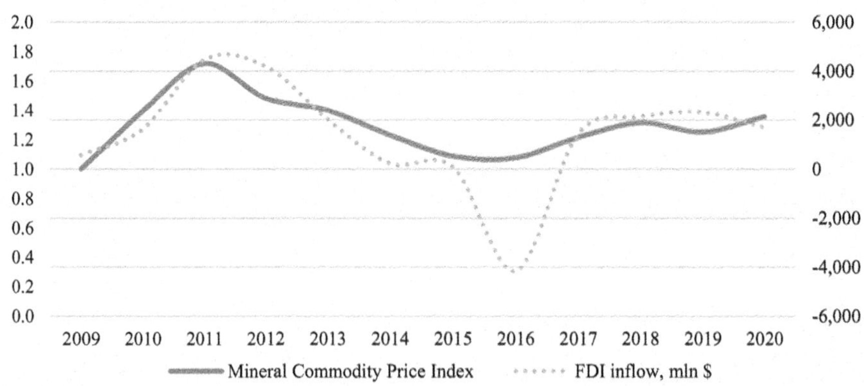


**Fig. 6** Commodity price index and FDI inflow in Mongolia, 2009–2020. *Source* Bank of Mongolia, NSO, World Bank, and research team's calculation

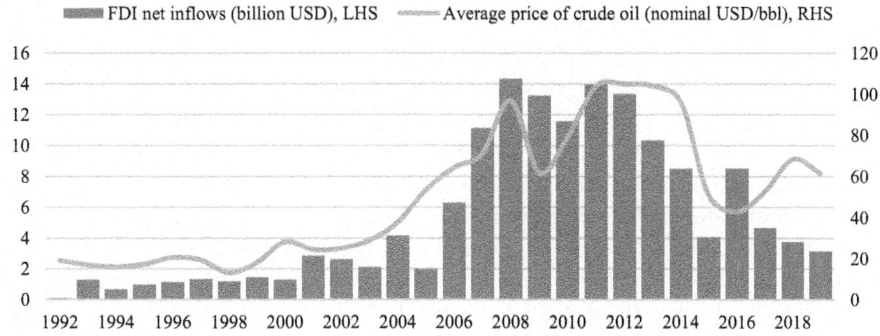


**Fig. 7** Kazakhstan FDI inflows relative to crude oil price, 2000–2019. *Source* World Bank and UNCTAD

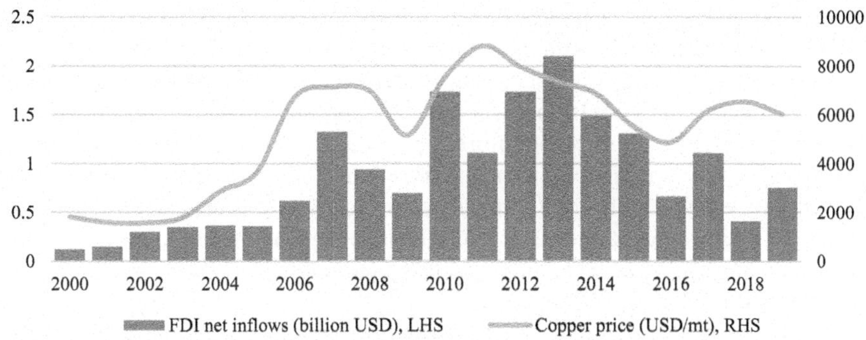


**Fig. 8** Zambia FDI relative to copper prices, 2000–2019. *Source* UNCTAD and World Bank

focus on improving its investment climate instead of relying on ambiguous changes in global commodity prices.

## 4.2 *Investment Climate in the Mining Sector*

According to the International Finance Corporation, a country's investment climate consists of a grouping of numerous factors, such as macroeconomic and political stability, traditions and culture, physical infrastructure, availability of capital, and human resources (IFC, 2016). Expanding on this, the EBRD defines it as "a wide range of factors that determine whether domestic and foreign investment happens", including the soundness of macroeconomic policies, the strength of economic and political institutions, the functioning of the legal and regulatory framework, the quality of infrastructure and other services (EBRD, 2021).

A country's investment climate plays a key role in alluring FDI since investors seek a predictable and acceptable return on their investment. Moreover, resource-rich countries can maintain a relatively stable FDI despite declines in mineral commodity prices if they have a favorable investment climate. Thus, defining Mongolia's investment climate is key to analyzing and bettering its FDI inflow in the future.

While there are several ways to estimate a country's investment climate, the Fraser Institute's Investment Attractiveness Index (IAI) is a good index to gain a general understanding. The IAI is especially useful in Mongolia's case as it takes into consideration Mongolia's mineral resource wealth. In particular, the IAI is a composite of the Policy Perception Index (PPI) and the Best Practices Mineral Potential Rank (MPI).

In most cases, approximately 40% of investment decisions are determined by policy factors. The Best Practices Mineral Potential Index shows the mineral potential of jurisdictions, assuming policies are based on "best practice" (i.e., world class regulatory environment, highly competitive taxation, no political risk or uncertainty, and a fully stable mining regime).

Despite the significant influence of mineral potential on investment decisions, a region's policy climate has become increasingly important in attracting and winning investments. The Policy Perception Index provides a comprehensive assessment of the attractiveness of mining policies in a jurisdiction. The Fraser Institute identifies 15 policy factors that influence a company's decision to invest and uses them in calculating the Policy Perception Index. These include legal and taxation regimes, trade barriers, labor and other regulations, security and political stability, infrastructure, and availability of skilled labor.[3]

The IAI scores, calculated out of 100, and the rankings of Mongolia compared to several chosen countries are shown below. As the jurisdictions and number of countries included in the study vary year to year, the total number of jurisdictions was included in the rankings. As previously stated, Chile was chosen as an investment role model, while Kazakhstan, Zambia and Peru were chosen for comparison due to their similar economic and mineral resource circumstances (Tables 9 and 10).

Mongolia's investment attractiveness was relatively high in 2012 owing to its superb mineral potential ranking. However, since then, its ranking has remained at approximately 80–90, largely due to weak policy factors. Mongolia's policy perception ranked 101 in 2016, for instance, due to deteriorating perceptions caused by uncertainty concerning disputed land claims, protection areas and the availability of labor and skills. Its ranking improved considerably in 2017, going from 81 to 53 as investors' concerns over geological databases, availability of labor and skills, and uncertainty concerning protected areas decreased.

Chile consistently ranks high in terms of investment attractiveness due to good policy perceptions coupled with high mineral potential. Although its rankings dipped in 2016 and 2020, due to uniform decreases in policy perception and mineral potential, it is still an attractive FDI recipient. Peru, on the other hand, has steadily improved

[3] For detailed description of the 15 policy factors that determine the PPI, please refer to the Fraser Institute's annual survey of mining companies (Yunis & Aliakbari, 2021).

**Table 9** Investment attractiveness index score (out of 100), select countries, 2012–2020[4]

| | Mongolia | | | Chile | | | Peru | | | Kazakhstan | | | Zambia | | |
|---|---|---|---|---|---|---|---|---|---|---|---|---|---|---|---|
| | IAI | PPI | MPI | IAI | PPI | MPI | IAI | PPI | MPI | IAI | PPI | MPI | IAI | PPI | MPI |
| 2012 | 67 | 42 | 84 | 79 | 84 | 75 | 63 | 61 | 65 | 63 | 56 | 67 | 63 | 68 | 60 |
| 2013 | 53 | 44 | 59 | 83 | 86 | 80 | 70 | 65 | 73 | 63 | 57 | 68 | 70 | 72 | 69 |
| 2014 | 49 | 29 | 63 | 82 | 83 | 80 | 75 | 68 | 80 | 51 | 46 | 55 | 76 | 75 | 75 |
| 2015 | 50 | 37 | 59 | 80 | 84 | 77 | 69 | 67 | 71 | 75 | 70 | 78 | 57 | 63 | 54 |
| 2016 | 49 | 28 | 64 | 70 | 79 | 64 | 73 | 70 | 76 | 54 | 39 | 64 | 73 | 74 | 72 |
| 2017 | 61 | 54 | 65 | 82 | 81 | 82 | 74 | 69 | 78 | 71 | 61 | 78 | 59 | 53 | 63 |
| 2018 | – | – | – | 85 | 89 | 82 | 82 | 80 | 83 | – | – | – | 64 | 65 | 63 |
| 2019 | – | – | – | 78 | 87 | 72 | 75 | 67 | 81 | – | – | – | 38 | 39 | 38 |
| 2020 | – | – | – | 72 | 83 | 65 | 70 | 75 | 67 | – | – | – | 61 | 65 | 58 |

*Source* Fraser Institute

[4] Unfortunately, Mongolia and Kazakhstan were removed from the Fraser Institute's jurisdiction starting from 2018.

**Table 10** Investment attractiveness index rank, select countries, 2012–2020

| | Total | Mongolia | | | Chile | | | Peru | | | Kazakhstan | | | Zambia | | |
|---|---|---|---|---|---|---|---|---|---|---|---|---|---|---|---|---|
| | | IAI | PPI | MPI | IAI | PPI | MPI | IAI | PPI | MPI | IAI | PPI | MPI | IAI | PPI | MPI |
| 2012 | 96 | 31 | 78 | 1 | 11 | 18 | 8 | 39 | 59 | 35 | 42 | 63 | 32 | 10 | 50 | 43 |
| 2013 | 112 | 80 | 95 | 51 | 4 | 21 | 4 | 34 | 60 | 19 | 53 | 76 | 31 | 33 | 49 | 28 |
| 2014 | 122 | 93 | 116 | 52 | 9 | 22 | 6 | 26 | 58 | 7 | 88 | 100 | 75 | 25 | 40 | 20 |
| 2015 | 109 | 85 | 94 | 59 | 11 | 26 | 11 | 36 | 55 | 25 | 20 | 50 | 10 | 68 | 61 | 73 |
| 2016 | 104 | 81 | 101 | 50 | 39 | 35 | 49 | 28 | 54 | 17 | 73 | 90 | 45 | 30 | 43 | 27 |
| 2017 | 91 | 53 | 70 | 36 | 8 | 25 | 7 | 19 | 43 | 14 | 24 | 59 | 15 | 58 | 71 | 39 |
| 2018 | 83 | – | – | – | 6 | 23 | 9 | 14 | 37 | 8 | – | – | – | 45 | 53 | 39 |
| 2019 | 76 | – | – | – | 17 | 15 | 27 | 24 | 45 | 12 | – | – | – | 71 | 69 | 66 |
| 2020 | 77 | – | – | – | 30 | 23 | 34 | 34 | 42 | 30 | - | - | - | 51 | 60 | 48 |

*Source* Fraser Institute

its investment attractiveness ranking from high 30 s in 2012 to 14 in 2018. Its rankings fell in 2019 and 2020, however, owing to a lower mineral potential index. Kazakhstan, similar to Mongolia, suffers from weak policy factors that ultimately reduce its overall investment attractiveness. Zambia's investment attractiveness has fluctuated considerably since 2012, with its policy perception index consistently falling behind its mineral potential index. Its policy perception, for instance, fell from a rank of 43 in 2016 to 71 in 2017 due to increased concern over its taxation regime and political instability.

These findings show that while shifting sentiment about a country's mineral potential may affect overall investment attractiveness, policy perception plays an equally, if not more, important role. Countries with weak policy perception rankings fail to gain favorable investment attraction rankings despite high mineral potential. This is particularly salient for Mongolia, as, despite its tremendous mineral resources, proximity to China, and agricultural endowment, its investment climate left investors wanting due to low mineral commodity prices, inadequate infrastructure, policy missteps, and a lack of responsiveness to foreign investors and economic diversification. This focus on investment climate was echoed by Kenneth Green, senior director of the Fraser Institute's energy and natural resource studies, who noted that "Rich mineral reserves, competitive taxes, efficient permitting procedures and certainty around environmental regulations will still attract significant investment—even with slumping commodity prices" (Dempsey, 2018).

## 4.3 *Other Institutional Dimensions*

The main determinant of FDI inflow in Mongolia, historically and currently, is mineral commodity prices. This trend has also been observed from data from other mineral-rich, developing countries, as shown above. However, in developed nations, the investment climate plays a key role in attracting FDI, since most have little-to-no mineral resources.

For instance, in recent years, nations without large mineral reserves have been attracting FDI through a favorable investment climate. In 2014, the Economist Intelligence Unit (EIU) ranked countries by their environments to invest and do business in. Even though the top three countries—Singapore, Switzerland, and Hong Kong—do not have mineral resources, these nations have attracted much foreign investment (Economic Intelligence Unit, 2014). Tan (1999) concluded that the reasons why foreign investors are attracted to Singapore are related to the country's political stability, absence of corruption in government and business, adherence to the rule of law, and the fact that the government keeps its promises (Tan, 1999).

To gain an overview of Mongolia's investment environment and those of comparable countries, we turned to the World Bank's Doing Business Index. The World Bank's Doing Business Index is an effective way to obtain a general understanding

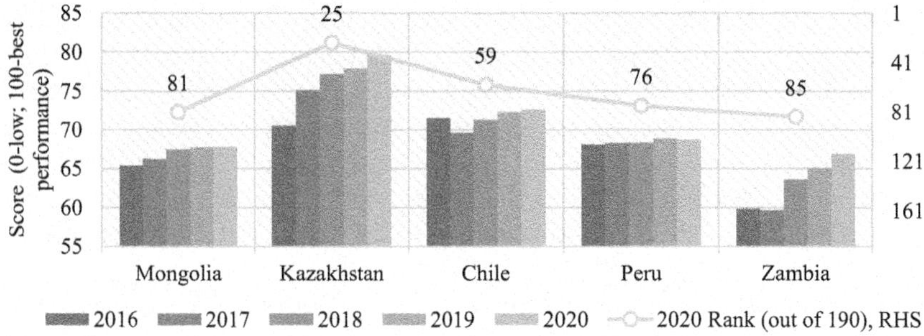


**Fig. 9** Ease of doing business, 2016–2020. *Source* World Bank

of a country's business environment.[5] Additionally, it is a useful indicator that can explain discrepancies in FDI inflows. Anderson and Gonzalez (2012) found that higher Doing Business rankings are associated with more foreign investment, which is believed to create jobs, bring in new technologies and processes and have other beneficial effects on the real economy (Anderson & Gonzalez, 2013) (Fig. 9).

Mongolia's ease of doing business score has improved consistently since 2016, although improvements have stalled since 2018. The improvements experienced in 2016 were due to reductions in the time required to start a business coupled with improving access to credit information, while the improvements in 2017 can be attributed to the introduction of an electronic taxation system that made paying taxes easier. In 2018, Mongolia further strengthened access to credit with the introduction of a new Law on Movable and Intangible Property Pledges along with establishing a new collateral registry. However, paying taxes became more difficult as VAT incurred by businesses could no longer be deducted as input credit (World Bank, 2018a, 2018b, 2018c).

Furthermore, Mongolia made enforcing contracts easier by reducing the fees that are required to enforce and judge in 2019 (World Bank, 2019a, 2019b, 2019c). No major changes were observed in terms of ease of doing business in 2020, although Mongolia was noted for its relatively limited labor regulations (World Bank, 2020). In general, Mongolia scored well in terms of starting a business, getting credit, and dealing with construction permits but was weak in terms of resolving insolvency, getting electricity, trading across borders and enforcing contracts.

Comparatively, Mongolia ranked 81st out of 190 countries in terms of ease of doing business in 2020. This is below similarly resource-rich countries such as Kazakhstan, Chile, and Peru but close to Zambia's rankings. More notably, Mongolia's improvements in bettering its business environment have stalled as in Peru, while Kazakhstan, Chile and Zambia continue to showcase significant reforms.

---

[5] The ten areas of business regulation that are measured include: starting a business, dealing with construction permits, getting electricity, registering property, getting credit, protecting minority investors, paying taxes, trading across borders, enforcing contracts and resolving insolvency. Labor market regulations and contracting with the government indicators are also measured but not included in the Doing Business Index rankings.

Overall, the top five problematic factors for doing business in Mongolia were foreign currency regulations, corruption, political instability, inefficient government bureaucracy, and government instability.

As identified in the World Economic Forum's Executive Opinion Survey 2017, corruption was a major factor in business deterrence. One index that examines corruption is Transparency International's Corruption Perception Index (CPI). The CPI is calculated using at least 3 data sources from 13 different surveys or assessments produced by independent organizations and ranges from 0 to 100 (Transparency International, 2021a, 2021b, 2021c). If a country's score is below 50, it means that a country has serious corruption problems, and a 100 means that a country is perceived as very clean.

Mongolia's CPI score increased significantly in 2012 before remaining stable and falling slightly in 2019. Its global ranking, on the other hand, fell consistently from 2010 to 2015 before ramping up again. Thus, Mongolia's fall in rank in 2016 and 2017 was largely due to the comparatively more significant improvements in governance in other countries. The improvements in 2018 can be attributed to the implementation of a new criminal code on 1 July 2017, which introduced stricter liability for corruption and corruption-related offenses for public servants and government officials (also extending to immediate families of government officials) (Fig. 10).

Additionally, in March 2017, the government developed a three-year action plan to implement the National Program Combatting Corruption, which was adopted in November 2016. The Anti-Corruption Law has been amended several times over the years; however, there is still no legislation that protects NGOs and other organizations investigating and reporting government corruption. Another measure implemented by the government since July 2017 aims to reduce the use of offshore bank accounts by government officials to combat corruption. In relation to this, the Independent Authority Against Corruption announced in early 2018 that several current and former public officials associated with offshore bank accounts were being subject to active investigation.

In 2019, Mongolia's score fell 2 points, as its rank also fell by 13. This seems to be the case for numerous countries, as Transparency International mentioned in its 2019 Corruption Perceptions Index report that while the collected data show some

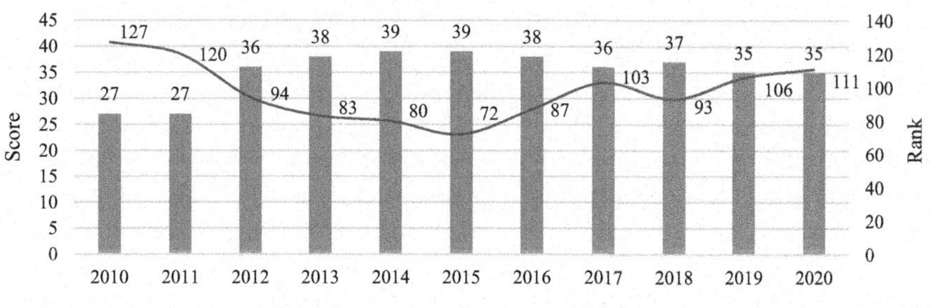


**Fig. 10** Mongolia's CPI, 2010–2020. *Source* Transparency International

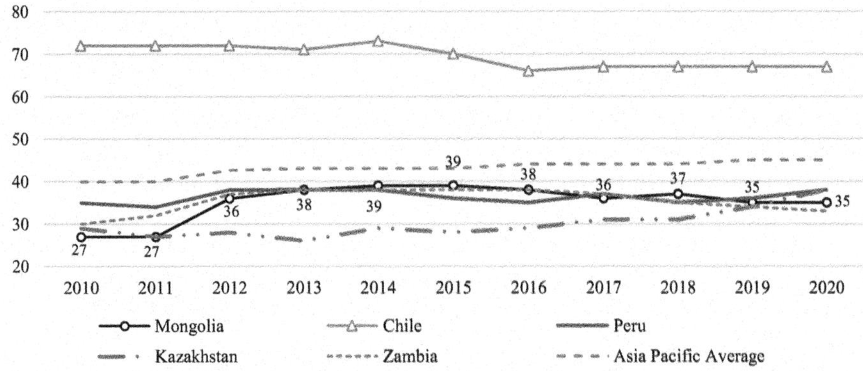


**Fig. 11** Corruption Perceptions Index scores, select countries, 2010–2020. *Source* Transparency International

progress, the majority of countries continue to fail to make any meaningful changes in combating corruption. Approximately 2 out of 3 countries scored below 50 points, with an average score of 43 points (Transparency International, 2020).

This continued into 2020 as the COVID-19 pandemic highlighted governance failures in many countries. Corruption was found to have undermined the global health response to the pandemic and was more pervasive in countries least equipped to handle the pandemic (Transparency International, 2021a, 2021b, 2021c). Most woringly, almost half of all countries included in the index have been stagnant for almost a decade.

As of 2020, Mongolia scored 35 out of 100, indicating the persistence of a corruption problem. Based on this score, it was ranked 111 out of 180 countries, with 69% of people considering government corruption in Mongolia to be a major problem according to the Global Corruption Barometer (Transparency International, 2021a, 2021b, 2021c) (Fig. 11).

Corruption and other aspects of governance are also tracked by the World Bank's Worldwide Governance Indicators (WGI). The WGI consists of aggregate and individual indicators for 6 dimensions of governance for over 200 countries. These include Voice and accountability, Political stability and absence of violence/terrorism, Government effectiveness, Regulatory quality, Rule of law, and Control of corruption. Countries are given a score on each indicator ranging from −2.5 to 2.5 based on numerous individual variables calculated from different data sources (Kaufmann, Kraay, & Mastruzzi, 2010). While topics such as governance are difficult to analyze quantitatively, the WGI offers an annual estimate that is beneficial for gaining a general understanding and tracking changes over time (Table 11).

Mongolia scores low in terms of its control of corruption, government effectiveness, rule of law and regulatory quality. Political stability and accountability scored comparatively well, although Mongolia does not score above 1 for any indicators. Thus, while Mongolia performs satisfactorily in terms of how it selects, monitors, and replaces its government, the government's formulation and implementation of

**Table 11** Mongolia's Governance Indicators, 2010–2020

| | Control of corruption | Government effectiveness | Political stability and absence of violence/terrorism | Regulatory quality | Rule of law | Voice and accountability |
|---|---|---|---|---|---|---|
| 2010 | −0.74 | −0.57 | 0.60 | −0.24 | −0.36 | 0.09 |
| 2011 | −0.69 | −0.59 | 0.61 | −0.22 | −0.27 | 0.05 |
| 2012 | −0.54 | −0.64 | 0.47 | −0.21 | −0.38 | 0.07 |
| 2013 | −0.48 | −0.55 | 0.49 | −0.32 | −0.37 | 0.11 |
| 2014 | −0.47 | −0.44 | 0.79 | −0.27 | −0.34 | 0.24 |
| 2015 | −0.49 | −0.42 | 0.72 | −0.35 | −0.38 | 0.27 |
| 2016 | −0.49 | −0.10 | 0.80 | −0.08 | −0.22 | 0.33 |
| 2017 | −0.45 | −0.27 | 0.79 | −0.12 | −0.31 | 0.29 |
| 2018 | −0.42 | −0.23 | 0.83 | 0.02 | −0.27 | 0.24 |
| 2019 | −0.43 | −0.20 | 0.63 | −0.01 | −0.27 | 0.32 |
| 2020 | −0.46 | −0.34 | 0.79 | −0.09 | −0.26 | 0.38 |

*Source* World Bank, Worldwide Governance Indicators

policies and actors' respect for the institutions that govern economic and social interactions are lacking.

The rule of law is particularly important in supporting the business environment and FDI in general, as legal consistency and predictability are key in mitigating some of the risks associated with investing.

**Box 2. Arbitration and Dispute Resolution**

One institutional dimension that effects a country's overall investment environment and is particularly salient in terms of FDI into the mining sector is the country's judicial system and its ability to resolve any disputes that may arise.

As contracts are the main mechanism through which interactions are managed in the mining sector, a country's ability to resolve issues pertaining to contracts and ensure their enforcement is vital. When analyzing this, the enforcing contracts indicator of the World Bank's Doing Business report is especially informative. The enforcing contracts indicator scores countries on 3 main factors: Time taken to enforce a contract through the courts, Cost of receiving any legal services as a percentage of the claim value and the Quality of Judicial Processes Index (QJPI). The QJPI in turn, is a comprehensive index that includes good practice areas under 4 broad categories: court structure and proceedings, case management, court automation, and alternative dispute resolution (ADR). The first 3 categories (court structure and proceedings, case management, and court automation) are largely linked to the domestic judicial system of the host country while ADR, which includes arbitrations, plays an important role in resolving international disputes in the mining sector.

In 2020, Mongolia scored 67.8 out of 100 in terms of ease of doing business. It scored 61.4 out of 100 in terms of enforcing contracts, an average litigation time of 374 days, an average cost of litigation of 22.9% of the claim and a QJPI score of 8.1. Mongolia boasts much lower time and cost of litigation results compared to the East Asia and Pacific region average. However, in terms of the QJPI, Mongolia has consistently ranked below average since the inception of the index. Thus, improvements in judicial quality, namely, court structure, case management, court automation and alternative dispute resolution are necessary.

To improve court structure and proceedings, Mongolia should conduct further research on whether it is beneficial to create a specialized commercial and small claims court. As for case management, the Mongolian courts should collect data and implement more performance measures in order to promote and enforce better judicial performance standards. Improving court automation, however, would require heavy government involvement to establish the necessary infrastructure needed and is not as salient as other factors. As for alternative dispute resolution, better utilization of Mongolia's mediation system and more comprehensive training of mediators and judges on how to best offer mediation services could reduce the workload of the courts and improve court efficiency.

These suggestions would lead to an overall improvement in Mongolia's legal environment, indirectly bolstering FDI. However, most FDI related disputes, particularly in the mining sector, depend on arbitration for its resolution. Arbitration is commonly used in the mining sector to resolve invest-state dispute settlements (ISDS). It is consensual, neutral, binding, private and is typically faster and more cost effective than domestic court proceedings (Luttrell & Murphy, 2019). From a theoretical standpoint, arbitration has the advantage of introducing and promoting principles of good governance in domestic judicial systems and providing investors an option to resolve conflicts without relying on the host country's domestic judicial system (Schreuer, 2015). Arbitration is distinct in that it does not depend on the domestic judicial system of the host country and requires the prior consent of participating parties. As Mongolia is already part of an ever-widening network of International Investment Agreements and Bilateral Investment Treaties, the issue of party consent does not occur often.

However, as more ISDS cases are likely to appear due to the increased FDI into Mongolia and its globalizing economy, its best to focus on preventing needless cases of ISDS moving forward. While an analysis of Mongolia' previous ISDS cases have highlighted improvements made in domestic legislation, the issue of their implementation and the government's adherence to due processes remain an issue. In fact, the majority of cases of ISDS involving Mongolia seems to be centered on indirect expropriation due to unlawful license nullification. Thus, it is key for Mongolia to focus on bettering its legal environment by improving the government's adherence to due processes while learning from past ISDS cases such as the Khan Resources case. This will lead to more stable government actions are in line with the government's policies to promote FDI.

## 5 FDI and Economic Diversification

Economic diversification has been put on the policy agenda of the Mongolian government since the early 2000s, following the initial recovery from transitional economic shock due to the collapse of the central plan. Several economic and export diversification government programs were developed in the course of the two decades, but none followed through. The more recent mining boom heightened the issue of economic dependence on very few mineral products, thus making economic diversification a pressing matter. As global tendencies elsewhere in the developing world show, FDI can potentially contribute to the economic diversification and thus long-term economic development of the country.

Economic diversification beyond the mining sector and the production of primary commodities has been linked to economic growth in the long run and is considered a safeguard against commodity price fluctuations (Hess, 2008). Commodity price fluctuations can destabilize an economy and are difficult to accurately predict, and countries such as Mexico, Venezuela and Nigeria have all been detrimentally affected by volatile oil prices (Gelb, 2010).

While many factors contribute to a country's ability to diversify its economy, Gelb found that the inability to successfully diversify is usually linked to a lack of two types of capital: human capital and governance/institutional capital. Institutional quality has also been linked to whether a country is likely to fall into or avoid a resource curse (Mehlum et al., 2006). The types of institutions needed to successfully diversify an economy depend on the chosen sector. To diversify into the manufacturing sector, for instance, countries should pay attention to the rule of law, contract enforcement and the overall business environment (Gelb, 2010). In general, economies with stronger institutions have a wider range of possible paths for diversification.

Similarly, human resources are also an indispensable factor of economic diversification. Countries that do not invest in human capital have more difficulty transitioning from an economy dependent on primary productions to the production of more value-added products (Maier & Wood, 1998).

Overall, countries should ensure macroeconomic stability, focus on bettering the endowment of certain factors such as institutions and human resources, employ countercyclical fiscal policies to smooth out boom-bust cycles, and implement measures to bring down the cost of production in newly traded sectors to bolster their development and encourage new entry. A handful of countries, such as China, South Korea and Malaysia, have implemented such measures to successfully diversify their economies from producing primary products to industrial products, becoming global industrial powerhouses. Other countries, primarily in Latin America, still rely on mineral commodities but have shifted from the production of primary ores to more value-added mineral products (Gelb, 2010).

As noted by the OECD and WTO, Chile, a country highly dependent on copper, exemplifies a successful two-track strategy to diversify its economy and exports. First, it diversified "within" industry by shifting from simple primary to more value-added processed products in the (same) copper industry. It also diversified "across" industries, developing fisheries and increasing exports of high value-added agricultural products such as salmon, fruits, and wine (OECD & WTO, 2019).

Zambia, on the other hand, is a landlocked country with high trade and transportation costs. FDI in the mining sector did not lead to inclusive growth. Growth has been primarily driven by mining, construction, and financial services. It created few jobs beyond the relatively small labor force employed in these industries. Thus, diversification still remains an essential objective to create wide-ranging opportunities for the poor in the country.

OECD and WTO argue that the role of FDI as an enabler of diversification depends on the type of investment. Positive spillovers to the rest of the economy depend on various factors, such as the recipient sector and joint venture versus foreign-only investment. FDI in the mining sector does not create as many jobs and economic linkages as agribusiness. Joint ventures between foreign and local entrepreneurs unleash greater spillovers than foreign-owned businesses.

Furthermore, foreign investors have different motivations when seeking to invest. This, in turn, has important implications for the rest of the economy. Following the framework developed by Dunning, there are four types of FDI: (i) natural resource-seeking (exploitation of natural resources); market-seeking (serving large domestic or regional markets); strategic asset-seeking (acquiring strategic assets through mergers and acquisitions); and efficiency-seeking investment (focusing on export-oriented production) (Dunning, 1980).

It is believed that the greatest benefit to the host country in terms of diversification comes from efficiency-seeking FDI. As a typical export-oriented investment, it focuses on lowering production costs, involves the transfer of know-how, improves access to distribution networks, and expands sources of finance (OECD & WTO, 2019). FDI thus can contribute not only to the overall economic diversification and long-term growth but also to export diversification, which makes the host countries less dependent on a few (highly volatile) primary products by providing more stable and sustainable sources of foreign exchange.

How can this be achieved in a resource-rich developing country such as Mongolia? As noted earlier, countercyclical fiscal policies to smooth out boom-bust cycles and prudent management of natural resource revenue are critical for creating a stable macroeconomic environment. Chile yet again provides a good example of setting up mechanisms that allowed us to save rents from mineral extraction and invest in critical growth expenditures. Structural fiscal surplus neutralizes copper price fluctuations and allows wealth to accumulate in good times. Chile spent its mineral proceeds on training a highly skilled labor force, building essential infrastructure, and financing high-growth start-ups. These all constitute a good foundation for attracting FDI into nonmining sectors.

A critical Fiscal Stability Law adopted in 2010 by the Mongolian Parliament was designed after a similar Chilean law and put in place an appropriate macro fiscal framework to prudently manage the mining revenue and circumvent boom-and-bust cycles. However, the law has been amended numerous times since its initial adoption, and the implementation of its critical clauses, such as maintaining fiscal balance and public debt within certain limits, has been pushed over for later periods. Thus, a good legal framework that has been in place of over a decade is now being wasted due to the lack of political will.

As Gelb noted, not all developing countries were able to grow into industrial powers, such as South Korea, Malaysia and Mexico. Several developing countries, Chile among them, have moved away from traditional simple primary exports to more complex yet still primary-based products and services (Gelb, 2010). This is especially plausible for countries with a very strong comparative advantage in a range of natural resources, such as Mongolia. Vast landmass, animal husbandry and a nomadic lifestyle provide a solid footing for diversifying the economy and exports in this direction. Cashmere production is the second largest earner of foreign exchange after mining, making Mongolia a significant player in the global cashmere market. There is also great potential in advancing agricultural production and tourism. The World Bank considers agriculture the most promising sector to promote diversification (World Bank, 2019a, 2019b, 2019c).

The OECD and WTO emphasize the need to promote policy coherence between FDI linkages to local firms and investment incentives, notably through well-designed supplier development programs. Supplier development programs connect large international firms with potential domestic suppliers and are an effective way to develop the domestic supply of value added. Investment promotion agencies are best equipped to implement these programs and can offer incentives and additional support to ensure that domestic suppliers meet the quality standards of large international firms. One example of this is Chile's Supplier development program, which focuses on improving the commercial links between SMEs and large foreign firms through matchmaking services in addition to offering subsidized credit and other fiscal incentives. The program was very effective in increasing sales, employment, and the overall survival rates of SME suppliers (Araiz, Henriquez, & Stucchi, 2013). Similar programs have also been implemented in El Salvador, Colombia, and Malaysia.

Tuvshintugs et al. (Chap. 4), in a recent ADB study on Mongolia, look at the economic diversification beyond mining. They site low institutional quality and poor business climate, poor infrastructure, seasonality of many inputs and the associated supply chain issues as the largest impediments to economic diversification (ADB, 2020). For instance, in 2020, Mongolia ranked 129th out of 167 countries based on its weighted aggregated scores of the World Bank's Logistics Performance Index (World Bank, 2019a, 2019b, 2019c).

Mongolia could not possibly compete with China or other mass exporters of manufactured goods in terms of economies of scale and the related low production costs. However, as the ADB study reveals, Mongolian companies are capable of producing small-batch, high-quality (e.g., organic) goods and supplying them in growing niche markets. These may include food, beverages, cosmetics, pharmaceutical products, etc., which use natural local ingredients and exclusive production technologies and can be sold at higher prices. The government needs to drastically improve the business environment, lower the cost of cross-border trade, address transport and logistics bottlenecks, and provide public goods and services, including internationally recognized standardization services. Coordination failures among small businesses and property rights issues also need to be addressed by the government.

## 6 Conclusion

FDI is an important source of financing for many developing countries. Mongolia has relied on FDI in the mining sector, which has provided a great boost to the economy. We looked at the sectoral distribution and country of origin of FDI. Unfortunately, there has been very little diversity on both accounts, with the mining sector being the dominant recipient of FDI and Canada and China providing the bulk of investment. In fact, in recent years, FDI dynamics have generally been determined by a sole investment in the Oyu Tolgoi project.

As a result, any changes in FDI inflow into the mining sector greatly affect the overall Mongolian economy. We estimated that an additional FDI injection equal to 1% of the mining output creates positive growth for all sectors. However, the magnitude differs substantially across the economic sectors, some such as utilities and services sectors, transportation, and storage as well as the construction sector, benefitting more through the higher domestic absorption of intermediate consumption. The foreign investment multiplier was estimated to be 0.87 and 1.04 in 2010 and 2015, respectively, the latter due to the higher share of intermediate consumption from the domestic market.

Structural economic shifts can also affect the multipliers, and in recent years, shifts have occurred due to a boom in the mining sector. Its impact is negative but not significant. The respective multipliers stand at 1.49 and 1.48 for the two years. As the mining sector is capital intensive, the aftershocks in the mining sector encourage increases in imports, as the domestic manufacturing sector cannot provide the equipment needed. As a result, the development of the manufacturing sector continues to be relatively weak. Thus, developing the Mongolian manufacturing sector that can benefit from increased FDI into the mining sector will improve investment multipliers.

Although highly volatile and closely connected with commodity prices, terms of trade have generally been positive for Mongolia since the early 2000s. The same trend is observed in Chile, another important copper exporter. The composite mineral commodity price index has also been positive. The price index and the FDI inflow go hand-in-hand, a phenomenon common to most resource-rich developing countries.

Commodity prices are thus crucial for foreign investment but cannot be controlled by individual countries such as Mongolia. A country cannot simply "hope" for higher or sustained commodity prices in the future. Thus, to achieve sustainable long-term growth, Mongolia should try to attract FDI inflow through efforts independent of global prices.

The impact that foreign investment exerts on the overall economy ultimately depends on the quality of the business environment. All things equal, countries with better business regulatory environments tend to be more attractive to FDI. It is believed that resource-rich countries can maintain a relatively stable FDI despite declines in mineral commodity prices if they have a favorable investment climate. The Fraser Institute's composite Investment Attractiveness Index (IAI) provides a good overview of the FDI attractiveness of individual jurisdictions. In most cases, approximately 40% of investment decisions are determined by policy factors, while the mineral potential accounts for the remaining 60%. Mongolia's PPI has always lagged behind the best practice MPI, suggesting that FDI is driven mostly by commodity prices, while policies and institutional quality are not conducive to attracting FDI. The country's rankings are significantly lower than those of resource-rich developing countries such as Chile, Kazakhstan, Peru, and Zambia. Other measures of institutional quality, such as the Doing Business Index, Corruption Perception Index, and Worldwide Governance Indices, corroborate this point.

As we noted, this is particularly alarming for Mongolia as, despite its tremendous mineral resources, proximity to China's vast markets, and agricultural endowment, its investment climate leaves investors wanting due to inadequate infrastructure, policy missteps, and a lack of responsiveness to foreign investors. These factors are the root causes of not only poor FDI inflow but also a generally volatile economic situation and lack of economic diversification.

FDI matters, but not all FDI is created equally. FDI in the extractive industries is focused on the utilization of mineral resources and capturing economic rents. It is very capital intensive, has weaker linkages to the rest of the economy and creates fewer jobs. In many developing countries, the extractive industries sector is both shaped by and, in turn, influences political dynamics. As the OECD and WTO argue, a focus by policymakers on short-term rents from resources and their allocation to ensure political survival has sometimes distracted from policies and investments necessary to sustain growth in the long term and has often been associated with increased internal conflict, with adverse effects for FDI and economic diversification (OECD & WTO, 2019). Mongolia could serve as a case in hand.

However, the mining sector is likely to remain the major source of foreign investment and hence high economic growth in Mongolia. Some resource-rich developing countries were able to capitalize on the natural resources moving away from simple primary exports to more value-added but still resource-based exports. For instance, Chile improved the quality of copper extraction and started exporting processed products, complementing this with the development of domestic ancillary/logistics services (OECD & WTO, 2019). Furthermore, a prudent macro fiscal regime smooths out commodity price fluctuations, and the surplus created was accumulated and used for strategic long-term development goals, such as enhancing the skills and building infrastructure. These developments have had a positive impact not only for the resources sector but also, most importantly, for further attracting FDI and diversifying the economic base.

Market and strategic asset-seeking foreign investors may not be interested in Mongolia. Mongolia's potential for mass production of internationally competitive low-cost products is low due to the small population, lack of a cheap labor force and related economies of scale. Studies show that efficiency-seeking FDI has a much greater impact on the economy. However, the country's strength may lie in the niche market export products rather than the mass market. This pertains to agricultural products and tourism, to name a few.

If prudent fiscal policies, public investment in education and much-needed infrastructure are realized, it can provide a good backdrop for both mining and nonmining sectors to attract more FDI and grow faster by narrowing the education and technology gap between the domestic factors of production and inward foreign investment. For a starter, the government could demonstrate the political will and start implementing the core principles of the fiscal regime outlined in the Fiscal Stability Law.

## References


ADB. (2020). *Mongolia's economic prospects: Resource-rich and landlocked between two giants.* Asian Development Bank.

Almfraji, M. A., Almsafir, M. K., & Uao, L. (2014). Economic growth and foreign direct investment inflows: The case of Qatar. *Procedia-Social and Behavioural Sciences*, 1040–1045.

Anand, A. (2011). *The impact of Foreign Direct Investment on the sectors: The case of Mongolia* (pp 155–177) (Working Paper-6) Bank of Mongolia.

Anderson, J., & Gonzalez, A. (2013). *Doing business 2013: Does doing business matter for foreign direct investment?* World Bank.

Anderson, J., & Gonzalez, A. (2012). Does doing business matter for foreign direct investment? *Doing Business*, 47–50, 2013. Washington, D.C: World Bank.

Araiz, I., Henriquez, F., & Stucchi, P. (2013). Supplier development programs and firm performance: Evidence from. *Small Business Economics*, 277–293.

Bidarkota, P., & Crucini, M. J. (2000). Commodity prices and the terms of trade. *Review of International Economics, 8*(4), 647–666.

Blomstrom, M., Lipsey, R. E., & Zejan, M. (1992). *What explains developing country growth?* (Working Paper, 1–36). The National Bureau of Economic Research.

British Geological Survey. (2011). *World mineral production 2005–2009.* Nottinghamshire.

Céspedes, L. F., & Velasco, A. (2012). Macroeconomic performance during commodity price booms. *IMC Economic Review*, 570–599.

Chowdhury, A., & Mavrotas, G. (2006). *FDI and growth: What causes what?* UNU-WIDER.

Dempsey, K. (2018, February 23). *Ontario's mining rankings improve dramatically.* Retrieved from Sudbury Star: https://www.thesudburystar.com/2018/02/24/ontarios-mining-rankings-improve-dramatically

Dunning, J. H. (1980). Toward an eclectic theory of international production: Some empirical tests. *Journal of International Business Studies*, 9–31.

EBRD. (2021). *What are investment climate and governance?* Retrieved from European Bank for Reconstruction and Development: https://www.ebrd.com/what-we-do/sectors-and-topics/investment-climate-governance.html

Economic Intelligence Unit. (2014). *Business environment rankings: Which country is best to do business in?* Economic Intelligence Unit.

Economic Research Institute. (2017a). *Coal market study.* Admon LLC.

Economic Research Institute. (2017b). *Copper market study.* Admon LLC.

Fernando, J. (2020, November 29). *What is investment multiplier?* Retrieved from Investopedia: https://www.investopedia.com/terms/i/investment-multiplier.asp

Fornero, J., Kirchner, M., & Yany, A. (2016). *Terms of trade shocks and investment in commodity-exporting economies* (Working Paper, 773–790). The Central of Chile.

Gelb, A. (2010). *Economic diversification in resource rich countries.* Center for Global Development.

Hansen, H., & Rand, J. (2005). *On the causal links between FDI and growth in developing countries.* UNU-WIDER.

Hansen, H., & Rand, J. (2006). On the casual links between FDI and growth in developing countries. *The World Economy*, 21–41.

Hess, H. (2008). *Export diversification and growth* (Working Paper No. 21, Growth Commission). World Bank.

IFC. (2016). *The investment climate.* World Bank.

Investopedia. (2018, February). *Terms of trade—TOT*. Retrieved from Investopedia: https://www.investopedia.com/terms/t/terms-of-trade.asp

Iqbal, M. S., & Shaikh, F. M. (2010). Causality relationship between Foreign Direct Investment, Trade and Economic growth in Pakistan. *Asian Social Science*, 82–89.

Javzandorj, A., & Dehong, L. (2012). Factors contributing to foreign direct investment in Mongolia. *European Researcher*, 1559–1565.

Kaufmann, D., Kraay, A., & Mastruzzi, M. (2010). *The worldwide Governance indicators: Methodology and analytical issues* (Working Paper No. 5430). World Bank Policy Research.

Kose, M. A. (2002). Explaining business cycles in small open economies 'How much do world price matter?'. *Journal of International Economics*, 299–327.

Luttrell, S., & Murphy, A. (2019, June 18). *Stabilisation provisions in long-term mining agreements.* Retrieved from Global Arbitration Review: https://globalarbitrationreview.com/guide/the-guide-mining-arbitrations/1st-edition/article/stabilisation-provisions-in-long-term-mining-agreements

Maier, J., & Wood, A. (1998). Africa's export structure in a comparative perspective. In *Study #4.* UNCTAD.

Mehlum, H., Moene, K. O., & Torvik, R. (2006). Institutions and the Resource. *Economic Journal*, 1–20.

Munkhtsetseg, D., & Gantumur, P. (2015). *The optimal policy applying on foreign investment* (pp. 655–724) (Working Paper-10). Bank of Mongolia.

Nnadozie, E. (2011). *Investment climate and foreign direct investment in Africa.* African Development Bank Group.

NRGI. (2015). *Country strategy note.* NRGI.

NSO. (2016). *Annual report.* NSO.

Obwona, M. B. (2001). Determinants of FDI and their Impact on Economic Growth in Uganda. *African Development Review*, 46–81.

Och, M., Baerbig, C., & Jadamba, T. (2017). Determinants of inward FDI in Mongolia: An application of the ARDL bounds testing approach to cointegration. *Asian Economic and Financial Review*, 307–333.

OECD & WTO. (2019). *Aid for trade at a glance 2019: Economic diversification and empowerment.* OECD Publishing.

OECD. (2008). *The social impact of foreing direct investment.* Policy Brief.

OECD. (2021). *Input-output tables (IOTs).* Retrieved from OECD: https://www.oecd.org/sti/ind/input-outputtables.htm

Popescu, G. (2014). FDI and economic growth in Central and Eastern Europe. *Sustainability*, 8149–8163.

Quazi, R. M., & View, P. (2007). Investment climate and foreign direct investment: A study of selected countries in Latin America. *Global Journal of Business Research*, 1–13.

Reuters. (2021, April 9). *Rio Tinto, Turquoise Hill reach deal on Oyu Tolgoi expansion.* Retrieved from Reuters: https://www.reuters.com/article/us-rio-tinto-oyu-tolgoi-turquoise-hill-idUSKBN2BW0P5

Rio Tinto. (2016, May 6). *Rio Tinto approves development of Oyu Tolgoi underground mine.* Retrieved from Rio Tinto: https://www.riotinto.com/en/news/releases/Oyu-Tolgoi-underground-approved

Schmitz, C. (1986). The rise of big business in the world copper industry 1870–1930. *The Economic History Review, 39*, 392–410.

Schreuer, C. (2015). Do we need investment arbitration. In J. E.-B. Kalicki (Ed.), *Reshaping the investor-state dispute settlement system* (pp. 879–889). Brill Nijhoff.

Tan, A. H. (1999). Official efforts to attract FDI: Case of Singapore's EDB. In *Conference on Industrial Globalization in the 21st Century: Impact and Consequences for East Asia and Korea* (pp. 1–22). Seoul: Korean Development Insitute.

The Bank of Mongolia. (2016). *Mongolia' foreign trade review*. The Bank of Mongolia. Retrieved from https://www.mongolbank.mn/documents/statistic/externalsector/tradebalancereview/2015/10e.pdf

Tiwari, A. K., & Mutascu, M. (2011). Economic growth and FDI in Asia: A panel-data approach. *Economic Analysis and Policy*, 173–187.

Transparency International. (2020). *Corruption Perceptions Index 2019*. Transparency International.

Transparency International. (2021a). *Corruption Perceptions Index 2020*. Transparency International.

Transparency International. (2021b). *Mongolia Corruption Perceptions Index Global Corruption Barometer*. Retrieved from Transparency International: https://www.transparency.org/en/countries/mongolia

Transparency International. (2021c). *The ABCS of the CPI: How the Corruption Perceptions Index is calculated*. Retrieved from Transparency International: https://www.transparency.org/en/news/how-cpi-scores-are-calculated

UNCTAD. (1998). *World investment report 1998 trends and determinants*. UNCTAD.

UNCTAD. (2017). *World investment report*. United Nations Publication.

UNTCAD. (2021). *World investment report 2021*. United Nations Publications.

World Bank. (2015, July 3). *China economic update*. Retrieved from World Bank: https://www.worldbank.org/content/dam/Worldbank/document/EAP/China/ceu_06_15_en.pdf

World Bank. (2018a). *Doing business 2018*. World Bank.

World Bank. (2018b). *Global investment competitiveness report 2017/2018 foreign investor perspectives and policy implications*. World Bank.

World Bank. (2018c). *World development indicators*.

World Bank. (2019a). *Aggregated LPI*. Retrieved from World Bank Logistics Performance Index: https://lpi.worldbank.org/international/aggregated-ranking

World Bank. (2019b). *Doing business 2019*. World Bank.

World Bank. (2019c). *Mongolia central economic corridor assessment: A value chain analysis of the cashmere-wool, meat and leather industries*. World Bank.

World Bank. (2020). *Doing business 2020*. World Bank.

World Bank. (2021). *Commodity market outlook April 2021 special focus causes and consequences of metal price shocks*. World Bank. Retrieved from World.
World Banks. (2020). *Global Investment competitiveness report 2019/2020 rebuilding investor confidence in times of uncertainty*. World Bank.
Yao, S. (2006). On economic growth, FDI and exports in China. *Applied Economics*, 339–351.
Yunis, J., & Aliakbari, E. (2021). *Survey of mining companies 2020*. Fraser Institute.

**Dr. Chuluunbat Narantuya** is the Chair and Associate Professor at the Economics Department of the National University of Mongolia (NUM). She teaches undergraduate and graduate courses in Microeconomics, Economic Development, Public Sector Economics, New Institutional Economics. Her research interests include political economy, transition, public finance, institutions and governance. Her most recent research is related to economic diversification and export promotion in the non-mining sectors in Mongolia. In 2013–2017 Dr. Chuluunbat Narantuya served as the Vice President for Finance and Development of the NUM. She also is a member and secretary of the national Doctoral Defense Committee in Economics. Chuluunbat Narantuya received her Ph.D. in Policy Studies from the University of Maryland, College Park, MD, USA. Her doctoral research was on the political and economic transition in Mongolia in 1990–1996. She also studied at the Moscow State University, Russia and obtained her Master of Economics degree from the University of Sydney, Australia.

**Manlaibaatar Zagdbazar** is a project manager and senior researcher at the Economic Research Institute (ERI) of Mongolia. He has a bachelor's degree in applied mathematics from the Khan-Uul Institute, Mongolia; a master's degree in economic policy from the Central European University, Hungary; and is currently a Ph.D. candidate in economics at the National University of Mongolia. He has abundant teaching and research experience, working as a lecturer at Khan-Uul Institute, Mongolia, and the National University of Mongolia. Previously, he worked as a researcher at the Development Strategy and System Research Centre in Mongolia; an assistant researcher at the Research Department of the Central Bank of Hungary; and a consultant at the Independent Research Institute of Mongolia. He has published in international and domestic peer-reviewed journals such as *Resources Policy* and *Sociology* and coauthored several economic textbooks in Mongolian.

**Khorol-Erdene Bayartsogt** is a researcher at the Economic Research Institute (ERI). She received her bachelor's degree from New York University in the USA and completed a double major in economics and political science. She also has an undergraduate law degree from the National University of Mongolia. Her research interests include governance and political economy.

**Dulguun Tuvshintugs** is a researcher at the Economic Research Institute (ERI). She received her bachelor's degree from Bentley University in the United States, where she majored in finance with a concentration in corporate finance and a minor in law. Her research interests include monetary policy, capital markets, and financial modeling.

**Bayarjargal Munkh-Ireedui** has worked as a researcher at the Economic Research Institute (ERI). He received his bachelor's and master's degrees in economics from the National University of Mongolia. He is currently completing his Ph.D. program at Concordia University in Canada. His research interests include labor economics and CGE modeling.

**Delgermaa Begz** worked as a researcher at the Economic Research Institute (ERI). She received her bachelor's degree from the University of Finance and Economics in Mongolia as well as a master's degree in environmental economics from the Central European University in Hungary. Her research area focuses on macroeconomics, financial markets, environmental and resource economics, education, and inequality.

# Mining Development Strategy

**Tuvshintugs Batdelger**

## 1 Introduction

The main objective of this study is to assess the national strategy of resource management. The Parliament of Mongolia adopted national strategic and policy documents such as "Vision 2050" (Parliament of Mongolia, 2020), "Sustainable Development Goals 2030" (Parliament of Mongolia, 2016), "State Minerals Policy 2025" (Parliament of Mongolia, 2014), and its follow-up programs. Since these strategic documents cover a wide range of issues, such as planning, taxation, environmental management, financing, labor, and education, our primary focus is to assess the gaps and overlaps in these documents.

Mongolia's national strategy in managing its natural resources recognizes the need to reduce reliance on commodity exports in the long term. Thus, our assessment primarily focuses on the issue of economic diversification and related policies while sustainably regulating the mineral sector.

Long-term management of the resources sector requires a proper legal and institutional framework. Therefore, our assessment also focused on whether the current legal and institutional framework adequately addresses the needs for long-term management of the sector.

This study used two pillars out of four of the benchmarking methods developed by the Natural Resource Governance Institute (NRGI). By this methodology, the country should address the following four issues in its national strategy:

- Cognizant of reality
- Considering the long-term approach
- Comprehensiveness—consideration of the full range of issues in the management of resource wealth

T. Batdelger (✉)
Economic Research Institute, Mongolia and the National University of Mongolia, Ulaanbaatar, Mongolia
e-mail: tuvshintugs@eri.mn



Y. Hosoi et al. (eds.), *Economic Dependence of Mongolia on Minerals*,
Contributions to Economics, https://doi.org/10.1007/978-981-19-5515-0_4

- *Coal-chemical, coal-energy, methane gas production and technological park;*
- *Steel factory;*
- *Fluorspar enrichment plant;*
- *Gold cleaning factory.*

*Mining deposits:*

- *Tavan Tolgoi coal deposit;*
- *Oyu Tolgoi underground mine;*
- *Dornogovi silicon deposit;*
- *Tsagaan suvarga deposit;*
- *Kharmagtain deposit;*
- *Lithium deposit;*
- *Step up exploration and survey work on rare earth elements.*

4.2.15 *Lay down the water pipeline to the Gobi area.*
4.2.16 *Build up an oil refinery plant, its infrastructure network, and oil chemical enterprise.*

The SDG document indicates that the country views the mining sector as of significant importance in the near term, which paves the way for the country's long-term development. The following are the objectives and phases of the development of the mining sector:

***Objective 1. Support Geological Sector Development***

- ***Phase I—(2016–2020)***: *Strengthen the capacity to undertake all types of comprehensive research in geology, geochemistry, and geophysics, update research methodologies, guidelines, and procedures conjunct with internationally accepted methods, draw a complete map of Mongolia with a 1:200,000 scale, and draw geological maps on a 1:50,000 scale for 40% of the territory, with ore zones and banks with mineral resources for general exploration.*
- ***Phase II—(2021–2025)***: *Create a geological information database, create a favorable environment for investment in the mineral exploration sector, and draw geological maps of 1:50,000 scale for 50% of the territory, with ore zones and banks with mineral resources for general exploration.*
- ***Phase III—(2026–2030)***: *Conduct in-depth explorations at all sites with mineral resource deposits and draw a geological map of 1:50,000 scale for 60% of the territory, with ore zones and banks, with mineral resources for general exploration.*

***Objective 2. Transparent and Accountable Extractive Industries Should Be Encouraged, and the Competitiveness of the Mining Sector Should Be Improved***

- ***Phase I—(2016–2020)***: *Ensure a stable investment environment for the mining sector, develop an environmentally friendly infrastructure and transportation network, and establish a high-capacity power plant in the Gobi region.*

- ***Phase II—(2021–2025)***: *Implement projects on reliable water supply sources and ensure full functionality of large mining projects.*
- ***Phase III—(2026–2030)***: *Start the development of large mining projects and develop the infrastructure.*

The next major piece of legislation on the mining sector's development strategy is a document entitled "State Minerals Policy (SMP) 2014–2025", adopted in 2014 by the Parliament. This minerals policy document is a more detailed long-term view of the sector's development.

It has four parts. The first part is the general motivation of the document, the second part stipulates principles for mineral sector policies, the third part specifies policy guidelines, and the final fourth part addresses minerals policy implementation stages and outcomes.

According to this document, the mineral policy strategy is to be implemented based on the following eight principles:

1. *No breach of parties' interests involved*
2. *Support for the adoption of modern machinery, technology, and innovation*
3. *Promotion of state organizations' and companies' transparency and responsibility*
4. *Promotion of good governance at companies*
5. *No discrimination in ownership type*
6. *Make available and transparent all levels of information on the geological survey, mining, and processing operations that are not prohibited by law*
7. *Improvement in safety and sanitary standards to the international levels and its implementation*
8. *Improvement in state regulations on registration, permit issuance, and supervision and maintaining state intervention in exploration and mining operations at the appropriate level.*

These guiding principles show how the country aims to achieve its long-term goals within these parameters. In other words, policies and strategies in the mining sector will be in line with these principles in achieving goals set out in the "Vision 2050", SDGs, and the Government action plan for 2020–2024.

In particular, SMP aims to achieve the following goals:

1. *To implement geological research and exploration in accordance with government policy and to increase national mineral reserves, providing a long-term sustainable development basis for the mining sector.*
2. *To mine mineral reserves exhaustively and at an appropriate level using technology with minimal environmental impact, the processing level should be deepened to increase the production level as well as a variety of products.*
3. *Adoption of integrated standards in mining and processing and to create safety and sanitary conditions in each step of production, which leads to fewer production accidents.*

4. *To be able to carry out long-term planning as a follow up to mining projects that bring infrastructure development (road networks, power plants, cities, and towns).*
5. *Creation of major industrial centers that will reduce overconcentration of the population.*
6. *Human resources of the minerals and infrastructure sector will be trained, and the number of professionally trained local workers and workplaces will decrease the unemployment level.*
7. *The activities related to environmental protection, mine closure, and rehabilitation, and long-term monitoring shall be done in accordance with laws and international standards in an orderly and responsible manner.*
8. *To restrict mining and processing operations near riverbed areas, out-flowing basins, forested areas, agricultural fields, fertile pastureland, Gobi oasis, lakes, and ponds to achieve ecological balance and to produce healthy eco-food products that will provide an environment for citizens to use healthy nutrition and a safe living environment.*
9. *All activities in the mineral sector shall be undertaken in accordance with applicable laws and regulations, be transparent to the public, and create an environment whereby public opinion should be received and reflected in the formulation of new laws and regulations and the implementation of large projects.*
10. *To create an environment whereby trading of mineral products is openly carried out at the minerals' market in compliance with international standards and accompanying improved business environment in the minerals sector will be established.*

It should be noted that the mining development strategy cannot be assessed by a single dimension. Rather, it is a complex set of policies that will consistently impact the economy and society. Specific to the mineral sector, SMP encompasses policies in the following areas:

1. Legal environment
2. Minerals sector management, organization, and human resource management
3. Environmental protection and reclamation
4. Support for local development, protection of interests of indigenous people
5. Downstream processing sector
6. Mining operations sector
7. Geological sector.

SMP specified detailed policies in each area, as well as corresponding follow-up regulations, programs, and policy documents that were enacted or still needed to be produced. We will assess the strategy in conjunction with these policies.

Another crucial piece of legislation is the government action plan for 2020–2024. The following actions are planned concerning the mining sector or related infrastructure development.

***In Mining and Heavy Industry***

3.2 ***The government will create a sustainable and multipillar economic structure and implement the principle of fair distribution of wealth by developing transparent and responsible mining and value-added industry and ensuring the growth of mineral revenues. We plan to commence the construction of heavy industries, including oil, coal-chemical, copper concentrate and metallurgy, and implement related infrastructure projects.***

- 3.2.1 *Increase the economic benefits of the following strategically important mines:*
  - 3.2.1.1 *Ensure that the Oyu Tolgoi project complies with the laws of Mongolia and commissions the underground mine.*
  - 3.2.1.2 *Resolve the issues related to ownership of the "Erdenet mining corporation" SOE, renovate and expand the open pit mine, concentration plant and repair and maintenance factory and increase its production capacity and returns.*
  - 3.2.1.3 *Commission the Tsagaan suvarga copper and molybdenum mine.*
  - 3.2.1.4 *Expanding the Baganuur and Shivee Ovoo coal mines increases their mining capacity and reduces costs.*
  - 3.2.1.5 *Carry out testing and research required for operationalization of the Asgat silver deposit and resolve issues related to the investment needed.*
  - 3.2.1.6 *Build the required infrastructure for the Tavan tolgoi group mines and commission a coal enrichment plant within the framework of establishing an Industry and Technology Park.*
- 3.2.2 *Commission the following major mines to increase exports:*
  - 3.2.2.1 *Operationalize the Salkhit silver mine up to its projected capacity.*
  - 3.2.2.2 *Commission the Zuun Tsagaan Del fluorspar underground mine.*
- 3.2.3 *Enhance geology and research works funded by the state budget and increase mineral revenues.*
- 3.2.4 *Develop an integrated National Geo-database, introduce an e-system and provide responsive public services.*
- 3.2.5 *Increase mineral revenues by boosting investment in the exploration of raw materials for high-tech industries, such as rare earth elements, precious, nonferrous, ferrous and mixed metals, nonmetallic minerals and oil.*
- 3.2.6 *Strengthen mining sector institutions, develop responsible mining, make licensing open to the public and revoke illegal permits.*
- 3.2.7 *Develop heavy industry, increase the level of mineral processing and produce value-added products:*

3.2.7.1 *Develop ferrous metallurgy (coke, cast iron, direct reduced iron) in Darkhan-Uul, Orkhon and Dornogovi aimags.*

3.2.7.2 *Set up an Industry and Technology Park based on the Erdenet Corporation. The park will include a copper concentrate processing plant and a cathode copper plant with heap leaching technology of oxidized ore.*

3.2.7.3 *Build a precious metal refinery plant.*

3.2.7.4 *Establish a branch laboratory for precious metal sampling, expand activities of sampling of precious stones and identify gemstones and increase the quality and accessibility of services provided to citizens.*

3.2.7.5 *Commence the construction of the copper concentrate processing plant based on the Oyu Tolgoi mine.*

3.2.8 *Develop an oil refinery plant based on local raw materials.*

3.2.8.1 *Accelerate the exploration and use of oil and nonconventional oil and increase reserves.*

3.2.8.2 *Resolve the issue of financing sources required for supplying raw materials to the oil refinery and construction of pipelines and carry out construction work.*

3.2.8.3 *Construct an oil refinery plant based on local raw materials in Altanshiree soum of Dornogovi aimag.*

3.2.9 *Implement the amendments made to the Constitution of Mongolia and create a system of equitable and fair distribution of benefits of mining to every citizen through the wealth fund.*

***In Transportation and Logistics***

3.6 ***The government will establish a national transportation and logistics network based on the smart transportation system that can ensure economic growth.***

3.6.1 *Expand road and transportation networks to enable economic growth and increase exports:*

3.6.1.1 *Complete the construction of the Tavan Tolgoi-Gashuunsukhait and Tavan Tolgoi-Zuunbayan bound railroads and commence the Saikhshand-Baruun Urt-Khuut; Khuut-Bichigt, Khuut-Choibalsan, and Zuunbayan-Khangi bound railroad construction projects.*

These policy actions align with the country's longer-term development strategy and are designed to achieve or provide steps to attain these goals in the medium term.

# 3 Assessments of Strategy Documents in Accordance with NRGI Benchmarking

The primary purpose of the strategic documents mentioned above is to ensure that all citizens benefit from the mining sector. To achieve the most significant possible benefit to citizens, these documents should be inclusive and comprehensive. Therefore, these documents should include the interests of all stakeholders and should address all phases of resource management.

## *3.1 Cognizant of the Reality*

Understandably, the country should be cognizant of reality. In other words, the country should have realistic expectations about the mining sector and its role in the economy.

### 3.1.1 About Resource Endowments and Commodity Price Scenarios

It is widely observed in resource-rich countries that the population and policymakers are too optimistic in assessing the mining sector. This leads to inefficient mining policies and makes the country susceptible to the resource curse. The country should make realistic assumptions about the size and scale of the mining sector and its effect on the economy.

The country's strategy in developing the mining sector must be based on a sound understanding of the fundamentals of resource wealth. The strategy should be based on a reliable and objective assessment of the country's resource endowments. Moreover, since Mongolia is a price taker in the world minerals market and the sector is greatly dependent on the prices of minerals, the strategy should also accommodate various scenarios of minerals' prices and their impact.

Thus, it is expected that strategy and policy documents such as "Sustainable development goals", "State minerals policy", and "Government action plan for 2020–2024" should be based on realistic assumptions about the reserves and prices of commodities.

It should be noted that these documents in themselves do not directly reveal the country's estimations of resource reserves and assumptions on pricing. These documents show that the authorities are cognizant that the country is endowed with rich natural resources but do not provide a specific estimate of its resource wealth. Therefore, we look at supporting documents of these policy papers for those assumptions.

Unfortunately, supporting documents of these major pieces of legislation do not reveal much about the estimation or assessment of resource reserves. The official estimate of resource reserves is primarily described in the "Annual bulletin of mining and geology".

The following is the official estimation of reserves of major commodities. It should be noted that resources or reserves are classified differently than JORC or NI43-101 methods since Mongolia has its country-specific regulations.[1] In brief, Mongolia has three types of resource reserves: Assessed mineral potential, Geological reserves, and Economic (commercial) reserves. "Geological reserves" are widely cited as the country's resource reserves.

Geological reserves are reserves determined by pre-feasibility studies of ore deposits, and these deposits are not required to have their economic viability assessed. After the economic viability of the ore deposit is assessed, reserves will be classified as "economic (commercial) reserves".

Therefore, we will use "geological reserves" as resource reserves. These reserves are shown below in the "Annual bulletin of mining and geology" (Table 1).

These reserves should not be treated as economic reserves, as we mentioned above. Nevertheless, these numbers show that the country possesses rich mineral endowments.

The country is endowed with rich mineral resources, and its economy is also increasingly becoming dependent on the mineral sector. There is little debate about whether the country is dependent on the mineral sector. A report titled "Study on Economic and Fiscal Policies in Resource-Rich Countries"[2] emphasizes that Mongolia's fiscal dependency is not as prominent as that of other comparable resource-rich countries. Nevertheless, it is above the threshold indicated in "Fiscal Frameworks for Resource-rich Developing Countries".[3]

The following Table 2 shows the production of minerals in the country and its forecast by the Mineral Resources and Petroleum Authority of Mongolia (MRPAM).

The table above shows that the production of the mineral sector is expected to expand until 2020 and thus increase in prominence in terms of its role in the economy.

Moreover, the following Table 3 shows how Mongolia's reserves measure up to the world's and neighboring countries' reserves. This is one of the indicators of how the country is cognizant of its reserves.

Noticeably, we can identify the following points:

- As of 2015, Mongolia's uranium resource was ranked in tenth place globally and holds 2% of the world's uranium resource (WNA, 2016).
- As of 2016, Mongolia's fluorspar reserves are ranked third globally and hold 8.5% of world reserves (USGS, 2017).
- As of 2017, Mongolia holds 1% of the world's molybdenum reserves (USGS, 2017).
- As of 2013, Mongolia holds 0.4% of the world's rare earth element resources (MRPAM, 2013).

[1] "Annual bulletin of mining and geology Mongolia 2016", The Mineral Resources Authority of Mongolia.

[2] "Study on Economic and Fiscal Policies in Resource-Rich Countries", JICA, KRI International Corporation and Mitsui Mineral Development Engineering Co. Ltd, 2016.

[3] "Fiscal Frameworks for Resource-rich Developing Countries", IMF Staff Discussion Note, IMF, 2012.

**Table 1** Mineral deposits

| Mineral type | Unit | □/Logical reserves/A + B + C/ | Number of deposits |
|---|---|---|---|
| Gold/hard rock/ | t | 2584.20 | 123 |
| Gold/placer/ | t | 237.2 | 727 |
| Copper/without copper in polymetallic deposits | mln t | 68.6 | 65 |
| Coal | mln t | 41,214 | 313 |
| Iron | mln t | 1888.80 | 101 |
| Zinc | mln t | 6.2 | 25 |
| Molybdenum | mln t | 1.5 | 38 |
| Fluorspar | mln t | 49.3 | 174 |
| Tungsten | ths t | 441.4 | 60 |
| Tin | ths t | 132.9 | 30 |
| Molybdenum | mln t | 1.5 | 38 |
| Fluorspar | mln t | 49.3 | 174 |
| Tungsten | ths t | 441.4 | 60 |
| Tin | ths t | 132.9 | 30 |
| Silver | ths t | 42.1 | 14 |
| Lead | mln t | 2.1 | 19 |
| Rare Earth elements/RE2O2/ | mln t | 2.4 | 10 |
| Uranium/oxide/ | ths t | 185.1 | 12 |
| Phosphorite | mln t | 54.1 | 4 |
| Limestone | mln t | 2205.40 | 95 |
| Crude oil | mln t | 332.6 | |

*Source* MRPAM (2016, 2017)

We can also look at the per capita resource wealth Mongolia is endowed with. The following Table 4 shows per capita geological reserves.

Since there is no clear indication of these kinds of assessments used in strategy documents, it is not clear whether the public has a deep understanding of the natural resource reserves or whether major pieces of development strategy documents such as "Vision 2050", "Sustainable development goals" and "State minerals policy" are based on a clear understanding of the endowment. Therefore, the consensus can be further improved by clearly conveying estimations and the potential scale of the mining sector and natural resource endowments and reflecting it in policy documents.

In particular, a gap needs to be addressed in terms of the country's estimated resource wealth and exploiting it consistent with the development strategy documents. Understandably, strategy documents reflect conceptual issues and thus lack

**Table 2** Mineral production

| | Unit | 2012 | 2013 | 2014 | 2015 | 2016 | 2017 | 2018 | 2019 | 2020 |
|---|---|---|---|---|---|---|---|---|---|---|
| Gold | t | 6.0 | 8.9 | 11.5 | 14.6 | 18.4 | 15.1 | 16.5 | 24.8 | 9.2 |
| Copper concentrate | ths t | 517.9 | 803 | 1080.4 | 1334.7 | 1445.1 | 1328.3 | 1067.1 | 1223.1 | 1258.2 |
| Coal/bituminous and lignite/ | mln t | 28.6 | 29.2 | 24.9 | 24.1 | 35.5 | 31.2 | 37.1 | 41.2 | 44.2 |
| Iron ore and concentrate | mln t | 6.9 | 5.0 | 6.3 | 4.3 | 4.9 | 11 | 11 | 11 | 11 |
| Zinc ore and concentrate | ths t | 119.1 | 104.1 | 93.2 | 89.6 | 100.2 | 94 | 90 | 90 | 90 |
| Molybdenum concentrate | ths t | 3.9 | 3.7 | 4.1 | 5.2 | 5.2 | 4.5 | 4.5 | 4.5 | 4.5 |
| Fluorspar ore and concentrate | ths t | 641.6 | 238.1 | 374.9 | 230.8 | 201.8 | 200 | 250 | 240 | 250 |
| Tungsten | t | 130.0 | 530.0 | 1,080 | 680 | 1460 | 298 | 330 | 280 | 240 |
| Tin* | t | 118 | 103.53 | 93.1 | 89.6 | 126 | 85 | 85 | 85 | 85 |
| Silver/concentrate/ | ths t | | | | | | 39 | 29.2 | 37.7 | 37 |

*Source* NSO (2017) and MRPAM (2017)

**Table 3** 2013 mineral reserves and percentage of world reserve by country

| Mineral type | Unit | World resource | | World resource | China | | Russia | |
|---|---|---|---|---|---|---|---|---|
| | | Quantity | % of world | | Quantity | % of world | Quantity | % of world |
| Copper 99% | mln t | 51.8[4] | | 690 | 30 | 4 | 30 | 4 |
| Coal | bln t | 27 | 3 | 892 | 115 | 12.8 | 157 | 17.6 |
| Gold | t | 200 | 0.4 | 55,000 | 1900 | 3.5 | 5000 | 9.1 |
| Iron ore | mln t | 600 | 1 | 87,000 | 7200 | 8.3 | 14,000 | 16.1 |
| Fluorspar | mln t | 38 | 9 | 240 | 24 | 10 | 6 | 2.5 |
| Zinc | mln t | 0.3 | 0.13 | 230 | 43 | 18.7 | 45 | 19.6 |
| Molybdenum | ths t | 160 | 1 | 11,000 | 4300 | 39.1 | 250 | 2.3 |
| Tungsten | ths t | 70 | 2.1 | 3300 | 1900 | 57.6 | 250 | 7.6 |
| Crude oil | bln barrel | 0.6 | 0.04 | 1688 | 18 | 1.1 | 93 | 5.5 |

*Source* Final Report (Power Open Pit, 2015) and "Data collection survey on the copper industry sector in Mongolia", JICA, Mitsubishi Materials Techno Corp. and Sumiko Resources Exploration and Development Co. Ltd. (2014)

clarity and details. However, an estimate of resource wealth will benefit the population and policymakers, investors, and other stakeholders in forming expectations about the sector and its role in the economy and society.

### 3.1.2 Addressing Resource Dependency

The dominant mining sector does not necessarily translate into sustainable economic growth and development. In other words, there are risks involved in terms of the "resource curse" and "Dutch decease". Since these topics were examined diligently in the past, as in Fisher et al. (2011), we will not focus on them in this assessment.

However, it should be stressed that if a country does not address its weaknesses in institutions dealing with the governance of policymaking and its implementations, the strong dependency on the mining sector will lead to slower economic growth and growing inequality. This phenomenon is known as a "resource curse". Moreover, even if the country builds good institutions, economic growth led by the mining sector may not allow the economy to diversify away from the mining sector, which is known as a "Dutch disease" effect. Therefore, the country's strategy should formulate a realistic approach to dealing with the risks that resource dependency poses.

The country's dependency on a sector can be measured in different ways. The following Table 5 shows that in 2016, the mining sector accounted for approximately

[4] Using data from "Annual bulletin of mining and geology Mongolia 2016", The Mineral Resources Authority of Mongolia.

**Table 4** Resource wealth per capita

| | Unit | Geological reserves (A + B + C)** | Per capita (ton)*** |
|---|---|---|---|
| Coal | bln t | 41.2 | 13,209.9 |
| Limestone | bln t | 2.2 | 706.9 |
| Iron | bln t | 1.9 | 605.4 |
| Copper/without copper in polymetallic deposits | mln t | 68.6 | 22.0 |
| Phosphorite | mln t | 54.1 | 17.3 |
| Fluorspar | mln t | 49.3 | 15.8 |
| Zinc | mln t | 6.2 | 1.99 |
| Rare Earth elements/RE2O2/ | mln t | 2.4 | 0.75 |
| Lead | mln t | 2.1 | 0.66 |
| Molybdenum | mln t | 1.5 | 0.49 |
| Tungsten | ths t | 441.4 | 0.14 |
| Uranium/oxide/ | ths t | 185.1 | 0.059 |
| Tin | ths t | 132.9 | 0.043 |
| Silver | ths t | 42.1 | 0.014 |
| Gold/hard rock/ | ths t | 2.6 | 0.0008 |
| Gold/placer/ | t | 237.2 | 0.0001 |

*Source* Mineral Resources and Petroleum Agency of Mongolia (MRPAM)
**Geological reserves as of September 2017
***Mongolia's 2016 population was 3,119,935.

20% of Mongolia's GDP and 71% of its gross industrial output. And, approximately 23% of the total investment is in mining and quarrying.

Mining is also an important sector in the government budget. The Mongolian government's budget revenue in 2016 was over 2 billion USD, and is still increasing. In 2015, the Future Heritage Fund (FHF) was established to collect a portion of mineral revenue for future generations' use, and the law was passed in February 2016. FHF started accumulating in 2017, along with the stabilization fund, which was set up to insulate the domestic economy from large fluctuations in revenue.

In 2016, the mining sector contributed approximately 14% to the Mongolian general government revenue. Businesses licensed for mineral extraction paid approximately 260 million USD in taxes to national and local governments. Figures 1 and 2 break down the taxes paid by tax type and mineral. Copper, coal, and gold producers paid approximately 170, 47, and 16 million USD in taxes, respectively. Of taxes, 35.1%, approximately 91 million USD, were paid as royalties.

Another way to look at the country's dependency on the mining sector is to look at the sector's share in the total exports. (see Table 6) Approximately 70% of Mongolian exports are mineral products, with approximately 80% of all commodities exported to China.

**Table 5** GDP by Industry, USD million

| Division | 2015 (%) | | 2016 (%) | |
|---|---|---|---|---|
| Total | 9435 | | 9755 | |
| Agriculture, forestry, and fishing | 1260 | 13.4 | 1140 | 11.7 |
| Information and communication | 202 | 2.1 | 207 | 2.1 |
| Financial and insurance activities | 505 | 5.4 | 508 | 5.2 |
| Real estate activities | 646 | 6.9 | 658 | 6.7 |
| Professional, scientific and technical activities | 207 | 2.2 | 185 | 1.9 |
| Administrative and support service activities | 89 | 0.9 | 88 | 0.9 |
| Public administration and defense; compulsory social insurance | 432 | 4.6 | 456 | 4.7 |
| Education services | 413 | 4.4 | 425 | 4.4 |
| Activities of households as employers | 193 | 2.0 | 192 | 2.0 |
| Arts, entertainment, and recreation | 43 | 0.5 | 44 | 0.5 |
| Other service activities | 77 | 0.8 | 72 | 0.7 |
| Mining and quarrying | 1612 | 17.1 | 1960 | 20.1 |
| Taxes net of subsidies on products | 768 | 8.1 | 810 | 8.3 |
| Processing industries | 721 | 7.6 | 707 | 7.3 |
| Electricity, gas, steam supply; water supply; sewerage, waste management, and remediation activities | 155 | 1.6 | 188 | 1.9 |
| Water supply; sewerage, waste management, and remediation activities | 42 | 0.4 | 43 | 0.4 |
| Construction | 399 | 4.2 | 386 | 4.0 |
| Wholesale and retail trade; repair of motor vehicles and motorcycles | 1088 | 11.5 | 1091 | 11.2 |
| Transportation and storage | 493 | 5.2 | 496 | 5.1 |
| Accommodation and food service activities | 88 | 0.9 | 99 | 1.0 |

*Source* National Statistical Office

Moreover, using computable general equilibrium (CGE) modeling, ERI calculated[5] the direct and indirect contributions of the mining sector to be 27.6% of GDP in 2015. In particular, the direct contribution of the mining and quarrying sector was 17.1%, and the mining-related contribution of other sectors was 10.5% of GDP.

We can see from these indicators that the country is highly dependent on the mining sector. Development strategy documents acknowledge this dependency and promote the diversification of the economy. In particular, SDGs aim to achieve the following:

> By 2030, Mongolia aspires to be among the leading middle-income countries based on per capita income. It hopes to be a multisector stable economy and a society dominated by

[5] "Assessment of the role of the mining sector in the economy", Economic Research Institute, 2017.

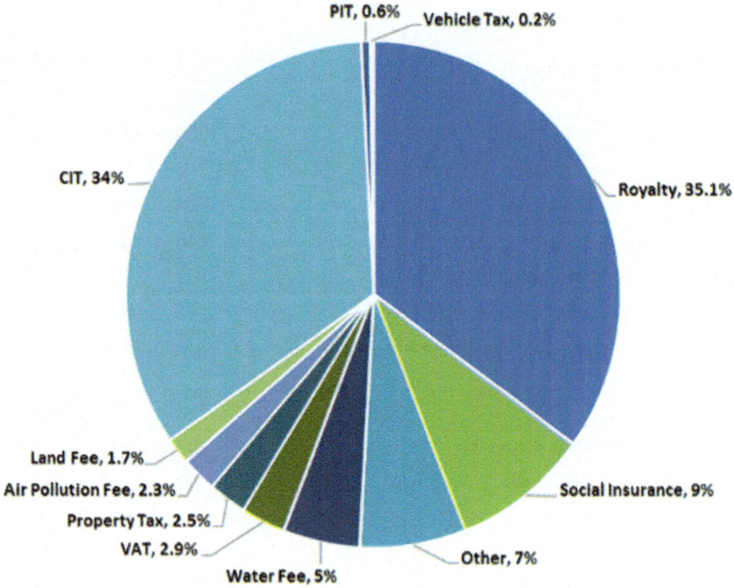


**Fig. 1** 2016 mining sector taxes paid by type. *Source* MRPAM

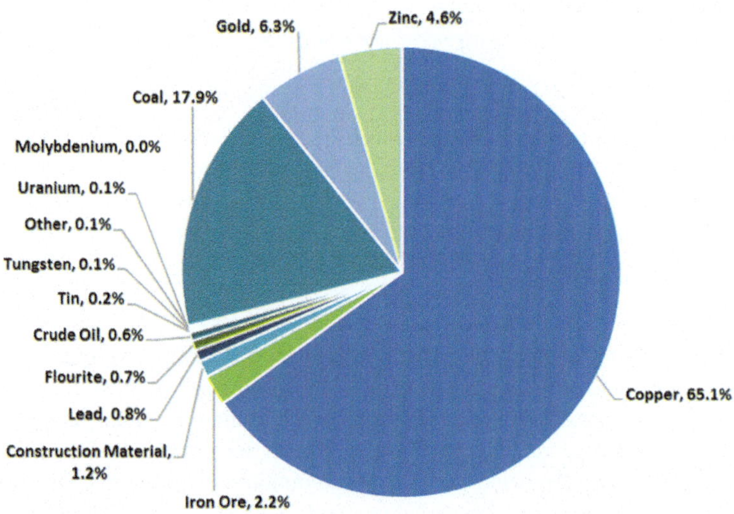


**Fig. 2** 2016 mining sector taxes paid by minerals. *Source* MRPAM

middle- and upper-middle-income classes, which would preserve ecological balance and have stable and democratic governance.

The strategy aims to develop an economy that is less reliant on one particular sector and promotes a diversified economy. Although SDGs specify goals for sectorial

**Table 6** Exports by commodity group in 2016, USD thousands and % of total exports

| Commodity group (%) | | |
|---|---|---|
| Total | 4,916,335 | |
| Wood and wooden articles | 429 | 0.0 |
| Cellulose, paper, cardboard and articles thereof | 56 | 0.0 |
| Textiles and textile articles | 300,224 | 6.1 |
| Footwear, headwear, umbrellas, feather and artificial flowers | 2034 | 0.0 |
| Articles of stone, plaster, cement, asbestos, glass, and glassware | 206 | 0.0 |
| Natural or cultured stones, precious metal, jewelry | 761,511 | 15.5 |
| Base metals and articles thereof | 86,178 | 1.8 |
| Machinery, equipment, electric appliances, recorders, TV, sets, and spare parts | 71,421 | 1.5 |
| Auto, air and water transport vehicles and their spare parts | 69,981 | 1.4 |
| Optical, photographic, cinematic-graphic, measuring control, medical, surgical, and musical instruments, watches | 1107 | 0.0 |
| Live animals, animals' origin products | 29,242 | 0.6 |
| Various industrial goods | 2670 | 0.1 |
| Other | 32 | 0.0 |
| Vegetable origin products | 55,108 | 1.1 |
| Animal and vegetable fat and oil | 701 | 0.0 |
| Food products | 11,920 | 0.2 |
| Mineral products | 3,484,055 | 70.9 |
| Chemical and chemical industry products | 1631 | 0.0 |
| Plastics, rubber, and articles thereof | 7619 | 0.2 |
| Raw and processed hides, skins, fur, and articles thereof | 30,210 | 0.6 |

*Source* National statistical office

developments, it, unfortunately, does not specify how priorities are decided and the costs associated with programs that promote the development of nonmining sectors.

In other words, there is a lack of clarity on how the prioritization of programs will be done and at what cost to achieve these goals. It is understood that follow-up policy documents will provide a clearer picture of these issues, but there is a lack of these follow-up documents showing a pathway to achieve the goals.

In the SMP paper, the government policy is described as follows:

> State mineral policy will be directed at increased reliance on the private sector, the development of a transparent, responsible mining sector, and the creation of a balanced and multipronged economic structure in the near and medium term, which serves fundamental national interests.

Thus, the SMP promotes a diversified economic structure. It should be noted that since this policy paper is directed at the development of the mining sector, policies and strategies for achieving diversification are not specified. The SMP document specifically articulates policies that promote value-added products and shift away from extraction and mining. Section 3.3 of the SMP document formulates policies directed at the processing sector. The following subsections of the document envision how the government will promote deeper processing in the sector and move away from extraction.

- *Conduct policies to promote improvement in the level of processing and produce value-added products*
- *To promote projects such as building coal processing, coke, and chemical factory, power plant near a coal mine, to get liquid fuel from brown coal and oil shale*
- *To promote processing factories through tax and financial policies and increase the processing level of minerals.*

More detailed goals and strategies for developing the mining sector are stipulated in the Government action plan for 2020–2024. The action plan specifies as follows:

> The government will create a sustainable and multipillar economic structure and implement the principle of fair distribution of wealth by developing transparent and responsible mining and value-added industry and ensuring the growth of mineral revenues. We will commence the construction of heavy industries, including oil, coal-chemical, copper concentrate, and metallurgy, and implement related infrastructure projects (Part 3.2).

Specifically, the Government of Mongolia aims to further develop downstream processing promoting value-added production. This will be achieved by increasing the economic benefits of current "strategically important" mines, operationalizing major new mines, and developing heavy industry and an oil refinery. Nevertheless, detailed plans and feasibility studies, and impact assessments have not yet been fully developed.

Generally, the lack of policy analysis has remained to be a challenging issue that needs to be addressed. Because of this lack of analytical background to the policy decisions, the Parliament approved the "Law on legislation", which requires policy proposals to have professional assessments attached to the benefits and costs of policy actions. It remains to be seen how this requirement is implemented in practice.

## *3.2 Considering the Long-Term Approach*

### 3.2.1 Do National Strategy Documents for the Extractive Industry Provide a Long-Term Vision that Considers the Impact of Resource Extraction on Future Generations?

As mentioned above, national strategy documents such as SDGs and SMPs are designed with a long-term view.

SDGs envision a high-growth economy with no poverty and a drastic reduction in income inequality by 2030, among other goals. Moreover, goals specific to the mining sector are designed to promote comprehensive research in geology and geophysics and to draw a geological map on a 1:50,000 scale of 40% of the entire territory by 2020 and 60% by 2030. The SDGs also stipulate that the goal is to create a favorable investment environment for explorations, conduct in-depth explorations of deposits, develop infrastructure with suitable power plants and water supply and transportation networks, and start developing large mining projects. From these goals, we can see that the country's strategy is to develop further and expand the mining sector so that future generations will benefit from the industry. This expansion will also allow the country to diversify its economy.

SMP specifically promotes policies whose positive effect should benefit all citizens. The very first principle of the minerals sector policy is directed at maintaining policies in the sector in the long run. In particular, it states that "to maintain minerals sector policies in the long run sustainably, decisions regarding legal and tax environment should be based on research and analysis and these should not harm the interests of stakeholders". Moreover, the policy paper stipulates the following:

> To mine mineral reserves completely and at an appropriate level and to increase the diversity and volume of final value-added products by promoting the processing level and using environmentally friendly technology;

In other words, the government's policy is to make sure the country benefits from the sector in the long run and avoids exhausting its reserves prematurely.

### 3.2.2 Does the Strategy Present a Pathway to Achieve this Vision? Is There Evidence That This Is Followed by the Government and Other Actors? (Areas of Particular Importance Include the Pace of Licensing, Fiscal Terms; Local Impacts; State-Owned Enterprises; Revenue Management; Private Sector Enabling Environment)

The long-term impact of the sector on future generations is dependent not only on developing and benefiting from current known resource deposits and projects but also on how the country handles the pace of exploration and mining licenses, the state's fiscal terms with mining companies on projects, the management of revenue from the sector and the promotion of the private sector.

**Licensing (from SMP)**

Licensing is partly reflected in the SMP. In particular, the policy is to align licensed areas with cadastral area units. In particular,

- *Licensed mining areas to be aligned with principles of cadastral area units in accordance with international benchmarks*
- *To create a legal environment for the usage of additional mineral deposits that are impactful at the national and local levels in an integrated manner (find out what legislation and regulations were adopted and its implementation. Additionally, look at whether assessments were made)*

- *To optimally plan the production and processing quantity in conjunction with the country's economic and industrialization development and domestic and foreign market outlook.*

The administration of the licensing process is regulated by the "Minerals Law" of Mongolia. This law regulates how the license will be issued and processed but does not address the pacing of the licensing. There are no follow-ups to the SMP document on pacing the licensing.

Currently, the government is evaluating various exploration and mining licensing policies and opening up new areas for more explorations. Multiple laws limit the expansion of new areas for explorations, such as

- Law on the prohibition of mineral exploration and mining activities in areas in the headwaters of rivers, protected water reservoir zones, and forested areas
- Environmental protection law of Mongolia
- Law of Mongolia on land
- Law of Mongolia on environmental impact assessment
- Law of Mongolia on subsoil
- Minerals law of Mongolia.

Moreover, in 2009, the President of Mongolia issued a decree suspending the issuance of exploration licenses for new areas. This suspension was lifted in 2014 since the exploration areas started lagging behind the mining areas, and the country needed to address the slowing economy by attracting investment in the mining sector.

According to the "Annual bulletin of mining and geology 2016", 8.9% of total areas are licensed for exploration and mining as of 2015, and almost 60%[6] of total areas are restricted by the abovementioned laws and cannot be opened for exploration. Thus, approximately 30% of the total area can potentially be opened for exploration licenses. However, there is a gap in the policy document that should address the pacing for exploration licensing.

The Ministry of Mining conducted a study on the "Optimal extraction model" in 2015. This was an attempt to determine how the country can pace its licensing for exploration and mining. Unfortunately, there are no follow-up policy documents for this study.

**Fiscal Terms**

Mongolia benefits from the mining sector by imposing royalties, taxes, tariffs on exports, and dividends from state ownership. Indeed, this is one of the most highly discussed topics in the public.

Historically, Mongolia set a model for how the country negotiated taxes, royalties, and state ownership policies during the Oyu Tolgoi negotiation. In general, the "Minerals law" imposes a royalty of 2.5% for coal and 5% for other mining products. The law was amended in 2014 to impose a royalty of 2.5% on gold sold to the Bank of Mongolia (the Central Bank) or banks permitted by the Bank of Mongolia. All other taxes and tariffs are similar to other industries.

---

[6] Source will be shown here.

"Minerals law" also identifies deposits that are deemed "strategically important" that can have a significant impact on national security, society, and the economy. Deposits become "strategically important" if they can contribute more than 5% of GDP per year. In these "strategically important deposits", the government can have ownership of up to 50% of the deposit, and if the deposit was discovered with private financing, then up to 34%. Moreover, for these deposits, royalties are negotiable along with provisions on environmental protection, infrastructure development, social responsibility, tax stabilization, workforce training, local workforce participation, and other issues.

In other words, policymakers declared that in the long term, the country would benefit from the mining sector through its state-owned mining companies. Indeed, one of the most significant contributors to the state budget is the state-owned copper mining company Erdenet JSC and a state-owned coking coal company Erdenes Tavan Tolgoi, the largest exporter of coking coal and operator of the largest coking coal deposit in the country.

In terms of implementation, there are ongoing contract negotiations on several "strategically important" deposits. The study titled "IGF Mining policy framework assessment: Mongolia" warned that there is a gap in terms of clearly determining what criteria constitute a "strategically important deposit", which still needs to be clarified.

Moreover, it is widely argued that the performance of state-owned mining companies must be further improved. In particular, the governance of state-owned enterprises needs to be significantly enhanced, as Erdenes Mongol, the parent company of state-owned mining companies, does not publicly provide its annual financial report, making it difficult to assess its performance and compare it against similar private companies (Namkhaijantsan 2017). The inefficiency and profitability of state-owned enterprises are widely believed to lag behind private mining companies. The regular turnover of the management team at state-owned companies indicates a strong incentive for politicians to influence these companies.

**Revenue Management**

Mongolia made great strides in terms of regulating the revenue from the mining sector. In particular, the "Fiscal stability law" was adopted in 2012 and went into full effect in 2013. According to this law, excess revenue from the mining sector will be accumulated into a "stabilization fund". The government can finance its expenditure from this fund when commodity prices are depressed. Four restrictions on expenditures were imposed to accumulate into the "Stabilization fund" when commodity prices are high and allow access to it when commodity prices are low. Namely, the law imposes ceilings on government expenditure growth, budget deficit, and total government debt and formulates commodity prices to be used for budgeting.

It should be noted that although rules for revenue management were set out in an exemplary fashion, the government found it hard to follow them through at the implementation level. In particular, major parameters such as budget deficit and debt level had to be amended frequently to accommodate ever-expanding government expenditure and debt levels. This practice of revising major parameters of this law shows a lack of government's commitment to the fiscal discipline.

One of the issues that still need to be addressed is the issue of revenue assurance. In other words, whether the government can make sure the country benefits from the mining sector as planned. For example, although the largest mining project Oyu Tolgoi greatly benefits the country, the project suffered from multiple cost overruns, which raised politically charged discussions on the project's benefits.

Furthermore, as mentioned above, the Parliament of Mongolia adopted a law titled "Future Heritage Fund" in 2016, which set up Mongolia's version of the sovereign wealth fund. This law provides the country with the possibility of accruing wealth from the mining sector to benefit future generations. Since this law is relatively new, for 2018, approximately 40 million USD will be transferred to the fund. It should be noted that the source of this fund is the same as that of the stabilization fund, but only after funds are transferred to the stabilization fund will 65% of the remaining funds be transferred to this wealth fund. This means that although the legal environment for accumulating proceeds from the mining sector is in place, failure to adhere to stabilization parameters will also hamper efforts to accumulate the wealth fund.

**Promotion of the Private Sector**

State minerals policy greatly emphasizes policies encouraging private sector participation in the mining sector. Namely, the State minerals policy envisions a private sector-based mining sector development and states its objective as

> The objective of the "State Minerals Policy" is to establish a stable investment environment, to improve the quality of mineral exploration, mining, and processing by encouraging the use of environmentally friendly and advanced techniques, technologies, and innovations, to produce final value-added products and strengthen the competitiveness of the country in the international market.

Thus, the government's strategy in the mining sector is to promote the private sector by providing better infrastructure in terms of a friendly investment environment and greater access to exploration data while encouraging more downstream processing and adoption of environmentally-friendly equipment, technologies, and innovations.

As we mentioned above, the mining sector's contribution to the economy is restricted by direct and indirect contributions through industries such as energy, transportation, and services. These indirect contributions are primarily provided by the private sector, except for electricity.

Another crucial area of interest for policymakers is the promotion of the downstream processing of mining products. Although understandably, the government's strategy is to promote private sector participation in downstream processing and attract foreign investment, it is not explicitly written in strategic and policy documents, and it is not clear how the government will promote private sector participation. Moreover, there is a lack of a detailed vision of how the government intends to create a favorable investment environment. Follow-up programs to achieve these strategic visions and policy actions are still missing.

### 3.2.3 Do Government Communications Set Reasonable Expectations About the Long-Term Nature of the Gains and Costs of Extraction?

Regarding calculating the long-term gains and losses from mining extraction, strategy documents such as SDGs, SMPs, and related programs and regulations do not reflect or convey such information.

In particular, there are no clear indications of whether gains and losses were assessed in the background documents of these policy and strategy documents.

It is becoming increasingly evident that economic impact assessments of changes in the laws and regulations need to be conducted and conveyed to the public. However, this situation was addressed by adopting the "Law on legislation". In particular, article 9.5 of this law articulates that opinions from professional and research organizations, analysts, and citizens should be taken into account in producing the draft law.

## 3.3 *Comprehensiveness and Inclusiveness—Consideration of the Full Range of Issues in the Management of Resource Wealth and Development, Implementation and Oversight Processes Must be Inclusive*

### 3.3.1 Governance of Planning; Environmental Management; Taxation; SOEs; Finance; Monetary Issues; Industrial Policy; Energy; Infrastructure; Labor and Education—This Chain is as Strong as its Weakest Link

**Does government ensure participation in resource strategy development, implementation, and oversight by all government bodies and actors outside the executive branch?**

Resource wealth management is not constrained only to the mining sector. Since the decision with regard to the resources is diverse, there are many players involved in the decision-making chain and its implementation. Decisions will have to be made at various stages of resource exploration, mining, and management of its proceeds. In particular, the chain of decision-making processes involves the governance of planning, environmental management, taxation, state-owned enterprises, finance and revenue management, industrial policy, energy, infrastructure, labor, and education.

Along this chain of decisions, many policy-making bodies conduct policies that should be consistent with the strategic and policy documents and its follow-up programs and regulations. This means that this chain of decision-making can be vulnerable at its weakest link and is suspect of breaking down in communication, coordination, and implementation.

It should be noted that the Minerals Law stipulates which government bodies are responsible for decision making, implementation, and oversight. In particular, the law specifies which government bodies are responsible for planning, implementation, and supervision in each of the steps.

At each step, we identify key players and their responsibilities as follows:

- Governance of planning: The Parliament of Mongolia is the highest decision-making body in terms of designing and adopting the strategy and policy on resource governance, and the Ministry of Mining is responsible for devising follow-up programs and regulations.
- Environmental management: Within the strategy and policy documents approved by the Parliament and respective laws on environmental protection, the Ministry of Environment is responsible for devising follow-up regulations and programs on environmental protection.
- Taxation: The Ministry of Mining and Ministry of Finance are responsible for collecting taxes and royalties and ensuring revenue assurance.
- State-owned enterprises: A government agency responsible for state-owned enterprises is in charge of appointing the management and overseeing the performance of these companies. Additionally, as we mentioned above, Erdenes Mongol is a state-owned mining company that is the parent company of state-owned mining companies.
- Financial and monetary issues: In accordance with the Minerals Law, the Parliament is responsible for deciding government ownership, taxes, and royalties for strategically important mines. The Ministry of Finance is accountable for managing proceeds from the resource sector.
- Industrial policy: As we mentioned above, the Mongolian government's strategy is to diversify the economy and develop the downstream processing of mining products. Currently, the Ministry of Mining and Heavy Industry is responsible for devising and implementing industrial policy in the country.
- Energy and Infrastructure: Policies in energy and infrastructure such as transportation are designed by the Ministry of Energy and Ministry of Roads and Transportation and implemented by these ministries.
- Labor and education: The Ministry of Education is responsible for devising policies for retraining labor for the mining sector and carrying it out through its TVET programs. It should be noted that with the intensity of the need for mining sector workers, mining companies themselves and international organizations such as the Millennium Challenge Corporation and Asian Development Bank played a crucial role in retraining workers.

As we can see, the management of mining resources encompasses decision making from diverse policy-making bodies. It should be noted that the Parliament of Mongolia is the highest strategy and policymaking authority responsible for overseeing the implementation and efficiency of these strategies and policies. Moreover, the Government of Mongolia is the crucial authority at the implementation and oversight stages. The NRGI strongly recommends that this decision-making chain should be strong and operational at every link.

Unfortunately, no assessment has been made on the decision-making process, implementation, and oversight along this chain. This is a critical issue for further analysis with significant policy implications.

### 3.3.2 Does the Resource Strategy Consider All of the Links Involved in Harnessing Extractive Resources for Development? Are There Any Notable Gaps?

As we can see, all the links along this chain of decision making are tied to corresponding decision-making bodies. There seem to be no obvious or notable gaps at the strategic and policy-making levels. However, per "IGF Mining policy framework assessment: Mongolia," the country scored "low" in implementation of Environmental Management and PostMining Transition, whereas it scored "medium" in implementation of Legal and Policy Environment, Financial Benefit Optimization, Socio-Economic Benefit Optimization, and Artisanal and Small Scale Mining.

It should be noted that this analysis is restricted to these six major issues in the mining policy, which does not cover all the links we discussed.

### 3.3.3 Does the Resource Strategy Identify Priority Areas in the Chain for Strengthening?

As mentioned above, strategic papers prioritize the extractive sector, but detailed follow-up policy papers do not prioritize areas that need to be strengthened along the policy decision-making chain. This is not because policymakers are unaware of gaps and omissions in their decision-making, but rather this chain analysis is a new concept, and because it is new, there has not been a proper assessment carried out along this chain of decision-making.

Therefore, it is highly advisable to assess each link of this decision-making process and identify weak links in this chain. This concept of identifying the weakest link in the decision-making chain is an attractive tool for policymakers and analysts for assessment and should be explored more comprehensively.

### 3.3.4 Does Policymaking Happen in a Joined-Up Way, or Does Decision-Making in Different Parts of the Chain Take Place in Isolation?

**Does the final strategy demonstrably take into account the inputs of these diverse actors?**

**Does the government recognize and enable strong oversight of the strategy? Does the strategy include oversight roles for actors within the executive and beyond?**

The Minerals Law identifies which ministries and agencies are responsible for corresponding decisions and how accountability works within this structure. This means that decisions are being made in a coordinated manner under this law.

However, NRGI emphasizes that the coordination of governance and decision-making should go beyond and suggests that there should be an overarching decision-making process that would cover all links in the decision-making process to ensure that weak links are addressed.

The strategy and policy documents assessed in this chapter are unclear about how the governance of decision making across diverse issues of managing the resource sector should be coordinated.

## 4 Conclusion

In this chapter, we used NRGI's benchmarking methodology to assess strategy and policy documents along the following four pillars: the policy documents should be (1) cognizant of reality, (2) consider the long-term approach, (3) comprehensive, and (4) inclusive.

We evaluated major pieces of legislation as well as its implementation and oversight. In particular, we concentrated on the first two pillars. The remaining two will be assessed in detail in this study's follow-up update.

The most overarching and long-term development strategy documents are "Vision 2050" and the Sustainable development goals adopted in 2020 and 2016 by the Parliament of Mongolia. These documents reveal the country's major developmental goals up to 2050 and 2030. The next sector-specific strategic document is "State Minerals Policy (SMP) 2014–2025", adopted in 2014 by the Parliament. The SMP details major principles and policies to develop the sector in the long run. In the medium term, we evaluated the government action plan for 2020–2024.

NRGI advises that these strategic documents should be cognizant of reality. These documents should set realistic expectations about the role of the mining sector. We noted that these documents do not directly reveal the country's estimations of resource reserves and assumptions on pricing. These documents show that the authorities are cognizant that the country is endowed with rich natural resources but do not provide specific guidance on its resource wealth. Furthermore, we look at supporting documents of these policy papers for those assumptions. We emphasized that the "Annual bulletin of mining and geology" is the primary document that conveys information about reserves and the sector's production. It should be noted that Mongolia is indeed a country richly endowed with natural resources. Nevertheless, we also noted that since there is a lack of supporting documents for the major development strategy documents, it is difficult to have a clear understanding of the endowment. Moreover, we noted an inconsistency that needs to be addressed regarding the country's estimated resource wealth and ensuring it is consistent with the development strategy documents. Estimate of resource wealth will benefit the population and policymakers, investors, and other stakeholders in forming expectations about the sector and its role in the economy and society.

Based on a clear understanding of the resource endowment, the country should address its dependency on the sector. We emphasized that all strategic documents promote a diversified economic structure. The diversification policies are supported by fostering the downstream processing of the mining products and promoting the development of nonmining sectors. Specifically, the Government of Mongolia aims to achieve these goals by conducting a series of policies by reducing production costs and formulating and implementing heavy industry development plans. However, we noted that officially ratified detailed programs that promote the economic diversification and development of nonmining sectors are not yet fully developed or are in the process of being developed. Moreover, the prioritization of specific plans and detailed feasibility studies and impact assessments are not yet clear, making it difficult to assess in what steps the goals will be achieved. Because of a lack of analytical background in policy decisions, the Parliament approved the "Law on legislation", which requires policy proposals to have a professional assessment of the benefits and costs of policy actions. It remains to be seen how this requirement is implemented in practice.

National development strategy documents should be devised with a long-term view. We noted that documents such as "Sustainable Development Goals" and "State Minerals Sector Policy" are designed with a long-term view. We noted that the long-term impact of the sector on future generations is dependent not only on developing and benefiting from the current known resource deposits and projects but also on how the country handles the pace of issuance of exploration and mining licenses, the state's fiscal terms with mining companies on projects, the management of revenue from the sector and the promotion of the private sector. Currently, the government is evaluating various policies on exploration and mining licensing and opening new areas for more explorations. It should be noted that although multiple laws limit the expansion of exploration areas, the policy is not clear what governs these openings of the new regions. In terms of fiscal benefit, Mongolia benefits from the mining sector by imposing royalties, taxes, tariffs on exports, and dividends from state ownership. Indeed, this is one of the most highly discussed topics in the public. We noted that policymakers declared that the country would benefit from the mining sector through its state-owned mining companies. Nevertheless, there is a gap in clearly determining what criteria constitute a "strategically important deposit" that defines the government's policy toward how the country will benefit from the sector.

We noticed that the "Fiscal Stability Law" adopted in 2012 and went into full effect in 2013 is a reasonable regulation in managing revenues from the mining sector. However, we also noted a lack of discipline in maintaining and implementing the law, which can be seen from numerous amendments to the law since the law was adopted. Moreover, the government's strategy in the mining sector is to promote the private sector by providing better infrastructure in terms of the investment environment and exploration data while encouraging more downstream processing and adoption of environmentally friendly equipment, technologies, and innovations.

In general, throughout this assessment, we emphasized a lack of detailed vision and follow-up programs on how the government intends to implement and achieve these strategic visions and policy actions.

## References

Fisher, B. S., Batdelger, T., Gurney, A., Galindev, R., Begg, M., Buyantsogt, B., Lkhanaajav, E & Chadraaval, B. (2011). *The Development of the Oyu Tolgoi Copper Mine: An Assessment of the Macroeconomic Consequences for Mongolia.* The National University of Mongolia and BA Economics.

Mineral Resources and Petroleum Authority of Mongolia (MRPAM). (2013, 2016, 2017). Annual bulletin of mining and geology.

National Statistical Office (NSO). (2017). National Accounting Dataset, www.1212.mn.

Namkhaijantsan, D. (2017). *Resource governance index points to state-owned enterprises as key Mongolia reform target.* Natural Resource Governance Institute.

Parliament of Mongolia. (2014). Adoption of State Minerals Policy, Resolution no. 18.

Parliament of Mongolia. (2016). Mongolia Sustainable Development Vision 2030, Resolution no. 19 annex.

Parliament of Mongolia. (2020). "VISION-2050" Long-Term Development Policy of Mongolia, Resolution no. 52 annex 1

Power Open Pit, LLC. (2015). *Preliminary feasibility study of mineral extraction model.* Research and Development Plan.

USGS (2017). Mineral Commodity Summaries, Fluorspar. United States Geological Survey

World Nuclear Association (WNA). (2016). http://www.world-nuclear.org/information-library/nuclear-fuel-cycle/uranium-resources/supply-of-uranium.aspx, Uranium Reserves.

**Tuvshintugs Batdelger** is the director of the Economic Research Institute (ERI) and an associate professor of economics at the National University of Mongolia. He has a bachelor's degree in economics from the National University of Mongolia; a master's degree in economics from the University of Manchester, UK; and a Ph.D. in economics from Boston University, USA. He has experience working at the Bank of Mongolia and was the head of the Economics Department of the National University of Mongolia from 2014 to 2017. He has been a member of the Economic Policy Council under the prime minister of Mongolia since 2012 and was a member of the Monetary Policy Committee from 2011 to 2016. He has been actively involved in policy discussions in the country through the establishment and operation of ERI since 2010, one of the longest-running think tanks in the country. Through ERI, he successfully contributed to policy discussions on wide-ranging economic and social issues by coordinating and implementing many projects by international organizations, such as the World Bank, Asian Development Bank, and JICA. In particular, he successfully led research teams conducting an economic assessment of big mining and industrial projects on the country's economy and society in general. He has successfully conducted and published policy research studies in international peer-reviewed journals and publications such as *Applied Economics, Resources Policy,* and *East Asia Forum* and has authored chapters on the Mongolian economy in numerous books. His current research interests are the role of mining in the economy and society, the role of monetary policy in regulating the Mongolian economy, and the impact of economic development on income distribution and the country's middle class.

# Budget Revenue Management

**Ragchaasuren Galindev, Tuvshintugs Batdelger, Esmedekh Lkhanaajav, Manlaibaatar Zagdbazar, Munkh-Ireedui Batjargal, Dulguun Tuvshintugs, Oyunzul Tserendorj, Nyambaatar Batbayar, Delgermaa Begz, and Ankhbayar Delgerchuluun**

## 1 Introduction

This chapter discusses the findings of the research carried out in the framework of the Budget Revenue Management project. Revenue Management is about setting up and managing Sovereign Wealth Funds (SWFs). In Mongolia, we have two such

R. Galindev (✉) · T. Batdelger · E. Lkhanaajav · M. Zagdbazar · D. Tuvshintugs · O. Tserendorj · D. Begz · A. Delgerchuluun
Economic Research Institute, Ulaanbaatar, Mongolia
e-mail: ragchaasuren@eri.mn

T. Batdelger
e-mail: tuvshintugs@eri.mn

E. Lkhanaajav
e-mail: esmedekh@eri.mn

M. Zagdbazar
e-mail: manlaibaatar@eri.mn

D. Tuvshintugs
e-mail: dulguun@eri.mn

O. Tserendorj
e-mail: oyunzul@eri.mn

D. Begz
e-mail: delgermaa@eri.mn

A. Delgerchuluun
e-mail: ankhbayar@eri.mn

M.-I. Batjargal · N. Batbayar
Concordia University, Montreal, Canada
e-mail: nyambaatar@eri.mn

 
Y. Hosoi et al. (eds.), *Economic Dependence of Mongolia on Minerals*,
Contributions to Economics, https://doi.org/10.1007/978-981-19-5515-0_5

funds—the Fiscal Stability Fund (FSF) and the Future Heritage Fund (FHF).[1] The Fiscal Stability Law (FSL) was adopted in 2010, and the FSF was established in 2011 to prevent economic fluctuations and promote sustainable economic growth. As the Mongolian economy became more dependent on the mining sector around 2008–2010, it was predicted that the highly volatile prices of our mineral commodities and the flow of FDI would be the main sources of economic fluctuations. Evidently, the economy has experienced severe ups and downs over the recent decade. The most recent economic slowdown followed the greatest boom in 2010–2012 when the price of coal fell significantly on the world market, and the first stage of the OT copper mining development approached the end. The budget expenditure increased, revenue fell, and the foreign public debt grew substantially. The prolonged economic slowdown led the government to accept the terms of the International Monetary Fund's (IMF) Extended Fund Facility (EFF)[2] program to keep fighting the economic hardship at lower borrowing costs.[3] Luckily, the coal market condition improved, and the flow of FDI increased from 2017 so that the economy started enjoying economic growth again until the COVID-19 pandemic. The idea of the FSL is that the country saves during good times when the mineral prices are higher than expected and uses the saving in bad times when the mineral prices are lower than expected. In this way, the disposable budget revenue and expenditure would grow in a more stable fashion, which would encourage stable economic growth in the long term. The FHF, on the other hand, was established by the government in 2016 to allocate the country's mineral wealth across the current and future generations. The philosophy behind the fund is that the mineral wealth explored by the current generation of Mongolians belongs to the current and future generations. The money accumulated in the FHF will not be spent until 2030 and assets will be invested.

Our studies discussed in this chapter use computable general equilibrium (CGE) models that we have developed in-house. CGE modeling is an extensively used and widely accepted tool for estimating the impacts of changes in economic conditions. They belong to the economy-wide class of models that provide industry disaggregation in a quantitative description of the whole economy (Dixon & Rimmer, 2010). CGE models are based on a comprehensive economy-wide database such as a national social accounting matrix (SAM), and can serve as a laboratory for policy analysis. The CGE framework helps capture interrelationships between economic sectors and agents captured by the database and accounts for the repercussion effects of policy (Dixon & Rimmer, 2002). Even if only one sector is directly involved,

---

[1] Parliament of Mongolia (2010, 2016).

[2] See International Monetary Fund (2017) and International Monetary Fund (2018) for the details of the program.

[3] In addition to granting a loan of approximately 5.5 billion USD in total, the program also assists in implementing policies and structural reforms. Some of these mandatory reforms are to enforce fiscal policy discipline, improve the central bank's independence and governance, strengthen the financial sector, foster economic diversification and inclusive growth, and protect the lower socioeconomic classes.

there will be indirect effects on other sectors, making economy-wide modeling a necessary tool to analyze these effects. For these reasons, CGE analysis has become a mainstream contributor to policy discussions (Anderson et al., 2012). A typical CGE model can be represented as a system of $m$ equations (entailing the demands, supplies, market-clearing conditions and macroeconomic aggregates) and $n$ variables (quantities, prices, price indices, values and aggregates):

$$F(X, Y) = 0$$

where $F$ is a vector of $m$ functions and $Y$ is a vector of $m$ endogenous variables to be solved for given $X$ which is a vector of $n-m$ exogenous variables. The idea is that $X$ can change exogenously and the model gives us the solution for $Y$. For instance, $X$ may contain the world price of mineral commodities that we export, productivity levels, FDI, the various tax rates, government spending on goods and services and real investment in some sectors. In assessing the impact of a shock (either external or policy), CGE modelers define scenarios. Certain values for $X$ chosen by a modeler and corresponding $Y$ values are considered as a base (baseline or business-us-usual) scenario. Then, considering a different value for one (or more) exogenous variable of $X$ yields a policy (or alternative) scenario. The results of the policy scenario are compared with those of the base scenario in terms of $Y$ to draw a conclusion about the impact of the shock, as shown in Fig. 1.

Our first study examines whether the imposition of the FSL can reduce economic fluctuations caused by oscillations in mineral commodity prices. In the second study, the sensitivity of economic performance to the changes in some of the key requirements in the FSL is analyzed. The third and final study examines the impact of the FSF and the FHF on the economy. The first and second studies use the same CGE

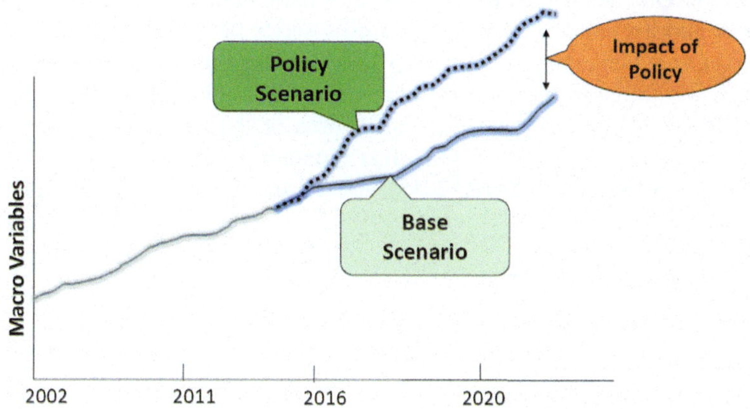


**Fig. 1** Policy impact analysis in CGE models

calibrated to a 2015 Mongolian database while the final piece uses a different CGE model calibrated to a 2017 SAM.[4]

Before moving onto the studies, we briefly discuss related literature, some sovereign wealth funds in the world including the Mongolian ones, the dynamics of the Mongolian economy in the past 20 years and the current state of the Mongolian government budget.

## 2 Literature Review

The related literature for Mongolia in this field can be divided into two broad groups. The first group addresses fiscal issues using different modeling tools. Galindev (2014) considers two scenarios with and without the FSL in a dynamic CGE model calibrated to a 2005 Mongolian database. It finds that in the presence of fluctuations in the prices of mining commodities, the average growth of macroeconomic variables in both scenarios is similar, but their volatilities are reduced suggesting that the law promotes economic stability.[5] The joint effort of the Natural Resource Governance Institute (NRGI) and Gerege Partners produced reports on fiscal sustainability in Mongolia for 2017 and 2018 by equipping a semi-structural macroeconomic model with a satellite fiscal model (known as the Mongolian Macro-Budget Model—MMM) with the IMF's EFF agreement and the common forecasts of mineral commodity prices (NRGI & Gerege Partners). This highlights the vulnerability of the economy to the decline in commodity prices. The second group of the literature develops and applies CGE models in Mongolia. ERI has developed two in-house CGE models over the years. Using the models, we have studied the economic impact of megaprojects in Mongolia—(1) an economic impact assessment of Erdenes Tavan Tolgoi (2014a), (2) the Iron Ore sector (2014b) and (3) the Coal-to-Liquid project (2016). ERI's Galindev and his colleagues have produced a series of working papers under the Partnership for Economic Policy (PEP) grant by adopting the PEP standard CGE models5—(1) the economic and environmental impact of FDI in the Mongolian coal sector (2018), (2) the effects of ups and downs of the Mongolian mining sector (2018), (3) uncertainties in the Mongolian economy in the near future (2019), (4) the impact of fiscal consolidation (2018), and (5) the economic impact of FDI in the coal sector (2019).[6]

---

[4] Our first CGE model operates in GEMPACK program while the second CGE model operates in GAMS program.

[5] The 2005 database can be considered as outdated as the structure of the economy changed after 2010. This is the reason why we carried out a series of research in this chapter with more recent data.

[6] Baatarzorig et al. (2018) and Galindev et al. (2020a, 2020b).

## 3 Fiscal Rules and Sovereign Wealth Funds

### *3.1 Fiscal Rules*

For resource-rich developing economies driven mainly by commodity exports, the issues are the volatility of commodity prices and depletion of natural resources in achieving stabilization and debt sustainability. Price volatility could create economic instability and the depletion of resources could undermine fiscal sustainability.

Fiscal rules place quantitative constraints on government finances by providing a numerical ceiling or target for key budget aggregates such as the budget balance, debt, revenue and expenditure. The successful implementation of fiscal rules may help overcome three macroeconomic challenges associated with sustainable management of natural resources: procyclical fiscal policy, boom-bust cycles and the Dutch disease. These challenges, especially the procyclicality of fiscal policy and boom-bust cycles, have been observed in Mongolia. During periods of economic boom, the Mongolian government had a tendency to increase spending, and then during periods of bust when revenues declined, the government became unable to finance its planned expenditure.

Mihalyi and Fernandez (2018) is an NRGI research paper that assesses the Resource Governance Index (RGI) in 79 countries and finds that 34 countries have at least one fiscal rule in place. Accordingly, the two most common fiscal rules are the budget balance and debt rules as 27 and 23 countries implement them, respectively. Chile, Colombia, Peru and the United Kingdom have structural budget balance rules similar to Mongolia, which allows for adjustments of targets depending on the economic cycle. Alternatively, Tanzania, Norway, Botswana and Ecuador apply a nonresource budget balance target that is the difference between expenditures and nonresource revenues. This rule ensures that the government follows the same budget plans irrespective of resource revenue fluctuations, thus stabilizing the economy. Twenty three countries have a debt rule in place, which limits government debt as a percentage of GDP. In the case of resource-rich countries, the debt rule restricts the government from borrowing during a slump in commodity prices. Some resource-rich countries consider expenditure rules to control spending stemming from expected future wealth. Revenue rules are ideal for resource-rich countries where the flow of resource revenues into the budget and sovereign wealth funds are limited and monitored. However, this rule is only effective if paired with limitations on borrowing or debt. Otherwise, governments may save the appropriate amount but borrow to achieve elevated levels of spending.

Most countries with fiscal rules have more than one type of rule implemented. Mongolia, for instance, combines these four main fiscal rules. The parliament of Mongolia approved the FSL in 2010, which initially set the following constraints:

1. Total budget revenue must be calculated using an equilibrated method /based on the average price of the main minerals within the last 20 years and the average price of the subsequent 3 years.

2. The growth rate of total expenditure must not exceed the maximum of the growth rate of nonmining GDP in the same year and the average growth rate of nonmining GDP in the past 12 years.
3. The budget deficit based on the equilibrated method must not exceed 2% of GDP in the same year or run a surplus.
4. The net present value of government debt must not exceed 60% of the GDP in the budget year.

## *3.2 International Sovereign Wealth Funds*

In addition to fiscal rules, another tool for budget revenue management is Sovereign Wealth Funds (SWF). As of 2018, there were 119 SWFs operating in the world and the overall size was above USD 8.1 trillion (SWF Institute, 2019). SWFs are defined as a special purpose investment fund or arrangement owned by the general government. In terms of policy purposes, the main types of SWFs are (i) stabilization funds that aim to stabilize the budget and economy against commodity price fluctuations (e.g., Russia and Chile), (ii) savings funds for future generations that aim to convert nonrenewable resources into a more diversified portfolio of assets (Kuwait and Norway), and (iii) reserve investment corporations (Singapore and Korea) for increasing the return on reserves (IWG, 2008).

In terms of their management, transparency and success, Chile's and Norway's SWFs are considered international best practices. Therefore, the past performance and fiscal rules of these funds are briefly covered in this section.

**Chilean Wealth Funds**

As one of the resource-rich counties and the leading copper exporter, Chile established two SWFs in 2006 and 2007. First, the Economic and Social Stabilization Fund (ESSF) has a role in supporting fiscal stability by accumulating fiscal surpluses during periods of economic boom and higher commodity prices. When commodity prices fall and the government has fiscal deficits, the cash is transferred from the Fund to the budget to maintain stable budget expenditures, especially on social programs. Second, the Pension Reserve Fund (PRF) receives contributions to accumulate savings for future pension payments (Chilean Ministry of Finance, 2019). As of 2018, these funds have an asset of USD 23.8 billion, approximately 8% of the country's GDP (World Bank, 2019).

In 2001, the Chilean government started implementing the fiscal structural balance rule in its budget law to keep its spending level consistent with structural budget income. Then, the Chilean government passed the Law on Fiscal Responsibility in 2006, which adopted the structural balance rule and created the regulations and institutional framework for the accumulation, management and operations of fiscal savings through the funds. By the law, the newly elected Presidential Administration should announce structural balance targets in its first year. In 2015, for example, the previous government announced that the structural deficit would be approximately 0.25% of GDP through 2018. However, the target was missed for the period from 2016 to 2018.

Depending on the effective fiscal surplus, the PRF must receive a contribution of at least 0.2% and at a maximum of 0.5% of the previous year's GDP. The accumulation should be continued until the fund asset reaches 900 million unidades de fomento (~USD 41 billion as of 2013). The PRF specifically finances state guaranteed solidarity pension benefits and contributions for the elderly and disabled (NRGI; Columbia Center, 2013). The ESSF must receive any remaining fiscal surplus after contributions to the PRF made, less the amortization of public debt or advance payments to the ESSF in the previous year.

Resources can be withdrawn from the ESSF at any time to finance fiscal deficits and pay public debt, but the spending is subject to the structural balance rule. Moreover, funds can be transferred from ESSF to the PRF by the decision of the Minister of Finance. Resources from the PRF can only be used to pay for pension and social welfare. Until 2016, spending from the PRF must not exceed the Fund's return in the previous year. Since then, annual spending can be increased up to an amount equal to one-third of the difference between the pension payment in the current year and inflation-adjusted pension payment in 2008. In 2017 and 2018, the first withdrawals were made from the PRF. After 2021, the PRF will cease to exist if the withdrawals in a current year are not greater than 5% of pension spending in that year and its remaining funds will be transferred to the ESSF.

The fiscal rules and the funds clearly stabilized the economy during the 2008–09 global financial crisis. Between 2003 and 2007, the average structural budget surplus was 1.1% of GDP, while the average effective budget surplus was 4.2% of GDP as copper prices increased by 220% in real terms. In other words, before the crisis, the government took advantage of higher copper prices and accumulated annual savings equal to 3% of GDP (Solimando & Guajardo, 2017). In 2009, USD 9.3 billion was withdrawn from the ESSF. Of this spending, USD 0.8 billion was used to finance the full contribution of the PRF, and the remaining fund was assigned to the economic recovery (Chilean Ministry of Finance, 2019). According to Solimando and Guajardo (2017), two SWFs along with an improved macroeconomic framework may have contributed to lower output volatility and the reduced country risk since their inception.

**Norwegian Wealth Funds**

The world's largest SWF, the Government Pension Fund Global (GPFG),[7] was set up in 1990 by the Norwegian government to avoid higher economic volatility caused by dependency on oil prices. However, in 1996, the fund received 2 billion kroner as its first contribution after the government ran a budget surplus. Since then, the value of the fund has been firmly increasing and reached USD 1099 billion as of November 2019 (SWF Institute, 2019). Over the period of 1998–2018, the fund generated an

[7] The Fund's original name was the Government Petroleum Fund and it aimed at safeguarding long-term considerations in the use of petroleum revenues (Ministry of Finance, 2001).

annual return of 5.5%, and approximately half of the fund's market value is a return on the fund's investments. As of the end of 2018, the fund's investment spanned 73 countries, 50 currencies, 9158 companies and 1254 fixed-income security issuers.

For several years after its inception, there was no rule related to the contributions and spending of the fund. In 2001, the Ministry of Finance introduced a strategy for the use of petroleum revenues of the fiscal budget over the following years in its Guidelines for Economic Policy (Ministry of Finance, 2001). It stated that the fund receives the transfer from petroleum income[8] remaining when the Parliament has decided the share to be used for consumption and investment over the central government budget. In addition, the return on the capital should be deposited in the Fund itself. If necessary, up to 4% of the fund, the estimated expected real (not actual) return, can be withdrawn to the central government budget to cover the nonoil budget deficit, and the fund's capital should be fully invested abroad. In 2017, the government tightened the threshold to 3% to increase the fund's long-term sustainability due to a decrease in the real return on the fund after the global economic crisis of 2008 (Wirth, 2019).[9]

## *3.3 Mongolia's Sovereign Wealth Funds*

As mentioned earlier, there are currently two SWFs in Mongolia—the Fiscal Stability Fund (FSF) and the Future Heritage Fund (FHF).

**Fiscal Stability Fund**

Government revenue mainly follows the fluctuations of the mineral commodity price index, which is calculated by using four major commodity prices (gold, iron ore, copper and coal) and their share in total exports as weights (Fig. 2).

To promote mining revenue management, the FSL was approved by the Parliament of Mongolia in 2010 and took effect in 2013. The FSF was established in 2011. This is essentially the same as the Chilean ESSF. The disposable budget revenue is estimated on the basis of equilibrated prices of main mining commodities, which account for more than 3% of the budget revenue of that year.

**Sources of the FSF**

- Additional revenue generated when the actual price of the main mining commodities exceeds the equilibrated price
- Unspent leftovers of the Government Reserve Fund and Risk Fund
- Net income of the FSF financial activity
- Other income allocated by the Parliament of Mongolia.

[8] It comprised of taxes, royalties, dividends from Statoil state-owned company and state oil fields.

[9] See Nordes Bank of Investment Management report (NBIM, 2019) for more.

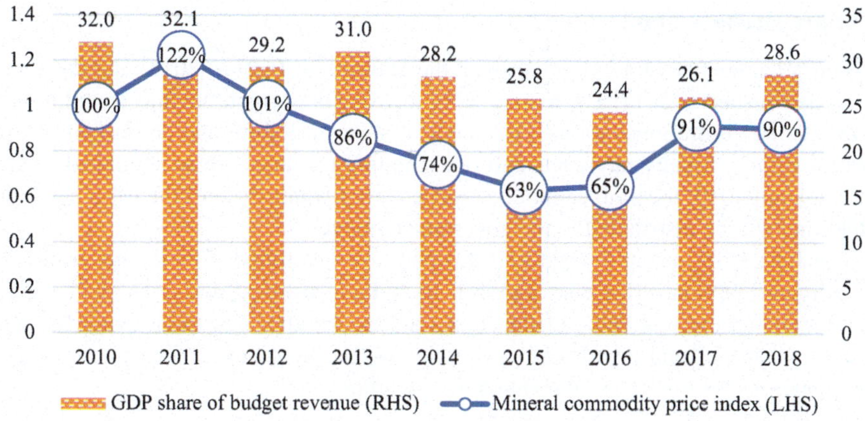


**Fig. 2** Government revenue and mineral commodity price index. *Source* Ministry of Finance and research team's calculation based on the World Bank and DIIS data

Accumulation in the fund can be transferred to the government budget in the following cases:

- The budget deficit is 4% of GDP higher than that in the Budget Plan
- Budget revenue disruption due to a decrease in major mineral commodity prices
- Budget revenue disruption due to a 20% or more decrease in the volume of major mineral commodities
- Recession, natural disaster or national emergency
- If the fund fails to address the second case, the government may borrow. This shall be within the scope of article 6.1.4 of the FSL (it will be implemented from 2024).

If the FSF exceeds 10% of GDP, an appropriate amount of investment in domestic and foreign financial markets can be made by joint decision of Bank of Mongolia and Ministry of Finance.

The revenue of the FSF has been volatile following fluctuations in commodity prices. Since 2011, except for 2016, the FSF has received revenue. Additionally, to finance the budget deficit, money from the FSF was allocated to the government budget in 2014, 2017, 2019 and 2020. As a result, the stock of the FSF is scarce as of 2020.

An important issue to note here is the implementation of the FSL. The Parliament of Mongolia has amended the law 12 times within 9 years since 2010. For instance, the requirement for net present value of government debt, which imposes a debt ceiling as 40% of GDP, has been amended three times. In February 2015, exemptions were added to the article that reflects the requirement for government debt before the exemptions were widened in May 2015. In 2016, the government debt ceiling rose from 40 to 60% of GDP.

**Future Heritage Fund**

The Parliament of Mongolia approved the law on the FHF in 2016, and the fund was established in 2017. The main goal of the fund is to create savings from mining revenue for future generations. Dividends of state-owned mining companies, most of the mining royalty payments and other mining revenues are accumulated in the fund. Until 2030, the fund cannot be touched, after which 10% of the net income of the fund will be distributed to the government budget.

In June 2019, a state-owned FHF Corporation was founded by the government. The main function of the corporation is to make investment decisions and to raise and maintain the real value of the fund's assets. Another important feature of the fund is that the fund invests only in foreign assets. Investing in foreign assets has implications for mitigating the Dutch disease effect.

**Source of the FHF**

- Dividends distributable to the state-owned shares of legal entities with state ownership participation or state-owned enterprises in possession of mining licenses
- Sixty-five percent of the mineral royalty payments collected in the budget after distribution to the FSF
- The remaining balance of the fund's net investment income after transfers to the government budget from 2030
- Starting from 2018, 20% of other mineral revenues to be collected to the state budget in excess of the base year outturn.

The FHF replaced the Human Development Fund (HDF), which was established in 2009. Both the FHF and HDF have similar income sources, such as 65% of mining royalty and dividends from the state-owned mining company, whereas the spending of the two funds is different—the money from the HDF has been distributed to citizens directly, while the money of the FHF has to be saved abroad for future generations.

According to the law on implementing the Future Heritage Fund Law, the FHF received an obligation to pay the accumulated debt of the HDF and transfers to the government budget until 2019 from its income. In particular, the FHF had a debt of 1071.9 billion MNT and transferred 160, 100 and 50 billion MNT in 2017, 2018 and 2019, respectively, to the government budget. By 2020, the FHF has savings of 1.4 trillion MNT after it has finished paying the debt of the HDF.

## 4 Dynamics of the Mongolian Economy

Mining sector development has been the driving force of the Mongolian economy in the past two decades. It has fundamentally altered the structure of the economy, social welfare and environment. At the peak of the mining boom around 2011, the resource industry became so pervasive that the nickname 'Mine-golia' was given to Mongolia

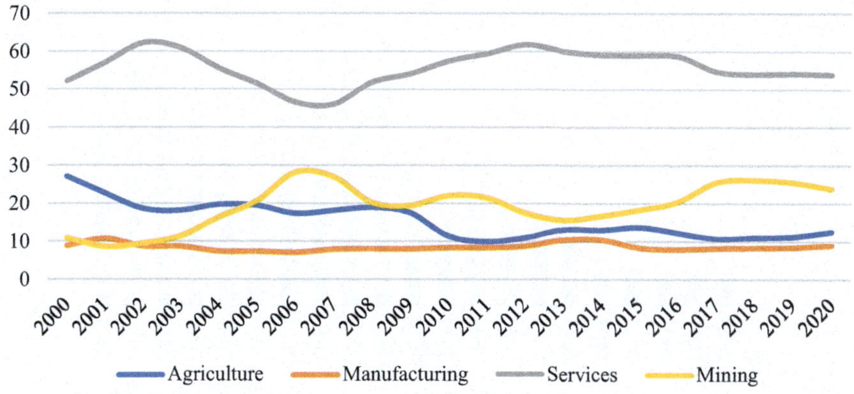


**Fig. 3** Sectoral shares of GDP (%). *Source* NSO

(Langfitt, 2012). This section briefly discusses the history of the Mongolian economy since 2000.

The Mongolian economy has become highly dependent on the mining sector. As shown in Fig. 3, the GDP share of the mining sector has increased from around 10% in 2000 to approximately 25% in 2020. On the other hand, the share of the agricultural sector declined. The shares of the service and manufacturing sectors sector have been more or less stable at approximately 55% and 10% of GDP, respectively.

The high dependency of the mining sector has made the economy vulnerable to changes in mining commodity prices. Figure 4 shows GDP per capita and economic growth between 2000 and 2020. The growth rates averaged 8.5% before 2009, so GDP per capita more than quadrupled. When the mining market boomed in 2011, GDP growth reached 17.3%. After that, economic growth slowed due to low commodities prices. Mongolia moved from low-income status to lower-middle-income in 2012 and upper-middle-income in 2015 according to the World Bank. However, the country experienced negative growth in 2016 before picking up again in the following years due to rising commodities prices until the COVID-19 pandemic.

As shown in Fig. 5, the export income of the Mongolian mining sector has increased sharply in recent years, owing to higher international prices and the utilization of the OT and TT mining developments.

The mining share of total exports has risen substantially since the early 2000s (Fig. 6). In particular, it has increased markedly since 2005, reaching almost 90% in 2011 and 2012. In contrast, the manufacturing share of total exports has fallen dramatically since 2005. During 2016 and 2020, the mining share of total exports fell, while the manufacturing share increased. This was due to the changes in the mining commodity prices and FDI.

Figure 7 shows the share of the mining sector in terms of total output, investment and employment. Investment in the mining sector rose from 5% of total investment in the early 2000s to 60% at its height in 2011. Since 2012, the investment share of the mining industry has fallen substantially due to the decline in FDI, which could

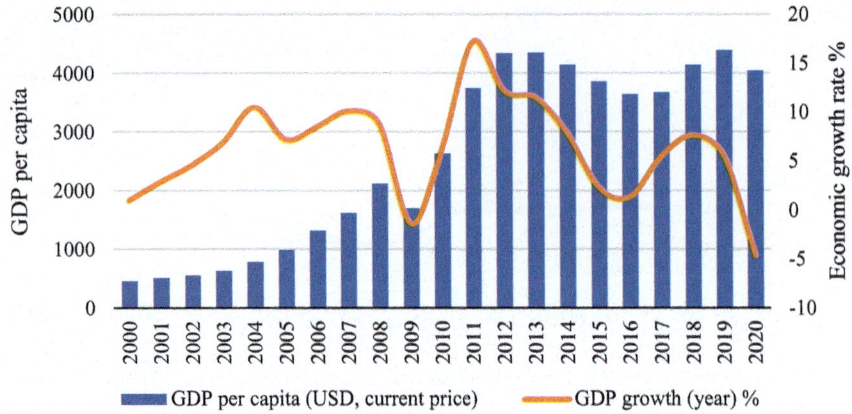


**Fig. 4** GDP per capita (USD, current price) and real GDP growth rate (%). *Source* National Statistical Office (NSO) and World Bank's database

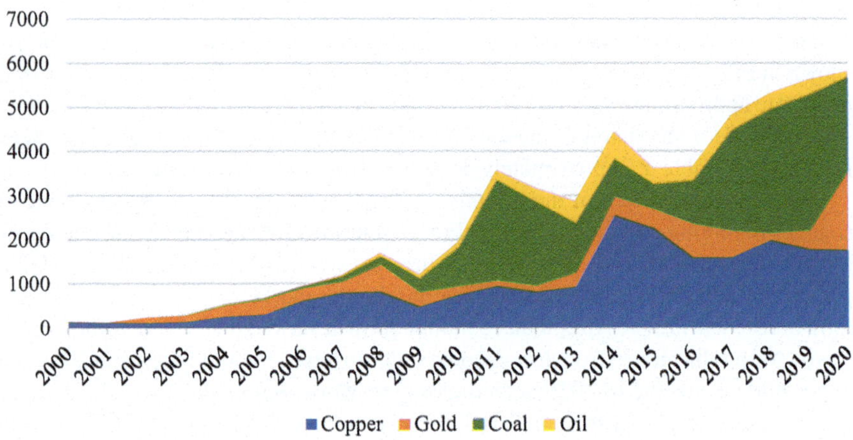


**Fig. 5** Value of mineral exports (USD million). *Source* NSO and Mongolian Customs General Administration

be explained by the harsh government policy toward foreign investment (Batdelger, 2014). The mining sector employs approximately 4% of the employment.

## 5 Current State of Budget Revenue Management in Mongolia

The FSL is a cornerstone of Mongolia's revenue management policy. The FSL came into effect in 2013. However, due to the postponement of FSL requirements, the

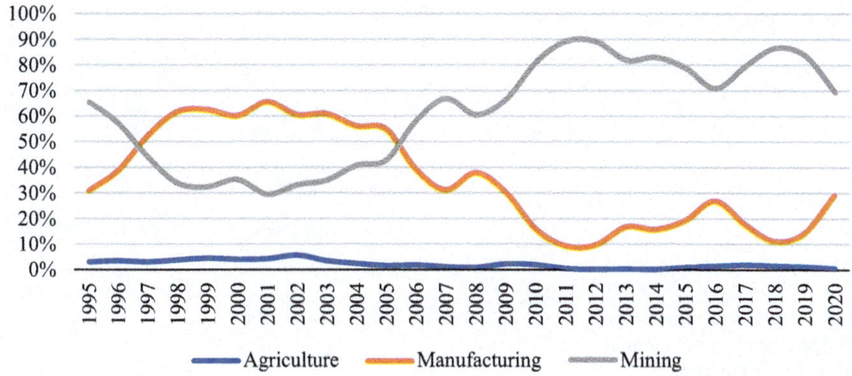


**Fig. 6** Export composition. *Source* NSO and Mongolian Customs General Administration

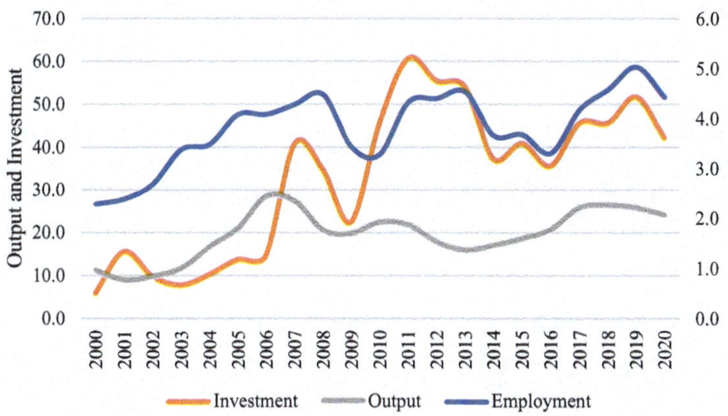


**Fig. 7** Share of mining activity, %. *Source* NSO

savings generated in the FSF were inadequate. Without sufficient savings in the fund, the government turned to loans to cover the budget deficit during the economic downturns. The increase in public debt prolonged the periods of deficit. For instance, by the end of 2020, public debt accounted for 77% of GDP (Fig. 8), and over 9% of the budget revenue was allocated to interest payments (Fig. 9).

The decrease in the ratio of interest payments to budget revenue after 2016 was mainly due to an increase in budget revenue. The budget revenue has grown steadily since 2017, reaching MNT 10 trillion by 2020. There is an increase of 1.8 times compared to 2016. The public debt-to-GDP ratio has declined rapidly since 2017 as well because of the implementation of the IMF's EFF program and a favorable economic condition.

As the simulations below will imply for the budget revenue and expenditure requirements of the FSL, an overview of past budget plans and performance may

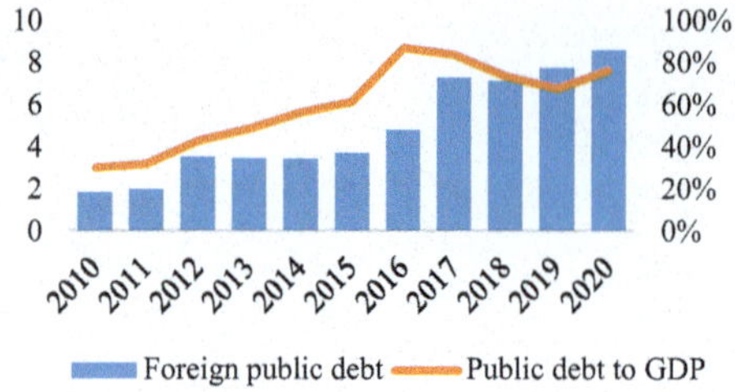


**Fig. 8** Public debt (bln USD, its ratio GDP). *Source* Bank of Mongolia

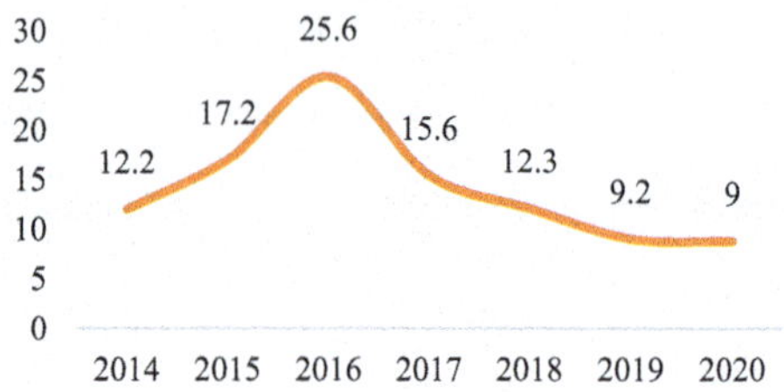


**Fig. 9** Interest payments to budget revenue ratio. *Source* Ministry of Finance

provide some helpful insights into the projection of revenue and expenditure. Table 1 provides a comparison of past planned versus actual performance of the budget.

As observed in the table above, the planned and actual budget revenues fluctuate more than the budget expenditure. Moreover, the actual revenue deviated from the

**Table 1** Planned and actual general budget revenue and expenditures from 2012–2020, billion MNT

| | 2012 | 2013 | 2014 | 2015 | 2016 | 2017 | 2018 | 2019 | 2020 |
|---|---|---|---|---|---|---|---|---|---|
| *Revenue* | | | | | | | | | |
| Planned | 5714 | 6449 | 7110 | 6076 | 5429 | 7113 | 8036 | 11,272 | 10,883 |
| Actual | 4976 | 5987 | 6316 | 5983 | 5835 | 7922 | 10,173 | 12,040 | 10,444 |
| Difference | 738 | 462 | 794 | 93 | −406 | −810 | −2137 | −768 | 439 |
| Diff/planned % | 13 | 7 | 11 | 2 | 7 | 11 | −27 | −7 | 4 |
| *Expenditure* | | | | | | | | | |
| Planned | 6474 | 6887 | 7612 | 7253 | 9992 | 9155 | 10,035 | 12,106 | 15,137 |
| Actual | 6018 | 6165 | 7145 | 7138 | 9495 | 8981 | 9317 | 11,662 | 13,904 |
| Difference | 456 | 722 | 467 | 115 | 497 | 174 | 718 | 444 | 1233 |
| Diff/planned % | 7 | 10 | 6 | 2 | 5 | 2 | 7 | 4 | 8 |
| Equilibrated balance | −1137 | −225 | −868 | −1157 | −3660 | −1742 | 856 | 379 | −3460 |
| % of GDP | 8.2 | 1.3 | 4.0 | 5.0 | 15.3 | 6.4 | 3.1 | 1.2 | −9.1 |

*Source* State budget 2012–2020 (Ministry of Finance, 2020) and ERI calculation

planned revenue more than the actual expenditure. Given the values for Diff/Planned %, the fluctuations in revenue and expenditure make it difficult to make appropriate projections about them.

Despite regulatory, fiscal and budget reforms, fiscal discipline in Mongolia has been weak. As a result, the budget revenue forecasts tend to be overly optimistic due to a political imperative to expand the budget expenditure leading to unexpected debt when the actual revenue falls below the planned value.

## 6 Imposition of the FSL

Mongolian economic cycles can be fully attributed to changes in the mining sector, such as changes in mineral commodity prices and FDI. The Mongolian fiscal rules set out in the FSL have a mission to stabilize the budget and the economy by adhering to the constraints on revenue, expenditure, budget deficit and public debt. The idea is that any budget surplus from when mineral commodity prices are higher than the equilibrated prices is deposited into the fund. The savings accumulated in the fund are then spent to stabilize the economy when prices are lower than the equilibrated prices.

This research examines whether the imposition of the FSL can reduce economic fluctuations caused by oscillations in mineral commodity prices for Mongolia. We use the ERI-CGE model, which embodies the characteristics of the Mongolian economy via calibrations to the 2015 Mongolian supply and use table (SUT) prepared by the National Statistics Office. It identifies 32 industries and 32 commodities. Three primary factors are identified (labor, capital and land). Labor is further distinguished by 9 occupational types, as in the International Standard Classification of Occupations 2008 (ISCO-08), one-digit major groups (International Labor Organization, 2012). The model has a representative aggregate household. Optimizing behaviors govern decision-making by industries and the household. Each industry minimizes its costs subject to given input prices and a constant-returns-to-scale output function. Household demands are modeled via a representative utility-maximizing household within a linear expenditure system. Units of new industry-specific capital are cost minimizing combinations of Mongolian and imported commodities. Imperfect substitutability between imported and domestic varieties of each commodity is modeled using the Armington constant elasticity of substitution assumption. The demand for any given Mongolian export commodity is inversely related to its foreign currency price. The model recognizes consumption of commodities by the government and a variety of direct and indirect taxation instruments. Purchasers' prices differ from producer prices by the unit value of indirect taxes and trade and transport margins. It is assumed that all sectors are competitive and all markets clear. As the mining sector has significantly expanded, the five main commodities are divided into subsectors, which are treated as individual sectors. The division of the mining sector into independent sectors allows for a more accurate estimate of the impacts of the megaprojects planned. Even though input output data provide the core data for CGE models, there are many other types of data and information concerning every aspect of the economy such as the government budget, balance of payment, public borrowings and debt.

### *6.1 Scenarios and Simulations*

In light of the discussion about CGE modeling in the Introduction, we carry out two simulations: a base scenario without the FSL and a policy scenario with the FSL. We make the following common assumptions about the exogenous variables in the model.

- Real GDP growth follows the IMF's forecast (Fig. 10);
- Population and the number of households are consistent with NSO's forecast made in 2010 (Fig. 11);
- Main mineral commodity production levels are consistent with the Medium Term Fiscal Framework Statement (Table 2);
- Five main mineral commodity prices follow the IMF forecasts (Fig. 12).

There are no commonly used theoretical models for grants, other capital expenditures, and other revenue components of the public-sector account. Therefore, their movements have been linked to that of GDP.

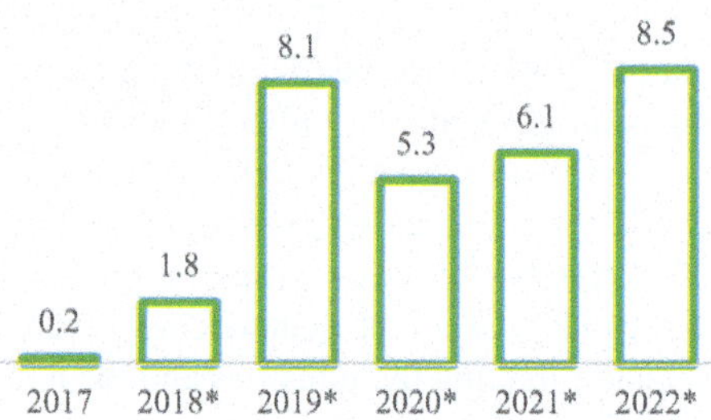


**Fig. 10** Economic growth, YoY %. *Source* IMF

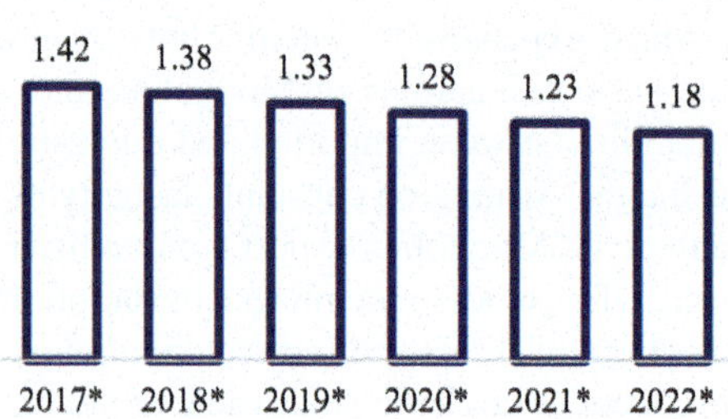


**Fig. 11** Population growth, YoY %. *Source* NSO (2012)

**Table 2** Mining sector's production by commodities

| | 2017[a] | 2018[b] | 2019[b] | 2020[b] | 2021[b] |
|---|---|---|---|---|---|
| Coal, mln tn | 33.24 | 36.23 | 38.76 | 40.74 | 40.74 |
| Copper concentrate, mln tn | 1.37 | 1.24 | 1.22 | 1.30 | 1.30 |
| Crude oil, mln barrell | 8.10 | 8.10 | 8.10 | 8.10 | 8.10 |
| Gold, tn | 17.00 | 20.00 | 20.00 | 20.00 | 20.00 |
| Iron ore, mln tn | 5.58 | 5.89 | 6.20 | 8.20 | 8.20 |

*Source* Ministry of Mining and Heavy Industry
[a] Preliminary performance
[b] Forecast

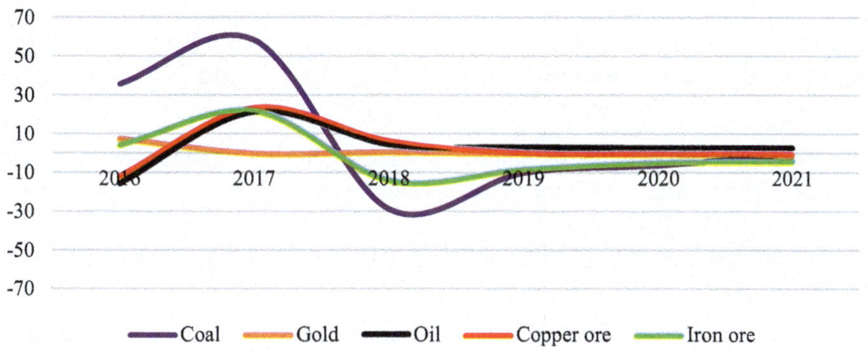


**Fig. 12** Price changes of 5 main commodities, YoY %. *Source* ERI estimation, IMF, WB, and other international institutes

**Base scenario**

The base scenario shows how the Mongolian economy could develop in the future without implementing the FSL. The main difference between this scenario and the policy scenario is that the budget expenditure follows the GNP (procyclical).

**Policy scenario**

In addition to the common assumptions regarding the exogenous variables, the policy scenario takes into account the implementation of the FSL. According to the law, the government budget must follow the following requirements.

- Total budget revenue must be calculated using an equilibrated method[10];
- The budget deficit derived from the equilibrated method must not exceed 2% of GDP in the same year or must become surplus;

[10] The Government must first calculate the average price of last 20 years for each main mining product as well as the average price of subsequent 3 years (including current year) predicted by the government approved international agency. The equilibrated price is the average of these two average prices.

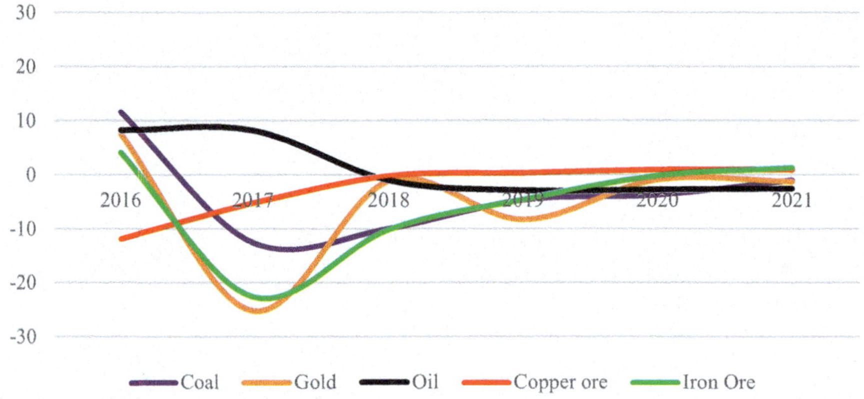


**Fig. 13** Equilibrated price changes of the main 5 commodities, YoY %. *Source* ERI estimation, IMF, WB, and other international institutes

- The growth rate of total expenditure must not exceed the maximum of the growth rate of nonmining GDP in the same year and the average growth rate of nonmining GDP in the previous 12 years;
- The present value of government debt must not exceed 60% of the GDP in the budget year.

We assume that the actual mineral commodity prices are the same as in the base scenario. However, the budget revenue and deficit must use the equilibrated prices, which are shown in Fig. 13.

Unlike the base scenario, the budget expenditure must meet the conditions of the FSL rather than being linked with GNP.

## *6.2 Simulation Results*

The results of the two scenarios are presented in Tables 3 and 4.

Given the results in the above tables, one may see that the magnitude of the volatility of the selected macroeconomic variables is smaller in the policy scenario than in the base scenario. Further investigation is revealed in Table 5, which compares the mean and standard deviation of those macroeconomic variables in the two scenarios to emphasize the impact of the FSL on the economy. Overall, although the mineral commodity prices fluctuate in both scenarios, the economy is slightly more stable in the policy scenario.

It is worth noting that the growth of the nonmining sector is higher under the policy scenario, illustrating the lessening impact of the FSL on the negative consequences of mining development, also known as deindustrialization. Both the magnitudes of changes in mining sector output and nonmining sector output are smaller in the

**Table 3** Results of the base scenario (macroeconomic variables)

| Macro variables, % | 2017 | 2018 | 2019 | 2020 | 2021 | 2022 | 2023 | 2024 | 2025 |
|---|---|---|---|---|---|---|---|---|---|
| Inflation | 9.5 | −0.7 | −6.5 | 6.2 | 6.4 | −8.5 | −6.2 | −4.7 | −3.5 |
| Real GDP | 0.2 | 1.8 | 8.1 | 5.3 | 6.1 | 8.5 | 8.0 | 7.0 | 6.0 |
| Real exports | 2.5 | 4.0 | 9.7 | 11.5 | 13.7 | 7.5 | 6.2 | 6.0 | 5.7 |
| Real imports | 0.3 | 1.5 | 3.5 | 4.0 | 5.3 | 2.8 | 1.4 | 1.1 | 1.3 |
| Mining sector output | 2.5 | 2.7 | 10.0 | 9.2 | 16.9 | 18.5 | 17.2 | 14.5 | 13.2 |
| Nonmining sector output | −1.4 | 1.2 | 7.2 | 3.7 | 1.3 | 3.9 | 4.0 | 6.8 | 7.3 |
| Real wage | −10.8 | 1.4 | 8.9 | −4.8 | −5.3 | 7.6 | 8.1 | 5.2 | 4 |
| Terms of trade (ToT) | 10.2 | −1.3 | −7.2 | −0.6 | −1.1 | −1.8 | 1.3 | −0.9 | −0.8 |

*Source* ERI estimation
[a] Forecast

**Table 4** Results of policy scenario (macroeconomic variables)

| Macro variables % | 2017 | 2018 | 2019 | 2020 | 2021 | 2022 | 2023 | 2024 | 2025 |
|---|---|---|---|---|---|---|---|---|---|
| Inflation | 9.0 | −0.7 | −6.8 | 6.3 | 5.3 | −7.2 | −5.9 | −4.8 | −3.6 |
| Real GDP | 0.2 | 1.8 | 8.1 | 5.3 | 6.1 | 8.5 | 8.0 | 7.0 | 6.0 |
| Real exports | 2.4 | 4.3 | 9.5 | 11.3 | 13.4 | 6.8 | 6.1 | 5.6 | 5.2 |
| Real imports | 0.3 | 1.3 | 3.0 | 5.7 | 3.4 | 3.2 | 2.1 | 1.5 | 1.6 |
| Mining sector output | 2.2 | 2.3 | 8.7 | 15.6 | 16.9 | 16.1 | 15.0 | 12.6 | 11.5 |
| Nonmining sector output | −1.5 | 1.3 | 7.6 | 3.9 | 1.4 | 4.1 | 4.2 | 7.2 | 7.7 |
| Real wage | −9.4 | 1.3 | 8.3 | −5.0 | −5.7 | 6.5 | 7.2 | 4.5 | 4.3 |
| Terms of trade (ToT) | 8.9 | −1.4 | −7.6 | −0.6 | −1.0 | −1.7 | 1.3 | −0.8 | −0.8 |

*Source* ERI estimation

**Table 5** Comparing the simulation results (macroeconomic variables), %

| | Mean | | Standard deviation | |
|---|---|---|---|---|
| | Base | Policy | Base | Policy |
| Inflation | −0.9 | −0.9 | 6.24 | 5.87 |
| Real GDP | 5.67 | 5.67 | 2.72 | 2.72 |
| Real exports | 7.42 | 7.18 | 3.39 | 3.33 |
| Real imports | 2.36 | 2.46 | 1.54 | 1.49 |
| Mining sector output | 11.63 | 11.21 | 5.66 | 5.36 |
| Nonmining sector output | 3.78 | 4.00 | 2.85 | 3.02 |
| Real wage | 1.59 | 1.34 | 6.60 | 6.08 |
| Terms of trade (ToT) | −0.24 | −0.40 | 4.28 | 4.01 |

*Source* ERI estimation

policy scenario. However, we can see that the variation in the mining sector output is relatively higher than that in the nonmining sector output.

The FSL implementation does not have a significant impact on the mean growth rates of the selected macroeconomic variables. However, the magnitudes of the cyclical variations of the selected variables are significantly reduced. For instance, the inflation rate is the same in both scenarios on average but is less volatile in the policy scenario. We can observe similar results for other macroeconomic variables. This suggests that if the government persistently follows the FSL, the Mongolian economy is likely to be more stable.

# 7 Sensitivity of Economic Indicators to the Changes in the FSL

The previous study considers Mongolia's mining revenue management by examining the economic impact of FSL implementation using the ERI-CGE model. The main findings are that the mean growth of the nonmining sector is higher under the FSL, implying deindustrialization, and the implementation of the FSL does not have a significant impact on the average growth rates of selected macroeconomic variables, while the cyclical volatility of the selected variables is significantly lower.

The implementation of the FSL should act as a countercyclical fiscal policy in the presence of fluctuations in mineral commodity prices—the FSF plays a role in the stabilization of the economy during times of economic ups and downs related to the mining sector. Ultimately, the stability of the economy depends on the government's implementation of the FSL and its fiscal discipline. However, as mentioned earlier, the FSL has been amended and modified multiple times to accommodate the government's failure to meet its original budget targets. The FSL set ceilings on four key budget indicators: budget revenue, budget expenditure, deficit, and public debt. Currently, there have been no analyses undertaken on how budget and economic performance are sensitive to changes in these targets. This study tries to fill that void. Specifically, the following two key benchmark parameters in the FSL are relaxed in order to determine its impacts on the budget as well as the economy: ceiling on the growth of the budget expenditure and restriction on the budget revenue.

## *7.1 Scenarios and Simulations*

This research examines the impacts of relaxing the budget revenue and expenditure requirements of the FSL on the Mongolian economy. In doing so, we carry out four simulations in the ERI-CGE model: (i) Base scenario with all four main restrictions of the FSL; (ii) Scenario 1 relaxes only the restriction on the budget expenditure; (iii)

Scenario 2 relaxes the restriction on the budget revenue; and (iv) Scenario 3 relaxes both the restrictions on the budget expenditure and revenue.

We make the following assumptions on the exogenous variables.

- Real GDP growth follows the IMF forecasts (Fig. 14)
- Population growth is consistent with the IMF's projection (Fig. 15)
- The same main mineral commodity production levels are considered as those in the previous section (Table 6)
- Mineral commodity prices are based on the estimates made by the World Bank and other international institutions.

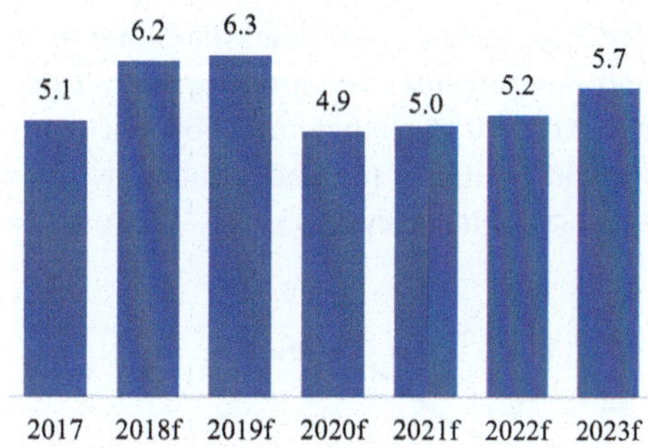


**Fig. 14** Economic growth, YoY %. *Source* IMF

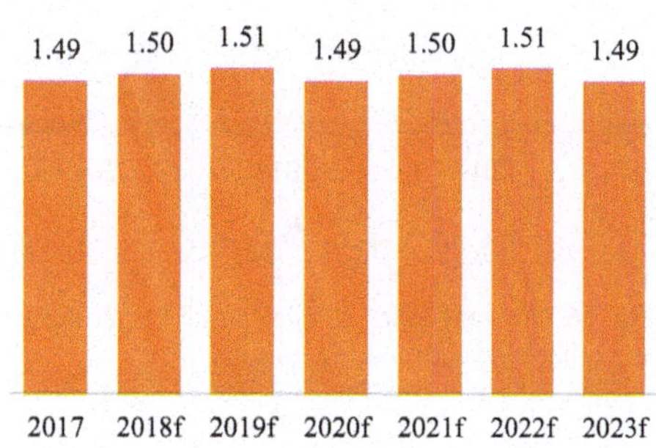


**Fig. 15** Population growth, YoY %. *Source* IMF

**Table 6** Mining production forecasts

| | 2017e | 2018f | 2019f | 2020f | 2021f |
|---|---|---|---|---|---|
| Coal, mln tn | 33.24 | 36.23 | 38.76 | 40.74 | 40.74 |
| Copper concentrate, mln tn | 1.37 | 1.24 | 1.22 | 1.30 | 1.30 |
| Crude oil, mln barrel | 8.10 | 8.10 | 8.10 | 8.10 | 8.10 |
| Gold, tn | 17.00 | 20.00 | 20.00 | 20.00 | 20.00 |
| Iron ore, mln tn | 5.58 | 5.89 | 6.20 | 8.20 | 8.20 |

*Source* Ministry of Mining and Heavy Industry

The production of the main mineral commodities, based on the forecasts made by the Ministry of Mining and Heavy Industry, are shown in Table 6. With the implementation of the "Gold-2" program by the Government of Mongolia and the Bank of Mongolia, the production of gold is expected to increase to promote economic recovery.

Utilizing various forecasts made by international institutions gives the average price forecasts for five commodities—coal, gold, crude oil, copper concentrate and iron ore (Fig. 16).

The equilibrated prices of the commodities are shown in Fig. 17.

**Base scenario**

The base scenario simulates the economy within the scope of the exogenous variables and the implementation of the FSL. Table 7 shows how macroeconomic variables are expected to change in the base scenario.

The results in the above table are different from those generated in the policy scenario of the previous study. The reason is simply due to the updated forecasts and

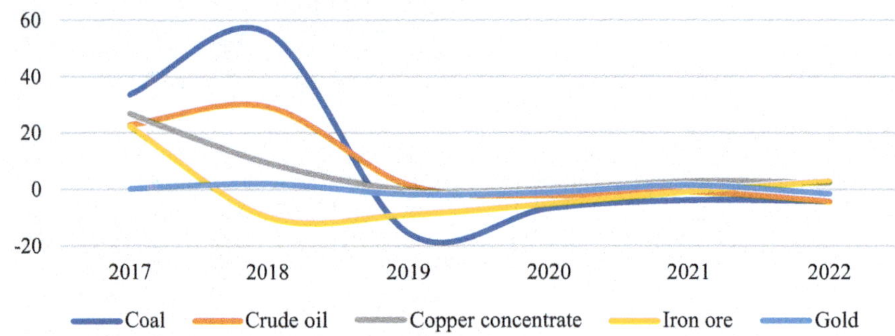


**Fig. 16** Average price forecasts of 5 commodities, YoY %. *Source* ERI estimation, World Bank, and other international institutions

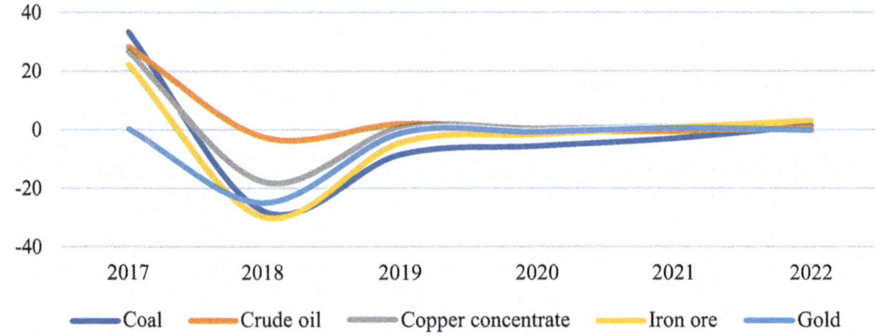


**Fig. 17** Equilibrated prices of 5 commodities. YoY %. *Source* ERI estimation, World Bank (2018) and other international institutions

**Table 7** Base scenario results under FSL

| Macro variables % | 2018 | 2019 | 2020 | 2021 | 2022 | 2023 | 2024 | 2025 |
|---|---|---|---|---|---|---|---|---|
| Inflation | 5.44 | 7.18 | 4.77 | 4.32 | 6.45 | 3.94 | 2.91 | 2.26 |
| Real GDP | 6.20 | 6.30 | 4.90 | 5.00 | 5.20 | 5.70 | 5.00 | 4.50 |
| Real exports | 8.23 | 9.63 | 10.74 | 9.39 | 8.57 | 6.31 | 5.43 | 4.55 |
| Real imports | 3.38 | 6.27 | 5.76 | 5.61 | 4.73 | 4.44 | 3.87 | 3.25 |
| Mining sector output | 11.43 | 13.38 | 9.52 | 16.06 | 17.18 | 15.43 | 15.15 | 13.55 |
| Nonmining sector output | 4.71 | 4.26 | 3.42 | 1.52 | 1.91 | 2.89 | 2.16 | 1.90 |
| Real wage | −1.55 | −4.02 | −0.35 | −0.71 | −1.11 | 0.70 | −0.35 | −0.43 |
| Terms of trade (ToT) | 1.18 | 3.96 | −0.39 | −0.69 | 2.19 | 0.42 | −0.23 | −0.25 |
| Gov't spending growth | 6.41 | 6.48 | 6.92 | 7.46 | 7.39 | 7.53 | 7.36 | 7.08 |

*Source* ERI estimation

assumptions about the exogenous variables. For instance, the economic growth rates, population growth rates and the forecasts of commodity prices have been updated to reflect the current positions.

**Scenario 1**

In this scenario, all the provisions of the FSL are included except the restriction on the budget expenditure. In other words, there is no constraint on the growth rate of the budget expenditure. The budget revenue is calculated utilizing the equilibrated method, the equilibrated budget deficit cannot exceed 2% of GDP, and the debt-to-GDP ratio cannot exceed 60%.

Under the FSL, the growth rate of the budget expenditure must not exceed the maximum growth rate of nonmining GDP or the average of the past 12 years. In contrast, in this simulation, the growth rate expenditure can exceed the limit or can be higher than the growth rate in the base scenario. For simplicity and demonstration purposes, we assume that the growth rate of expenditures follows the growth rate of nominal GNP (procyclical). Under this assumption, the budget expenditure grows in the period of 2018–2025 by 18.84, 16.22, 14.16, 12.83, 11.13, 13.56, 11.77 and 12.81%.

Table 8 exhibits the economic impact of the FSL without the expenditure constraint.

Although we assume that the growth rate of the budget expenditure should be equal to that of GNP, this does not happen given the results in the last row of the table. This is due to the budget deficit being 2% of GDP, which constrains the growth rate of the expenditure. If the expenditure follows GNP, the budget deficit-to-GDP ratio would exceed 2%. Thus, to ensure that the other three rules are met, the growth of the expenditure is at the maximum rate allowed under the 2% budget deficit rule. This implies that when expenditures grew at a rate of 10.32% in 2018, the maximum growth rate under the 2% budget deficit rule was to be violated.

**Table 8** Results without expenditure constraint

| Macro variables % | 2018 | 2019 | 2020 | 2021 | 2022 | 2023 | 2024 | 2025 |
|---|---|---|---|---|---|---|---|---|
| Inflation | 9.04 | 10.20 | 6.49 | 5.60 | 8.11 | 4.65 | 2.91 | 3.78 |
| Real GDP | 6.20 | 6.30 | 4.90 | 5.00 | 5.20 | 5.70 | 5.00 | 4.50 |
| Real exports | 5.75 | 8.78 | 11.30 | 7.12 | 8.84 | 5.97 | 4.77 | 3.79 |
| Real imports | 5.54 | 7.98 | 8.69 | 6.95 | 6.43 | 5.75 | 2.76 | 4.51 |
| Mining sector output | 11.32 | 13.75 | 9.02 | 16.83 | 17.02 | 14.34 | 16.53 | 13.02 |
| Nonmining sector output | 4.82 | 4.02 | 3.95 | 1.31 | 2.02 | 3.06 | 3.21 | 2.48 |
| Real wage | −2.50 | −4.73 | −1.35 | −0.94 | −2.52 | 0.93 | 2.44 | 1.41 |
| Terms of trade (ToT) | 2.84 | 4.66 | 1.88 | −0.69 | 1.19 | 0.42 | −0.44 | −1.22 |
| Gov't spending growth | 10.32 | 9.83 | 8.91 | 9.37 | 9.12 | 8.21 | 6.20 | 8.59 |

*Source* ERI estimation

## Scenario 2

In the second scenario, the rules placed on the budget expenditure, deficit and government debt are included, while the budget revenue rule is relaxed. Specifically, the growth rate of expenditures is constrained by the growth rate of nonmining GDP, and the budget deficit-to-GDP ratio cannot exceed 2%. To calculate the budget revenue, the maximum price forecasts of the commodity prices are used instead of the average prices in Fig. 16. The simulation results are given in Table 9 for selected macroeconomic variables.

Despite projecting the budget revenue at the maximum possible commodity prices, all price fluctuations are stabilized through the FSF in such a way that during periods

**Table 9** Results without revenue constraint

| Macro variables % | 2018 | 2019 | 2020 | 2021 | 2022 | 2023 | 2024 | 2025 |
|---|---|---|---|---|---|---|---|---|
| Inflation | 6.12 | 7.83 | 7.35 | 6.36 | 5.77 | 3.49 | 3.39 | 2.65 |
| Real GDP | 6.20 | 6.30 | 4.90 | 5.00 | 5.20 | 5.70 | 5.00 | 4.50 |
| Real exports | 8.71 | 9.98 | 11.07 | 9.73 | 8.91 | 6.38 | 5.54 | 4.70 |
| Real imports | 3.18 | 6.04 | 5.58 | 5.41 | 4.54 | 4.39 | 3.79 | 3.15 |
| Mining sector output | 11.66 | 13.14 | 9.90 | 16.22 | 16.96 | 15.14 | 15.48 | 13.58 |
| Nonmining sector output | 4.61 | 4.33 | 3.29 | 1.51 | 1.94 | 2.95 | 2.12 | 1.90 |
| Real wage | −1.49 | −3.52 | −0.28 | −0.64 | −1.31 | −0.12 | −0.33 | −0.44 |
| Terms of trade (ToT) | 1.50 | 3.77 | 1.58 | 0.32 | −1.00 | −0.75 | −0.61 | −0.23 |
| Gov't spending growth | 6.41 | 6.48 | 6.92 | 7.46 | 7.39 | 7.53 | 7.36 | 7.08 |

*Source* ERI estimation

**Table 10** Results without expenditure and revenue constraints

| Macro variables % | 2018 | 2019 | 2020 | 2021 | 2022 | 2023 | 2024 | 2025 |
|---|---|---|---|---|---|---|---|---|
| Inflation | 13.30 | 15.34 | 10.31 | 10.11 | 8.74 | 6.62 | 5.30 | 5.10 |
| Real GDP | 6.20 | 6.30 | 4.90 | 5.00 | 5.20 | 5.70 | 5.00 | 4.50 |
| Real exports | 4.24 | 8.21 | 9.15 | 6.70 | 7.25 | 3.62 | 2.51 | 2.54 |
| Real imports | 6.24 | 8.12 | 9.20 | 7.91 | 6.43 | 5.75 | 2.76 | 4.51 |
| Mining sector output | 10.50 | 14.05 | 8.11 | 16.79 | 12.00 | 15.40 | 14.72 | 13.06 |
| Nonmining sector output | 4.56 | 5.78 | 3.90 | 2.32 | 3.02 | 3.05 | 3.16 | 2.45 |
| Real wage | −3.68 | −7.11 | −2.14 | −1.70 | −2.72 | 1.32 | 4.45 | 1.91 |
| Terms of trade (ToT) | 4.17 | 7.01 | 2.98 | −1.25 | 1.28 | 0.59 | −0.79 | −1.65 |
| Gov't spending growth | 18.84 | 16.22 | 14.16 | 12.83 | 11.13 | 13.56 | 11.77 | 12.81 |

*Source* ERI estimation

of low mineral commodity prices, the amount needed is withdrawn from the fund and vice versa during periods of high mineral commodity prices.

If the FSF balance is negative, there is no way to channel the impact of this on the economy. Additionally, as observed by the results, the growth rate of the budget expenditure is equal to that exhibited in the base simulation as the government expenditure limitations are in place.

**Scenario 3**

In the third scenario, both the budget revenue and expenditure rules are relaxed in the model. As in Scenario 2, the budget revenue is based on the higher forecasted mineral commodity prices. The expenditure growth rate follows the growth rate of nominal GNP. This is not constrained by the budget deficit rule of 2%, as the budget revenue is not constrained either. Table 10 presents the simulation results.

## 7.2 *Simulation Results*

The three simulations compare the impact of the revenue and expenditure provisions of the FSL on the economy. Overall, in all the simulations, removing even one constraint on the budget destabilizes the economy in such a way that the standard deviation of most macroeconomic variables increases relative to the base simulation. Table 11 shows the average and standard deviation of the macroeconomic variables calculated for each simulation from 2018 to 2025.

In the first simulation, the growth constraint of the expenditure is relaxed. However, the budget deficit constraint limits expenditure growth. Relative to the base simulation, expenditure growth is significantly higher in the first simulation, resulting in an increase in real imports and a decrease in real exports. Government spending positively affects demands for domestic and imported products. As the demand for

**Table 11** Comparison of results

| | Mean | | | | Standard deviation | | | |
|---|---|---|---|---|---|---|---|---|
| | Base | Sim-1 | Sim-2 | Sim-3 | Base | Sim-1 | Sim-2 | Sim-3 |
| Inflation | 4.66 | 6.35 | 5.37 | 9.35 | 1.57 | 2.43 | 1.82 | 3.45 |
| Real GDP | 5.35 | 5.35 | 5.35 | 5.35 | 0.61 | 0.61 | 0.61 | 0.61 |
| Real exports | 7.86 | 7.04 | 8.13 | 5.53 | 2.05 | 2.32 | 2.16 | 2.45 |
| Real imports | 4.66 | 6.08 | 4.51 | 6.37 | 1.06 | 1.77 | 1.03 | 1.95 |
| Mining sector output | 13.96 | 13.60 | 14.01 | 13.08 | 2.37 | 2.48 | 2.25 | 2.63 |
| Nonmining sector output | 2.85 | 3.11 | 2.83 | 3.53 | 1.10 | 1.08 | 1.09 | 1.09 |
| Real wage | −0.98 | −0.91 | −1.02 | −1.21 | 1.30 | 2.23 | 1.05 | 3.40 |
| Terms of trade (ToT) | 0.77 | 1.08 | 0.57 | 1.54 | 1.50 | 1.86 | 1.52 | 2.81 |
| Gov't spending growth | 7.08 | 8.82 | 7.08 | 13.92 | 0.41 | 1.17 | 0.41 | 2.36 |

*Source* ERI estimation

domestic products increases, it creates the pressure to raise market prices. This can be easily shown from the mean and standard deviations of inflation.

As seen in the past, Mongolia tends to spend considerably during economic upturns, later spiraling the economy into debt when the cycle flips. This later forces the government to pay down previous debt by accumulating more debt. In this case, the government expenditure does not increase as much as expected due to the other provisions, such as the revenue and the budget deficit, still in place. As revenue is calculated using the equilibrated method, the revenue is limited, as the budget deficit cannot exceed 2% of GDP, limiting the growth of the expenditure. However, if the other provisions are not in place, expenditures would skyrocket and greatly destabilize the economy. This can be observed from the standard deviations of most of the macroeconomic variables.

At the sectoral level, mining sector output decreases slightly, while its standard deviation increases slightly, and nonmining sector output increases, while its standard deviation remains relatively stable. The increase in nonmining output is associated with government spending. In other words, the government demand for nonmining products increases, leading to growth in sectoral output. However, as can be observed in the comparison table, the magnitude of the impact is not considerable. Real wages are affected as the standard deviation of inflation is greater compared to the base simulation.

In the second simulation, the restriction on the budget revenue is omitted, which affects the economy significantly less than the first simulation. The reason for the subdued effect on some of the macroeconomic variables is due to the FSF. This simulation considers the budget income shortfall, which the fund plays a central role in covering. The magnitude of variation for most macroeconomic variables remains relatively stable to the base simulation. The shocks mainly affect imports and exports, but their standard deviations are miniscule. The small fluctuations in exports and imports decrease real wages slightly and barely any impact on the outputs of the mining and nonmining sectors.

In the third simulation, both revenue and expenditure restrictions are relaxed. This impacts the economy the most compared to the previous two simulations. As the expenditure growth is not capped by the budget deficit constraint of 2%, the mean growth of government spending is approximately 14%, the highest of all simulations run. High government spending positively impacts demand for domestic products and imported goods, whose market prices are reflected in inflation. Revenue, on the other hand, has a lesser impact on the economy as the FSF is being implemented. Therefore, during periods of high mineral commodity prices, the amount over the equilibrated price is being put into the fund and is withdrawn during periods of low mineral commodity prices. This is why the standard deviation of imports and exports are slightly more muted than otherwise.

## 8 An Assessment of the Potential Impact of SWFs on the Mongolian Economy

The Mongolian sovereign wealth funds, the FSF and FHF, are designated to smooth business cycle fluctuations that occur in budget expenditures that would contribute to achieving economic stability in the long term as well as allocating mineral wealth over generations. To examine the funds' impact, we first develop a long-term baseline economic projection for the next 20 years using a dynamic CGE model. Then, we introduce the FSF and FHF into the model as alternative scenarios. Comparing the results of the alternative scenarios with the result of the baseline scenario, we can assess the economic impact of the two funds. In the previous two studies, we assume that the FSF implements as reflected in the FSL and do not consider the effect of the FHF.

The CGE model we consider in this analysis is quite different from the ERI CGE model developed for the previous two studies. We extend the recursive dynamic CGE model of ) as a main tool for this analysis.[11] The model is calibrated to a 2017 Mongolian SAM (social accounting matrix), which we built for this study using the 2017 supply and use tables, balance of payments and government budget data.[12] The SAM is a square matrix with 47 columns and rows. Its accounts consist of 12 sectors/commodities, three types of institutions, three types of taxes and saving (investment) accounts divided into public investment and changes in inventories. Table 12 has the Macro-SAM, which is the aggregated version of the detailed SAM. This gives a snapshot of the Mongolian economy in 2017. As seen, there are 15 accounts. The SAM is similar to a double-entry book keeping so that each cell represents a payment from the column account to the row account.

---

[11] This model is a version of the PEP-1-t model of Decaluwé et al. (2013b) adopted for Mongolia.

[12] We followed the same approach in Galindev et al. (2019a, 2019b) (which complied the Mongolian SAM for 2014.

**Table 12** Macro-SAM 2017 (percent of GDP)

| | | 1 | 2 | 3 | 4 | 5 | 6 | 7 | 8 | 9 | 10 | 11 | 12 | 13 | 14 | 15 |
|---|---|---|---|---|---|---|---|---|---|---|---|---|---|---|---|---|
| 1 | Labor | | | | | | | | 0.6 | 45.2 | | | | | | 46 |
| 2 | Capital | | | | | | | | 0.1 | 45.4 | | | | | | 45 |
| 3 | Households | 44.8 | 33.6 | | 11.6 | | | | 2.1 | | | | | | | 92 |
| 4 | Government | | | 3.2 | | 13.1 | 1.7 | 7.4 | 0.2 | 0.4 | | 0.0 | | | | 26 |
| 5 | Direct taxes | | | 13.1 | | | | | | | | | | | | 13 |
| 6 | Import duties | | | | | | | | | | 1.7 | | | | | 2 |
| 7 | Commodity taxes | | | | | | | | | | 7.4 | | | | | 7 |
| 8 | World | 0.9 | 11.9 | 0.7 | 2.0 | | | | | | 56.3 | | | | | 72 |
| 9 | Sectors | | | | | | | | | | 126.2 | 53.8 | | | | 180 |
| 10 | Commodities | | | 53.5 | 12.7 | | | | | 89.1 | 15.2 | 4.9 | 18.7 | 5.9 | 6.7 | 207 |
| 11 | Export | | | | | | | | 58.7 | | | | | | | 59 |
| 12 | Pri. investment | | | 17.4 | (0.3) | | | | 8.3 | | | | | | | 26 |
| 13 | Pub. investment | | | 4.0 | (0.1) | | | | 1.9 | | | | | | | 6 |
| 14 | Stock changes | | | | | | | | | | | | 6.7 | | | 7 |
| 15 | Total | 46 | 45 | 92 | 26 | 13 | 2 | 7 | 72 | 180 | 207 | 59 | 25 | 6 | 7 | |

*Source* SAM 2017

## 8.1 Scenarios and Simulations

Similar to other CGE models, the number of variables exceeds the number of equations in our model so that some variables must be fixed as exogenous. The potential labor supply grows 1.83% per annum for the first 3 years and 1.6% in the following years, reflecting the population growth rate projected by the NSO. Total factor productivity (TFP) is another exogenous variable, and its growth rate is a weighted average of sector-specific productivity growth rates, which are the historical averages estimated from a Solow residual analysis. We assume that the TFP growth rate is at the historical value of 3.4% per annum, which applies to all sectors. The following exogenous variables are assumed to grow at the sum of population and the average TFP growth rates:

- Government spending on goods and services
- Government capital expenditure
- Current account balance
- Remittances from the rest of the world
- Investment expenditure on the livestock sector
- Inventory changes of all commodities except for other mining and livestock
- Real investment in the public, mining and livestock sectors.

We consider arbitrary series for the main commodity prices to reflect the mining cycles. In particular, coal and copper prices are assumed to fluctuate around their equilibrated levels. In generating the artificial price series, we also consider the correlation coefficient of 0.77 between the changes in coal price and copper price. The equilibrated prices are calculated as the average of historical prices of the last 12 years and the expected prices of the subsequent 3 years. The arbitrary and equilibrated prices are given in Fig. 18.

The above assumptions are applied in all the scenarios. However, each scenario has different assumptions specific to wealth funds.

We simulate the model from 2019 to 2040 in the following four scenarios:

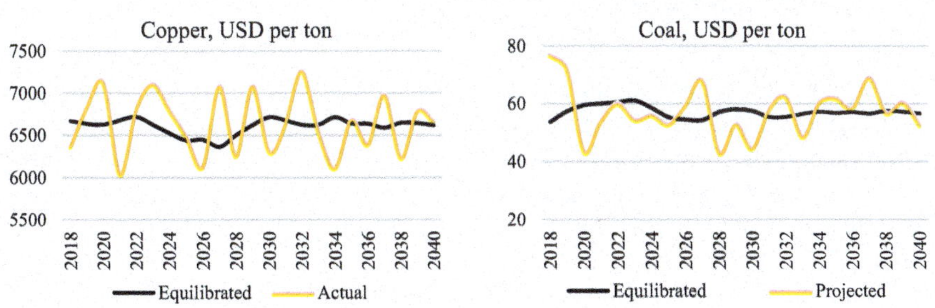


**Fig. 18** Coal and copper price projection. *Source* NSO, Authors' calculations

***Baseline scenario***: No FSF or FHF

It is assumed that there are no wealth funds—i.e., the Mongolian government spends all its revenue on its consumption of goods and services, transfers and investment. There is no equilibrated budget revenue. Naturally, there exists a budget deficit.

***Scenario 1***: FSF is present, FHF is absent

In addition to all the assumptions imposed in the baseline scenario, the FSF (not the FHF) is operational. In doing so, we introduce new equations related to the FSF. First, the fund's stock accumulates through the interest income of its financial activities and net change (the difference between the actual and equilibrated budget revenue). We also assume that the fund is invested abroad.

***Scenario 2***: FSF is absent, FHF is present

This scenario takes the implementation of the FHF into account (excluding the FSF), while all the assumptions in the baseline scenario remain the same. According to the FHF law, there will be no disbursement from the fund until 2030 but 10% of the net interest income of the fund after 2030 for budget purposes. In implementing this in the model, the stock of the FHF increases with interest income of financial activities of the fund and its net change until 2030. From 2030, on the other hand, the fund will receive 90% of net interest income from its financial activity so that the remaining 10% will be transferred to the government budget. The net change of the fund is sourced by 65% of the royalty from the mining sector and the government's dividend income from state-owned mining companies. Additionally, the fund stock is invested abroad.

***Scenario 3***: Both FSF and FHF are present

This scenario is designed to show the impact of both funds simultaneously, which is a combination of Scenarios 2 and 3.

## 8.2 Simulation Results

The revenue and spending of the FSF are generated when the actual price of the main commodities deviates from the equilibrated price. Figure 19 shows the dynamics of the fund stock, which follows the movement of the prices of the main mineral commodities chosen randomly for this analysis. Given the series of prices, the stock of the fund is estimated to reach approximately 2.17 trillion MNT by 2040 in Scenarios 2 and 4.

The purpose of the FHF is to allocate the revenue from mineral resources across the current and future generations, and the fund shall receive a certain share of the royalty income of the mining sector each year, which means that the net change of the fund is always positive and depends on the mineral commodities prices' fluctuations. Therefore, the stock of the FHF will increase (Fig. 20). It is estimated that the stock

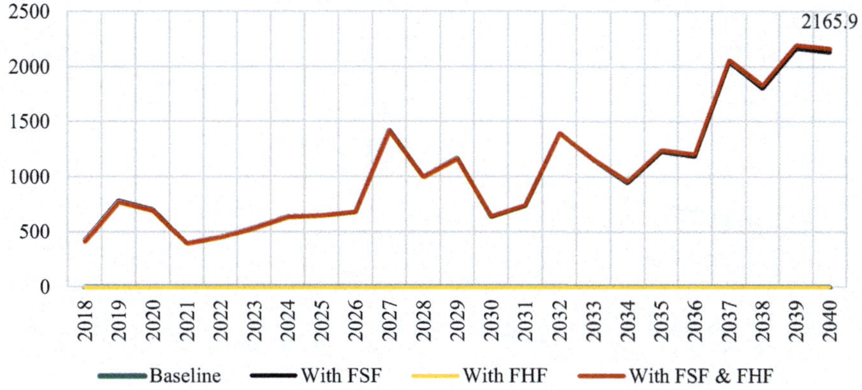


**Fig. 19** Stock of FSF, billion MNT. *Source* ERI estimation

of the FHF will reach 24.4 trillion MNT and 23.6 trillion MNT by 2040 from 1.4 trillion in 2019 in Scenarios 3 and 4, respectively. On the other hand, the stock of the FHF is zero in the other two scenarios, as the FHF is absent in those scenarios.

**Wealth funds' impact on government accounts**

The operation of the funds has the following impacts on the government revenue. Figure 21 shows the equilibrated budget revenue for the four scenarios. For the baseline scenario, the budget revenue is equal to the equilibrated revenue because there are no funds in this scenario. On the other hand, when the FSF is active, the volatility of the budget revenue is smaller as the FSF absorbs the price fluctuations. Furthermore, the equilibrated budget revenue is smaller when the FHF is active because the difference between the budget revenues in scenarios with the FHF and without the FHF is saved in the FHF for future generations.

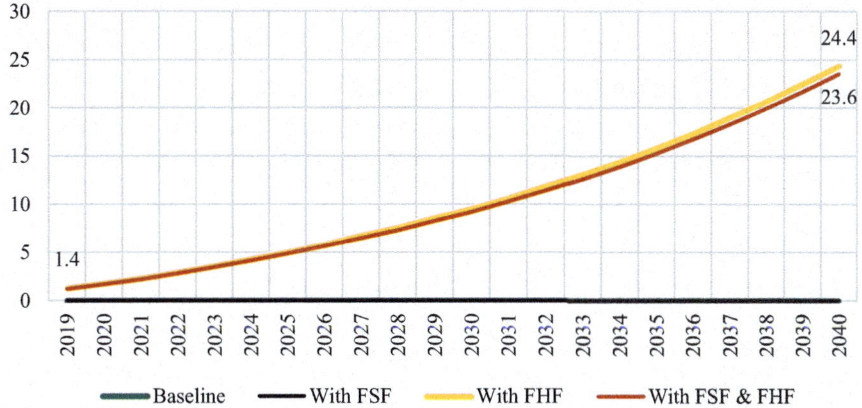


**Fig. 20** Stock of FHF, trillion MNT. *Source* ERI estimation

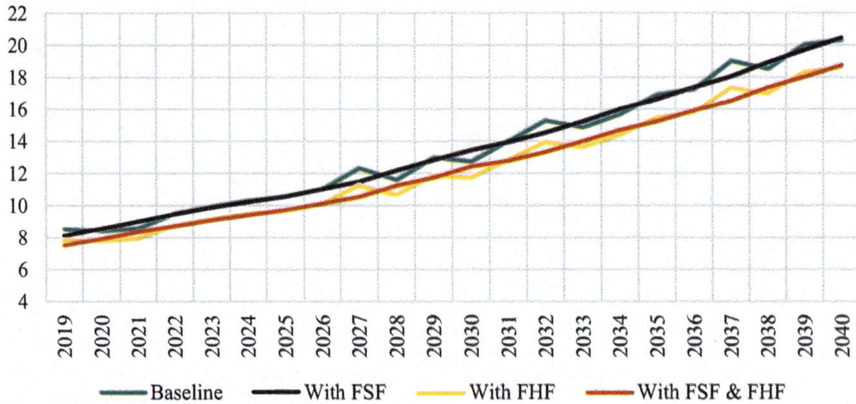


**Fig. 21** Equilibrated budget revenue, trillion MNT. *Source* ERI estimation

The trends of the budget expenditure follow the equilibrated revenue in the corresponding scenarios. In particular, the budget expenditure is more stable in the scenarios with the FSF, while it is lower in levels in the scenarios with the FHF. Furthermore, the effect of the funds on the budget expenditure is mainly through the government capital expenditure (public investment), as other expenditures (spending on goods and services and transfers) are determined exogenously. The volatility of capital expenditure is larger without the FSF, while FHF implementation lowers capital expenditure.

The impact of the FSF and the FHF on the budget can be seen more clearly from Table 13, which compares the average growth rates and standard deviations of the budget items. The funds have no significant impact on the average growth rates of the main budget variables other than capital expenditure, while the FSF reduces the growth rate of capital expenditure. In terms of their volatility, the FSF stabilizes all the budget variables significantly, while the FHF does not have much dampening effects.

**Table 13** Comparing the scenarios: government accounts

| | Average growth rates | | | | Standard deviations | | | |
|---|---|---|---|---|---|---|---|---|
| | Baseline | FSF | FHF | FSF & FHF | Baseline | FSF | FHF | FSF & FHF |
| Budget revenue | 4.3 | 4.4 | 4.2 | 4.3 | 5.1 | 0.8 | 4.6 | 1.0 |
| Budget expenditure | 4.3 | 4.4 | 4.2 | 4.3 | 4.7 | 0.7 | 4.3 | 0.9 |
| Capital expenditure | 4.8 | 4.2 | 4.8 | 3.3 | 20.3 | 6.4 | 27.8 | 13.5 |

*Source* ERI estimation

The government debt increases in absolute terms in all scenarios, but the debt-to-GDP ratios decrease gradually to 63.6% in the scenarios with the FHF and 61.7% in those without the FHF by 2040 (Fig. 22).

**Wealth funds' impact on macroeconomic variables**

This subsection discusses the impact of wealth funds on macroeconomic variables.

Figure 23 illustrates the real GDP growth rates under the four scenarios. The GDP growth rate slows down gradually and stabilizes at approximately 4% in the next 23 years in all four scenarios. However, the GDP growth rate is lower in the scenarios with the FHF and more stable in the scenarios with the FSF.

The impact on the macroeconomic indicators can be seen from Table 14. The FSF does not have a significant impact on the average growth rates of those macroeconomic variables. However, it reduces the magnitudes of their standard deviations.

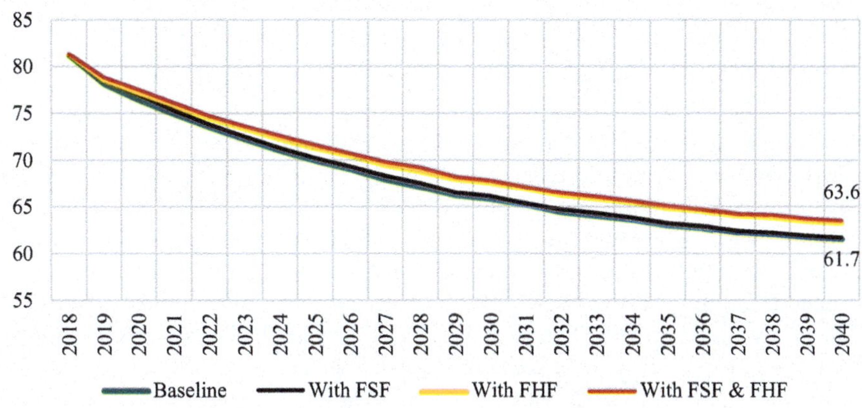


**Fig. 22** Government debt to GDP ratio, percent. *Source* ERI estimation

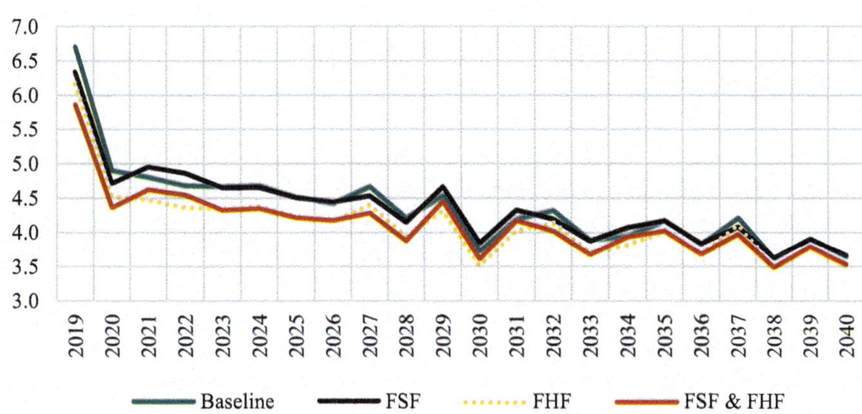


**Fig. 23** Real GDP growth, percent. *Source* ERI estimation

**Table 14** Comparing the scenarios: Macroeconomic variables

| Macro variables | Average growth | | | | Standard deviation | | | |
|---|---|---|---|---|---|---|---|---|
| | Baseline | FSF | FHF | FSF & FHF | Baseline | FSF | FHF | FSF & FHF |
| Real GDP | 4.38 | 4.37 | 4.16 | 4.15 | 0.64 | 0.57 | 0.54 | 0.50 |
| Nonmining GDP | 4.21 | 4.24 | 4.10 | 4.13 | 3.36 | 2.35 | 3.31 | 2.37 |
| Household consumption | 4.22 | 4.23 | 4.07 | 4.07 | 3.76 | 3.64 | 3.80 | 3.70 |
| Government consumption | 3.87 | 3.83 | 3.93 | 3.90 | 2.92 | 2.32 | 2.88 | 2.33 |
| Total Investment | 3.77 | 3.77 | 3.59 | 3.58 | 7.18 | 3.58 | 7.04 | 3.61 |
| Export | 4.41 | 4.41 | 4.34 | 4.35 | 6.87 | 7.20 | 6.99 | 7.29 |
| Import | 4.15 | 4.16 | 4.08 | 4.09 | 5.02 | 3.43 | 4.95 | 3.46 |
| CPI | -0.01 | 0.01 | 0.06 | 0.08 | 2.03 | 1.55 | 2.00 | 1.55 |

*Source* ERI estimation

On the other hand, the FHF does not have a stabilization effect on the macroeconomic variables, yet the average growths of the variables except for government consumption and CPI are lower.

In summary, the results suggest that the FSF tends to mitigate economic fluctuations generated by mineral commodity prices, while the FHF can help allocate revenue from mineral resources across current and future generations, although it reduces economic growth slightly as it is saved abroad. If the government implements the funds persistently, it could reduce the vulnerability of the economy to the fluctuations in mineral commodity prices. In addition, if the government is able to accumulate the FHF stock according to the current law, the FHF stock will reach approximately 30% of GDP by 2040.

## 9 Conclusions

Over the last decade, the Mongolian economy has experienced booms and busts initiated by changes in mineral commodity prices and FDI. The mining boom around 2010 made the economy vulnerable to commodity price slumps and an adverse shock to FDI. The economy slowed down from 2013 and even entered a recession in 2016 as the mineral prices fell and FDI to the first stage the OT project dried out. The public foreign debt grew substantially as a result of increased budget deficits. The inability to borrow at low interest rates on the world financial market led the government to negotiate with the IMF in 2017. Upon implementing the IMF program, the price of coal started to rise, and FDI started to increase because of the politically controversial Dubai agreement regarding OT's investment plan. The economy enjoyed a brief recovery until it faced the COVID-19 pandemic.

The fiscal and monetary policies were procyclical in Mongolia, which in turn exacerbated the fluctuations in the economy. The FSL is meant to play an important role in restraining fluctuations in the government budget and thereby reducing cyclical uncertainty. The law contains four main requirements related to budget revenue, expenditure, deficit and public debt. However, the caps on public debt and the budget deficit have changed a few times since they came into effect in 2013 due to economic difficulties and political unwillingness.

This chapter summarizes the research that we carried out under the Budget Revenue Management project. Assessing the economic impact of the FSL is the main objective of the research by developing and simulating various scenarios in our in-house CGE models calibrated to the Mongolian database. Three closely related but considering different aspects of revenue management studies were carried out, and each is discussed in a section. The remaining sections of the chapter discuss background information such as the brief history of the Mongolian economy, the government budget dynamics, the literature review and the SWFs of Chile and Norway as the best practices of revenue management among resource-rich countries.

The first and second studies use the same CGE model and 2015 database. The former considers two scenarios—a base scenario without the FSL and a policy scenario with the FSL. The simulation results show that adhering to the FSL leads to the economy experiencing a more stable path and could lessen the deindustrialization effect of developments in the mining sector. On the other hand, the latter examines the sensitivity of the economic performance to the changes in some of the key requirements in the FSL in four scenarios—a base scenario with the fully active FSL, scenario 1 with a relaxed constraint on the budget revenue only, scenario 2 with a relaxed constraint on the budget expenditure only, and scenario 3 with relaxed constraints on budget revenue and expenditure. It finds that removing even one constraint of the law destabilizes the economy in such a way that the standard deviation of most macroeconomic variables increases relative to the base simulation.

The third and final study assesses the economic impacts of the FSF and FHF using our second CGE model calibrated to the 2017 SAM. These two SWFs are essentially Budget Revenue Management for Mongolia as being a resource dependent economy. While the FSF aims to mitigate economic fluctuations stemming from mineral commodity prices and encourages sustainable economic growth, the FHF is designed to allocate mineral revenues for the benefit of future generations. The study considers four scenarios—a base scenario with no FSF or FHF, scenario 1 with FSF but without FHF, scenario 2 with FHF but without FSF and scenario 3 with both FSF and FHF—in an environment with randomly generated series of mineral prices reflecting volatility. The results of the simulations indicate the significance of the funds. The FSF could play a crucial role in mitigating the economic fluctuations by smoothing the budget expenditure, while the FHF reduces the dependence of the economy on the mining sector by placing some of the revenue from the mining sector. These results suggest that the government should implement those funds persistently.

## References

Anderson, K., Martin, W. J., & Mensbrugghe, D. V. (2012). *Estimating effects of price-distorting policies using alternative distortions databases* (CEPR Discussion Paper DP9083).

Baatarzorig, Ts., Galindev, R., & Maisonnave, H. (2018). Effects of ups and downs of the mongolian mining sector. *Environment and Development Economics, 23*(5), 527–542.

Batdelger, T. (2014). *Mongolias's economic prospects and challenges*. East Asia Forum. http://www.eastasiaforum.org/2014/03/23/mongolias-economic-prospects-and-challenges/

Chilean Ministry of Finance. (2019). *Annual Report Sovereign Wealth Funds-2018.*

Decaluwé, B., Lemelin, A., Robichaud, V., & Maissonnave, H. (2013a). *The PEP standard single-country, static CGE model*. Partnership for Economic Policy.

Decaluwé, B., Lemelin, A., Robichaud, V., & Maisonnave, H. (2013b). *PEP-1-t: The PEP standard single-country recursive dynamic CGE model*. Partnership for Economic Policy.

Dixon, B. P., & Rimmer, M. T. (2002). *Dynamic general equilibrium modelling for forecasting and policy: A pratical guide and documentation of MONASH*. North-Holand/Elsevier.

Dixon, P. B., & Rimmer, M. T. (2010). *Validating a detailed, dynamic CGE model of USA*. The Economic Society of Australia.

Economic Research Institute. (2014a). *Impact assessment of Erdenes Tavan Tolgoi.*

Economic Research Institute. (2014b). *Impact assessment of iron ore sector.*

Economic Research Institute. (2016). *Impact assessment of the coal-to-liquid project on the Mongolian economy.*

Galindev, R. (2014). *Impact of fiscal stability law* (Discussion Paper Series, 1-33). Economic Research Institute.

Galindev, R., Baatarzorig, Ts., Batbayar, N., Begz, D., Davaa, U., & Tserendorj, O. (2019a). *Impact of fiscal consolidation on the Mongolian economy* (Working Papers MPIA 2019-20). Partnership for Economic Policy.

Galindev, R., Baatarzorig, Ts., Batbayar, N., Begz, D., Davaa, U., & Tserendorj, O. (2019b). *The economic and environmental impact of foreign direct investment on Mongolian coal-export sector* (Working Papers MPIA 2019-21). Partnership for Economic Policy.

Galindev, R., Batbayar, N., Beyene, L, M., Davaa, U., & Tserendorj, O. (2020a). *Impact on the Mongolian economy of foreign direct investment in the coal-export sector* (Working Papers MPIA 2019-25). Partnership for Economic Policy.

Galindev, R., Baatarzorig, Ts., Batbayar, N., Begz, D., Davaa, U., & Tserendorj, O. (2020b). *Uncertainties in the Mongolian economy in the near future* (Working Papers MPIA 2019-26). Partnership for Economic Policy.

International Labor Organisation. (2012). *International Standard Classification of Occupations.*

International Monetary Fund. (2017). *Country Report No. 17/140.*

International Monetary Fund. (2018). *Mongolia: Fourth review under the extended fund facility arrangement.*

International Working Group of Sovereign Wealth Funds. (2008). *Sovereign wealth funds: Generally accepted principles and practices "Santiago principles".*

Langfitt, F. (2012). *Mineral-rich Mongolia rapidly becoming Mine-golia.* https://www.npr.org/2012/05/21/152683549/mineral-rich-mongolia-rapidly-becoming-minegolia

Mihalyi, D., & Fernandez, L. (2018). *How did fiscal rules hold up in the commodity price crash.* Natural Resource Governance Institute.

Ministry of Finance. (2001). *Guidelines for economic policy, Report no. 29 to the Storting.*

Ministry of Finance. (2020). *Annual budget performance 2010–2020.*

National Statistical Office. (2012). *Population projections 2010–2040.*

Natural Resource Governance Institute & Columbia Center on Sustainable Investment. (2013). *Chile: The pension reserve fund and the economic and social stabilization fund.* Natural Development Funds. https://resourcegovernance.org/sites/default/files/NRF_Chile_August2013.pdf

Natural Resource Government Institute & Gerege Partners. (2017). *Fiscal sustainability in Mongolia.* https://resourcegovernance.org/analysis-tools/publications/fiscal-sustainability-mongolia
Natural Resource Government Institute & Gerege Partners. (2018). *Fiscal sustainability in Mongolia.* https://resourcegovernance.org/analysis-tools/publications/fiscal-sustainability-mongolia-2018
Norges Bank of Investment Management. (2019). *Government Pension Fund Global Annual Report-2018.*
Parliament of Mongolia. (2010). *Fiscal stability law.* https://www.legalinfo.mn/law/details/503
Parliament of Mongolia. (2016). *Future heritage fund.* https://www.legalinfo.mn/law/details/11707
Solimando, A., & Guajardo, D. C. (2017). *The copper sector, fiscal rules, and stabilization funds in Chile: Scope and limits* (WIDER Working Paper 2017/53) (pp. 1–20).
Sovereign Wealth Fund Institute. (2019). *Top 86 largest sovereign wealth fund Rangins by total assets.* https://www.swfinstitute.org/fund-rankings/sovereign-wealth-fund
Wirth, E. (2019). The coherence between sovereign wealth funds and fiscal and monetary policies: The Norwegian case (2001–2017). *Fiscaoeconomia, 3*(1), 39–87.
World Bank. (2018). *Commodity markets outlook.* World Bank.
World Bank. (2019). *Chile.* https://data.worldbank.org/country/chile

**Ragchaasuren Galindev** worked as the managing partner of Gerege Partners LLC, a professional services consultancy firm in Mongolia. He has a bachelor's degree in economics from the National University of Mongolia as well as a master's degree and a Ph.D. from the University of Manchester, UK. He was an associate professor in economics at Queens University Belfast, UK; an assistant professor at Essex University, UK; and a part-time lecturer at the National University of Mongolia. He has published his research on economic growth, business cycles, and demographic transitions in international peer-reviewed journals such as the *Journal of Economic Growth, Journal of Economic Dynamics and Control*, *Oxford Economic Papers*, and others. His current research interest is computable general equilibrium (CGE) modeling in the case of Mongolia.

**Tuvshintugs Batdelger** is the director of the Economic Research Institute (ERI) and an associate professor of economics at the National University of Mongolia. He has a bachelor's degree in economics from the National University of Mongolia; a master's degree in economics from the University of Manchester, UK; and a Ph.D. in economics from Boston University, USA. He has experience working at the Bank of Mongolia and was the head of the Economics Department of the National University of Mongolia from 2014 to 2017. He has been a member of the Economic Policy Council under the prime minister of Mongolia since 2012 and was a member of the Monetary Policy Committee from 2011 to 2016. He has been actively involved in policy discussions in the country through the establishment and operation of ERI since 2010, one of the longest-running think tanks in the country. Through ERI, he successfully contributed to policy discussions on wide-ranging economic and social issues by coordinating and implementing many projects by international organizations, such as the World Bank, Asian Development Bank, and JICA. In particular, he successfully led research teams conducting an economic assessment of big mining and industrial projects on the country's economy and society in general. He has successfully conducted and published policy research studies in international peer-reviewed journals and publications such as *Applied Economics*, *Resources Policy*, and *East Asia Forum* and has authored chapters on the Mongolian economy in numerous books. His current research interests are the role of mining in the economy and society, the role of monetary policy in regulating the Mongolian economy, and the impact of economic development on income distribution and the country's middle class.

**Esmedekh Lkhanaajav** as a researcher at the Economic Research Institute (ERI) and as a lecturer in the Economics Department of the National University of Mongolia. He received his bachelor's degree in economics from the National University of Mongolia and his master's degree in economics from the University of Manchester, UK. His research interests include economics modeling and Bayesian econometrics.

**Manlaibaatar Zagdbazar** is a project manager and senior researcher at the Economic Research Institute (ERI) of Mongolia. He has a bachelor's degree in applied mathematics from the Khan-Uul Institute, Mongolia; a master's degree in economic policy from the Central European University, Hungary; and is currently a Ph.D. candidate in economics at the National University of Mongolia. He has abundant teaching and research experience, working as a lecturer at Khan-Uul Institute, Mongolia, and the National University of Mongolia. Previously, he worked as a researcher at the Development Strategy and System Research Centre in Mongolia; an assistant researcher at the Research Department of the Central Bank of Hungary; and a consultant at the Independent Research Institute of Mongolia. He has published in international and domestic peer-reviewed journals such as *Resources Policy* and *Sociology* and coauthored several economic textbooks in Mongolian.

**Munkh-Ireedui Batjargal** has worked as a researcher at the Economic Research Institute (ERI). He received his bachelor's and master's degrees in economics from the National University of Mongolia. He is currently completing his Ph.D. program at Concordia University in Canada. His research interests include labor economics and CGE modeling.

**Dulguun Tuvshintugs** is a researcher at the Economic Research Institute (ERI). She received her bachelor's degree from Bentley University in the United States, where she majored in finance with a concentration in corporate finance and a minor in law. Her research interests include monetary policy, capital markets, and financial modeling.

**Oyunzul Tserendorj** is a researcher at the Economic Research Institute (ERI). She received her bachelor's degree in economics from the National University of Mongolia and is currently pursuing her master's from the same institution. Her research area of focus includes macroeconomics, development economics, and CGE modeling.

**Nyambaatar Batbayar** was a visiting researcher at the Economic Research Institute (ERI). He graduated from the National University of Mongolia and obtained a bachelor's degree in economics. He is currently completing his master's degree in economics from the Corvinus University of Budapest. His research interests include macroeconomics and CGE modeling.

**Delgermaa Begz** worked as a researcher at the Economic Research Institute (ERI). She received her bachelor's degree from the University of Finance and Economics in Mongolia as well as a master's degree in environmental economics from the Central European University in Hungary. Her research area focuses on macroeconomics, financial markets, environmental and resource economics, education, and inequality.

**Ankhbayar Delgerchuluun** worked as a junior researcher at the Economic Research Institute (ERI). He received his bachelor's in economics from the National University of Mongolia. His research interests include institutional economics.

# Impact of Mining on Local Livelihood and Social Licensing in Mongolia

**Tuvshintugs Batdelger, Dulguun Tuvshintugs, Enkhsaikhan Usny-Ekh, Khorol-Erdene Bayartsogt, Manlaibaatar Zagdbazar, Oyuntugs Davaakhuu, Oyunzul Tserendorj, and Unurjargal Davaa**

## 1 Introduction

Social license to operate (SLO) is a relatively new concept for mining sector stakeholders and the general public in Mongolia. Before 1990, mines under central planning were automatically granted the social acceptance of mine operations and public participation and voices were absent in the policy-making process. However, after the collapse of the Soviet Union, assistance from socialist countries wholly halted, and the Government of Mongolia faced an economic crisis and a large cash deficit.

T. Batdelger (✉) · D. Tuvshintugs · E. Usny-Ekh · K.-E. Bayartsogt · M. Zagdbazar · O. Davaakhuu · O. Tserendorj · U. Davaa
Economic Research Institute, Ulaanbaatar, Mongolia
e-mail: tuvshintugs@eri.mn

D. Tuvshintugs
e-mail: dulguun@eri.mn

E. Usny-Ekh
e-mail: enkhsaikhan@eri.mn

K.-E. Bayartsogt
e-mail: khorol-erdene@eri.mn

M. Zagdbazar
e-mail: manlaibaatar@eri.mn

O. Davaakhuu
e-mail: oyuntugs@eri.mn

O. Tserendorj
e-mail: oyunzul@eri.mn

U. Davaa
e-mail: unurjargal@eri.mn

T. Batdelger
National University of Mongolia, Ulaanbaatar, Mongolia

 
Y. Hosoi et al. (eds.), *Economic Dependence of Mongolia on Minerals*,
Contributions to Economics, https://doi.org/10.1007/978-981-19-5515-0_6

To overcome this financial crisis, the government introduced the "Gold Program" to promote gold mine production in 1992, when the new Constitution was approved.

A new Minerals Law was adopted in 1997 and significantly relaxed the rules and processes for obtaining a mining license, permitting full foreign ownership of mining ventures and easing gold export restrictions (Byambajav, 2015). However, the growth of the gold sector brought with it extensive environmental degradation and other detrimental social impacts, as miners almost entirely ignored environmental rehabilitation during mining operations and closures. As gold mines increased, many artisanal miners began prospecting near gold mines. As of 2006, approximately 20% of the local workforce or 100,000 people were in informal gold mining (UNICEF Mongolia, 2017). Artisanal miners usually operate in poor health and safety conditions and contribute to environmental degradation.

These harmful consequences provoked local community grievances against mine operations and eventually led to local movements against mining operations. Growing local community opposition against irresponsible mining pushed the government to introduce new laws and amendments toward stricter environmental requirements, local community participation, and requirements for regional development and employment of local citizens. In 2006, the government adopted a new Minerals Law, which includes essential provisions such as mandatory local-level agreements, local revenue sharing, and voluntary community consultation. In 2009, the "Law on the Prohibition of Mining Operations in the Headwaters of Rivers, Protected Zones of Water Reservoirs and Forested Areas" was approved. Under the law, mining exploration in protected headwater, watershed, and forestry areas was prohibited. In 2012, the government approved another important law, the Law on Environmental Impact Assessments, and amended the Minerals Law to be consistent with this new Law. Public participation in environmental impact assessments is outlined in the law.

Another primary source of public concern was the minimal local benefits from mining projects despite the negative environmental impacts of mining operations. The collection of taxes and payments for local benefit was discouraged under the Budget Law. The Local Development Fund (LDF) was established in 2011 to promote local development with local citizen participation to boost the local benefit of mining projects. The LDF is a fund used to redistribute a particular portion of mineral resource revenue accrued to rural districts to support infrastructure and human development in local areas. According to the Budget Law, the LDF is financed from 5% royalties, 30% crude oil royalty payments, and 5% VAT.

Additionally, according to 2018 amendments to the Law on the State Budget, starting from 2020, all revenue from mineral exploration license fees and half of the revenue from mineral extraction license fees will be transferred to the LDF. The funds are distributed to local governments based on the local development index, population, territory, and tax incentives (PoM, 2011). Between 2013 and 2017, the LDF allocated MNT 655.0 billion to rural districts (ERI, 2020).

The local governor has a vital role in facilitating company-community relations. The local governor has the authority to grant a range of permissions, including land and water use under the Law on Land and the Law on Water. Moreover, according to the Minerals Law, the provincial governor has the right to oppose mining operations in case of violations and declare certain areas of land for use for local special needs, prohibiting it from mining use. However, there have been numerous cases where local governors used their power to request donations or financial aid from mining companies. To overcome this issue, in 2012, some restrictions on the local governor's power were included in the Law on Conflicts of Interest. Notably, under Article 17 of this Law, "a public official, or a state or local institution, is prohibited from requesting or accepting any form of donation or financial aid for public use from a natural or legal entity."

In 2014, the GoM also declared important SLO goals in the State Policy on the Minerals Sector. In particular, the GoM included a goal to promote transparent local-level agreements between mining companies and the local governor inclusive of public participation and a goal to establish a Policy Council to make recommendations and support the implementation of the policy. The Policy Council is made up of representatives from government agencies, investors, professional associations, and civil society organizations.

The most crucial legal amendment made toward promoting SLO in the mining sector is Article 6.2 of the Constitution of Mongolia, adopted in November 2019. The Constitutional amendment reflected the current social requirements of the mining sector. Moreover, the amendment is a significant legal measure taken toward the equitable distribution of the benefits from natural resources, increasing public awareness of mining companies' environmental impact and environmental responsibility and cementing the importance of the SLO in the Mongolian mining sector. Associated with the Constitutional amendment, relevant laws, regulations, and long-term policies are expected to be amended in the near term. Subsequently, in 2020, the government set a policy goal to promote responsible mining in the "Vision 2050" long-term policy document.

Communities continue to become more aware of and concerned about how mining activities can affect local livelihood. Moreover, sustainability and the environmental impacts of industrial activities are also becoming more salient. In some instances, the mining sector's detrimental social and environmental impacts have provoked community grievances against mining operations. There have been several cases where mining developments have been delayed, interrupted, or even shut down due to opposition from local communities in Mongolia. In other words, mine operations were halted since they could not earn an SLO from local communities and other stakeholders.

Therefore, obtaining an SLO is becoming an essential issue in the mining sector. While there is no set definition for SLO, it is understood as the ongoing acceptance of a company or industry's standard business practices and operating procedures by its employees, stakeholders, and the general public. Thus, it is not enough for mining companies to only obtain a legal license from the government and other regulators. An SLO is increasingly needed to operate mining activities in the country. This trend has already been observed globally.

This study aims to assess the current relationship between the Mongolian mining sector and the local community by determining the key challenges the companies and community face and analyzing how they are coping with these challenges. This analysis also covers the government actions implemented to address the problems related to social licensing and the sustainable mining sector. In addition, it includes domestic case studies that reflects developments of SLO. Finally, the study assesses the level of SLO of a specific project by applying the evaluation methodology suggested by Moffat and Zhang (2014).

## 2 Mining Impact in Mongolia and Cases of SLO

The mining sector strongly influences the Mongolian economy through direct and indirect factors. As of 2019, the mining sector accounted for 23.2% of GDP, 83.7% of total exports, and 48.6% of total investment. As of 2018, the mining sector's contribution to the state budget was approximately 22% (ERI, 2019a). In 2019, the mining sector employed 4.7% of the total workforce with an average wage of MNT 2.6 million, 2.3 times higher than the national average wage. In addition to taxes and fees, mining companies donate money to promote local and national development. According to EITI Mongolia, between 2013 and 2018, mining companies donated MNT 173.3 billion at the national level, which accounts for about 0.4% of mining GDP (EITI Mongolia, 2018).

Mining activities also have a significant impact on the local economy. For instance, local governments receive income from taxes and fees and the Local Development Fund. Mining provinces' per capita budget expenditure has been higher than that of nonmining provinces over the past decade (except 2013).

Mining companies implement local development projects by establishing a joint fund with local governments. Oyu Tolgoi LLC, the largest mining company in the country, established the Gobi Oyu Development Support Fund (Gobi Oyu DSF) in line with the Community Cooperation Agreement with the local government in 2015.

According to the Provincial Competitiveness Index, Orkhon and Umnugobi provinces, the two largest mining regions, are ranked first and second in the country (EPCRC, 2019). This ranking confirms that the impact of mining is significant at the local level. Provinces are measured and ranked against 180 criteria across four main categories: economic performance, governance efficiency, business efficiency, and infrastructure. The provinces with major mining projects tend to perform better than other provinces. According to the index, the most improved provincial economies are mining provinces such as Umnugovi (#1), Dornod (#2), and Orkhon (#4), and the most improved provinces for a standard of living are also mining provinces such as Umnugovi (#1), Dornod (#2) and Darkhan-Uul (#4). For bank deposits per capita, Orkhon, Umnugovi, and Darkhan-Uul provinces are the top 3.

Mining activities have a more significant impact on living standards even at the rural district level (ERI, 2017). For instance, in rural districts with mining activity, the average household income was about 7.2% greater than in rural districts without substantial mining sector activity between 2010 and 2016. Mining sector activities also have a considerable effect on other livelihood indicators. For example, household

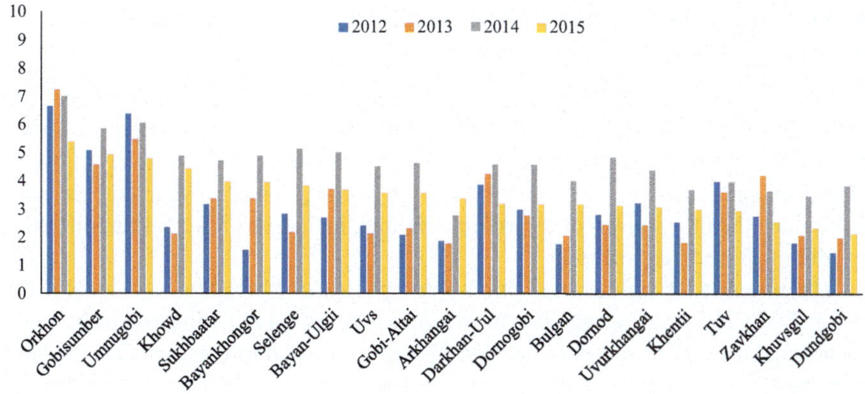


**Fig. 1** Citizen's opinion of the impact of mining on the economy by province. *Source* EPCRC (2015)

consumption is 11% higher in mining districts, and poverty is eight percentage points lower than in nonmining districts. In addition, individual wages in mining areas were 9.4% greater than individual wages in rural districts without mining.

Although the mining sector positively impacts the national economy and standard of living, local citizens and small businesses tend to disagree with that impact. In the annual surveys conducted by the EPCRC, small businesses were asked about their opinion on the effects of the mining sector on their local economy and other sectors (EPCRC, 2015). The survey covers 50 business executives from each province. Respondents were asked to rate the impacts of mining on a scale of 1–10, with 1 being the most negative score and 10 the most positive score. The impact of mining on the economy has been assessed as low or negative except in mining provinces such as Orkhon, Umnugovi, and Govisumber (Fig. 1).

The mining sector has positively impacted the country's economy and local living standards, but public perceptions of mining activities are likely lower or negative. Therefore, it is essential to improve the legal and cultural environment of SLO in the mining sector. In addition, mining companies should adopt and implement global and local good practices such as inclusiveness, transparency and accountability, civic engagement, and communication strategies with local communities to be accepted by and to obtain approval from the local communities.

However, there have been significant conflicts between the local community, the government, and mining companies. For instance, the number of arbitration cases in Mongolia was 41 in 2014, 70 cases in 2015, and 58 cases in 2016 (Lkhagvaa, 2017). In addition, according to the UNTCAD's Investment Dispute Settlement Navigator, Mongolia has had five known treaty-based investor-state dispute settlements cases since 2004 (ERI, 2019b).

- Alstom Power v. Mongolia (2004), Settled.
- Paushok v. Mongolia (2007), Pending.
- Beijing Shougang and others v. Mongolia (2010) decided to favor Mongolia.

- Khan Resources v. Mongolia (2011) decided to favor the investor, Settled.
- Munshi v. Mongolia (2018), Pending.

In Mongolia's case, SLO has become more and more relevant to the mining sector in the last two decades. Before 1990, due to socialism, SLO was not a salient issue, and from the 1990s to the mid-2000s, Mongolia's mining sector was relatively stagnant. However, since then, several foreign-invested mining companies have been established, and the first notions of responsible mining, including the social responsibility of mining, have been formed.

The majority of state-owned mining companies in Mongolia were established before 1990. However, since 1990, most newly established mines have been privately owned and foreign-invested. In the case of state-owned mining companies, information transparency is poor, and their social responsibility activities are political. For instance, Erdenes Mongol LLC, a state-owned holding company, is ad hoc in projects such as the research subcenter at the Ministry of Foreign Affairs and the Mongolia National Branding Council (Bauer & Namhaijantsan, 2019). Overall, state-owned mining companies established before 1990 do not face any public opposition, and state-owned mining companies established after 1990 face relatively lower public opposition than privately owned and foreign-invested mining companies.

In contrast, issues related to the SLO are most common in privately owned and foreign-invested mines. There have been several instances where privately owned and foreign-invested mining companies successfully obtained SLO for those mining companies. Oyu Tolgoi LLC and Energy Resources LLC are one of them. On the other hand, there have been several instances where mining developments have been delayed, interrupted, or even shut down due to opposition from local communities.

An example of mining projects that have faced strict community protest in Mongolia is Aspire Mining Ltd's Ovoot project, located in Khuvsgul Province. Aspire Mining Ltd. has been conducting explorations since 2008 and acquired the 30-year coal mining license in August 2012, although no mining has yet begun. The company has been continuously trying to gain an SLO through various local-level activities, such as student scholarship programs, operating heavy machinery training programs, and constructing a new hospital in a rural district. However, the company has not established a favorable relationship with the local community. This was one of the reasons for delaying the construction of a coal exporting railway. Ultimately, the company decided to construct a 560-km paved road between the Ovoot coal mine and Erdenet instead of a railway (Asia Mining, 2019). However, there is still a lack of consensus on the project at the local level. For instance, the Governor of Khuvsgul province detailed the implementation of the "No Mining Khuvsgul" program, which prohibits additional exploration or mining licenses and mentions plans to revoke existing licenses (Mongolian Mining Journal, 2019).

Centerra Gold LLC's Gatsuurt gold project in Selenge Province is another controversial case. Following exploration efforts, in 2005, Centerra Gold LLC conducted a feasibility study and began constructing necessary infrastructure and making other investments in the project. However, they have not begun mining production, as the company has not reached an explicit agreement or consensus with the local community and the central government. The Gatsuurt mine is located close to Noyon Mountain National Park, a landmark of both historical and natural significance. Moreover, mining operations at the Gatsuurt mine were prohibited by the "Law on the Prohibition of Mining Operations in the Headwaters of Rivers, Protected Zone of Water Reservoirs and Protested Areas" in 2009. However, the Gatsuurt mine was designated as a strategically important mineral deposit, allowing for legal mining in the area in 2015. As a mineral deposit of strategic importance, the Parliament resolution approved Mongolian state ownership in the Gatsuurt mine at 34% in 2016. Following this decision, the operation of the Gatsuurt mine officially commenced. Opposing these decisions, the "Rescue Noyon Mountain" NGO has been working to revoke the four mining licenses held by Centerra Gold LLC. The organization filed a lawsuit with the Ulaanbaatar Administrative Court in 2016, with the dispute continuing for almost four years. Finally, in 2019, the Supreme Court of Mongolia ruled to revoke the four mining licenses held by Centerra Gold LLC (Supreme court of Mongolia, 2019).

The Bayan-Khundii project in Bayankhongor Province is a recent case to gain SLO. In August 2019, Erdene Resource Management Corporation secured a mining license for the Bayan Khundii gold mine, and operation will start in early 2022 (Bayan-Khundii project, 2019). Erdene Resource is a member of the International Finance Corporation's VCP for sustainable water management in the Gobi region. The company cooperated with local herders, elected officials, and other stakeholders to reduce competition for scarce water resources and signed a local-level cooperation agreement with Bayankhongor Province, Shinejinst and Bayan-Under districts where the gold mine is located. In addition, the company provided some assistance to those districts to improve their potable water supply and commissioned hydrogeological work to source a water supply. As a result, Erdene Resource was listed on a foreign stock exchange and became the first company to list its shares on the Mongolian Stock Exchange (MSE). As part of the cross-listing, the company worked with local government officials from the two rural districts and gave a portion of the shares listed on the MSE to more than 5,000 people in the two districts. As a result, local people will benefit financially from the project in the future.

These cases show that a social license is not tangible and is ever-changing with the attitudes and perceptions of the community. Although a mining company may gain its SLO through community engagement and programs, the environmental impacts of the mining operation can set this back. Long-lasting discord can permeate relations to the extent that an SLO can never be fully attained.

# 3 Understanding the SLO and Its Evaluation

## *3.1 What is the SLO, and What Studies Recommend for the Mining Sector?*

Currently, there is no universally accepted definition of SLO. It is broadly understood as the ongoing acceptance of a company and its operations by the local community and other stakeholders. The concept evolved from the notions of "corporate social responsibility" and "social acceptability" and is also linked to the concept of sustainability (Allen, 2019). Many studies on the topic accept that the SLO can mean:

- **Ongoing acceptance and approval** of mining development by local community members and other stakeholders that can affect its profitability (Boutilier & Thomson, 2011; Moffat & Zhang, 2014; Prno & Slocombe, 2012).
- **Improved risk management**, as the inability to gain and maintain an SLO, can lead to conflicts, delays, and additional costs associated with a project (IFC, 2021).

Interestingly, an SLO is not a formal agreement between the operating company and stakeholders but is "the real or current credibility, reliability, and acceptance of organizations and projects" (Allen, 2019). It is also particular in that it must be slowly earned and constantly maintained. The notion of earning or gaining the SLO gained traction in the twenty-first century due to increased public concern over extractive operations. It acted as a form of risk management for businesses (IFC, 2021). Since then, this term has been adopted in many industries and sectors, including mining companies, civil society and nongovernment organizations, government, consultants, pulp and paper manufacturing, and alternative energy generation.

Moreover, an SLO cannot be gained from a government ministry or by simply paying a fee (Lassonde, 2003). It demands far more effort and resources to become a part of its community. Without local community acceptance, a project cannot be implemented efficiently, if at all.

Lack of public acceptance can cause delays in obtaining funding and government approvals for projects and lead to additional costs. According to Ernst and Young (2021), maintaining the SLO is the third-largest business risk facing the mining and metals industry. Therefore, gaining and maintaining an SLO is becoming increasingly crucial to long-term business viability.

The IFC (2021) defines the features of the SLO as follows:

- It takes time to earn but can be lost very quickly. It is responsive to changes in perceptions of the company and the project and susceptible to outside influences.
- This does not mean that every individual stakeholder or group supports the project (or consensus among the network of stakeholders) but broad social acceptance of the project.
- It is rooted in the beliefs, perceptions, and opinions held by the local population and other stakeholders about the project.

- It is dynamic and nonpermanent. It is responsive to company and project perceptions and is susceptible to outside influences. Therefore, the SLO must be earned, strengthened, and maintained.
- It is usually granted on a site-specific basis; hence, a company may have an SLO for one operation but not for another.

Overall, to obtain an SLO, a company must be seen operating responsibly, taking care of its employees and the environment, and being an excellent corporate role model. By doing so, the company will create a mutually beneficial relationship with stakeholders affected by the project. The following section will detail specific studies related to SLO and the mining sector.

Boutilier and Thomson (2011) is considered to be the first researchers to propose measuring and analyzing the SLO. They identified four levels of SLO based on extensive interviews with villagers on their relationship with a Bolivian mine over 15 years. Their latest model has four levels of SLO: Refusal, Acceptance, Approval, and Identification. In the theoretical model shown below, the level of SLO rises as we go up the model. Lower SLO levels indicate higher risks for the company. The lowest level of SLO is Refusal. At this level, the project is in danger of restricted access to essential resources such as financing, legal licenses, raw materials, labor, and public infrastructure. The next level of SLO is Acceptance of the project. Acceptance occurs when the community tolerates the operations of the company. If the stakeholders are satisfied and enthusiastically favor the activities, the SLO could rise to the level of Approval. Over time, if trust is established, the SLO could achieve Identification.

Only a few survey-based studies have been successful in quantitatively assessing the factors that influence SLO and their interactions with each other. One of these studies is the work of Moffat and Zhang (2014) on a large Australian coal seam gas company. The study developed a model in which community trust in the mining company is central to obtaining an SLO and a strong predictor of community acceptance. They proposed the following hypotheses: (i) the impacts of mining on the social infrastructure of a community negatively affected trust, acceptance, and approval of the company; (ii) procedural fairness, quantity, and quality of contact between the company's staff and the community strengthened trust in the company; and (iii) trust in the company positively influenced its acceptance and approval by communities. Their path analysis found that all of the factors mentioned earlier, except the quantity of contact, had statistically significant influences on project acceptance mediated through trust. Trust, in turn, was most influenced by perceived procedural fairness, contact quality, and impact on social infrastructure. The influence of the quantity of contact was not significant.

Their results showed that contact quality and procedural fairness played crucial roles in gaining and maintaining an SLO. Conversely, most mining companies focus on social infrastructure to mitigate the negative impacts of their operations. In other words, many mining companies attempt to buy trust from the local community. Instead, it is more effective to focus on creating a relationship with community members and including them in its decision-making process. For example, the study mentioned one oil company that spent USD 7 million per year on community programs but could not obtain community goodwill. As a result, the oil company consistently faced interruptions from the communities they work with (Moffat & Zhang, 2014).

Mining companies have a significant impact on the economy and the environment they operate. However, the economic and environmental impacts of SLO levels have not been adequately studied. To fill this literature gap, Cruz et al. (2020) tested the following hypotheses on the Brazilian S11D mining project:

(i) Procedural fairness and company-community interactions directly and positively influence trust in the company and the project.
(ii) Economic and environmental impacts directly and negatively affect trust, acceptance, and approval. Conversely, social infrastructure such as health and education facilities, housing affordability, infrastructure for mobility, and flow of merchandise, people, and vehicles improvements directly and positively affect trust, acceptance, and approval (Cruz et al., 2020).

They also employed path analysis to assess the relationship between the variables and found that procedural fairness and company-community interactions have a significant positive effect on trust. The perception of negative economic impact did not directly predict community trust in the company but significantly affected acceptance and approval. There was a positive and significant effect between improvements in social infrastructure and trust. However, improvements in social infrastructure did not significantly influence acceptance and approval. The relationship between environmental impacts and trust was negative and significant, as was the relationship between acceptance and approval and environmental impacts. Last, they also confirmed trust as a significant and robust predictor of acceptance and approval of the company and mining project.

These studies provided a theoretical basis on levels of SLO, the factors that influence whether a company can obtain an SLO, and the broader economic and environmental impacts of a mining project on SLO. Finally, we applied the methodology to evaluate SLO in a selected local mining project (please see Sect. 3 of this chapter).

## 3.2 Evaluation of SLO and Application of Methodologies

Maintaining an SLO involves continuous assessment of the community's attitudes toward a mining project and other influencing factors based on the literature and practices of mining-dependent countries. Robinson et al. (2020) assessed the SLO of mines in Western Australia according to the following pillars:

- Social Impact Assessment (SIA)
- Social Acceptance Survey (SAS)
- Social Media
- Protesting and Blockading.

**Social Impact Assessment (SIA)**

SIA emerged as a regulatory responsibility imposed by governments and international financial institutions in the latter half of the twentieth century (Harvey & Bice, 2014). SIA generally includes measures of the social and economic impacts generated by mining on service provisions, infrastructure and housing availability, socio-economic well-being (i.e., welfare, unemployment rates, % of low-income households), and the reliance of mining companies on the non-residential workforce (Robinson et al., 2020).

Studies conducted in Western Australia have shown significant differences in methodology. For example, some studies relied solely on the Australian Bureau of Statistics census data and did not include any direct participation. In contrast, other studies included workshops and survey interviews with stakeholders and individuals in the local community (Robinson et al., 2020). However, most surveys did not actively involve public participation in the evaluation and decision-making process of the mining project. Therefore, the evaluation showed a low level of public participation in the SIA of the Western Australia mining sector.

In Mongolia, large mining projects such as Oyu Tolgoi (2009) and Gatsuurt Gold Mine (2016) conducted SIAs. Oyu Tolgoi in the South Gobi region is one of the world's largest known copper and gold deposits. Gatsuurt Gold is an open-pit mining site located in Selenge Province in northern Mongolia. Social scoping issues identified by SIAs are demography, local economy, employment, social infrastructure, community health, education, cultural heritage, land use, and natural resources. These SIAs used survey methods such as household questionnaires, key informant interviews, and focus group discussions with local citizens, soum officials, business owners, and civil society representatives. Secondary data were also collected and analyzed to describe the current socio-economic conditions of the project areas.

**Social Acceptance Survey**

The most important and widely used tool when evaluating SLO is the Social Acceptance Survey. This survey measures the impact and benefits of mining operations and the level of trust, the acceptance of an operation, and interaction quality between community members and a mining company. Studies on the social acceptance and approval of mining operations have been used as an avenue for understanding and measuring SLO.

Boutilier and Thomson (2011) aimed to measure the SLO level using a revised set of 15 items (Table 1), which loaded on four latent factors: economic legitimacy, socio-political legitimacy, interactional trust, and institutionalized trust. They use a five-point Likert scale for responses to each item (1 = strongly disagree; 5 = strongly agree).

The average of the measures indicates the degree of SLO (Table 2). Mining companies can use the 15 items above to conduct a survey to determine their level of SLO, as shown in Fig. 2.

In another social acceptance survey, Moffat and Zhang (2014) surveyed over a hundred local community members near a coal seam gas project in Australia twice,

**Table 1** Items for measuring social license to operate

| Item | Statement |
|---|---|
| 1 | We can benefit from a relationship with the company |
| 2 | We need the cooperation of the company to reach our most important goal |
| 3 | The company keeps its promises |
| 4 | We are pleased with our relationship with the company |
| 5 | The presence of the mining project is a benefit to us |
| 6 | The company listens to us |
| 7 | In the long term, the project will contribute to the well-being of the whole region |
| 8 | The company respects our way of life |
| 9 | The company treats everyone fairly |
| 10 | Our group and the company have a similar vision for the future of the region |
| 11 | The company gives support to those who it negatively affects |
| 12 | The company shares decision-making with us |
| 13 | The company's decisions are fair and take into account our interests |
| 14 | The company concerned about our interest |
| 15 | The company openly shares information that is relevant to us |

*Source* Boutilier and Thomson (2011)

**Table 2** SLO levels and scores

| Level | Score |
|---|---|
| Identification | 4.5–5.0 |
| Approval | 4.0–4.49 |
| Acceptance | 2.5–3.99 |
| Withdraw | 1.0–2.49 |

*Source* Adapted from Boutilier and Thomson (2011)

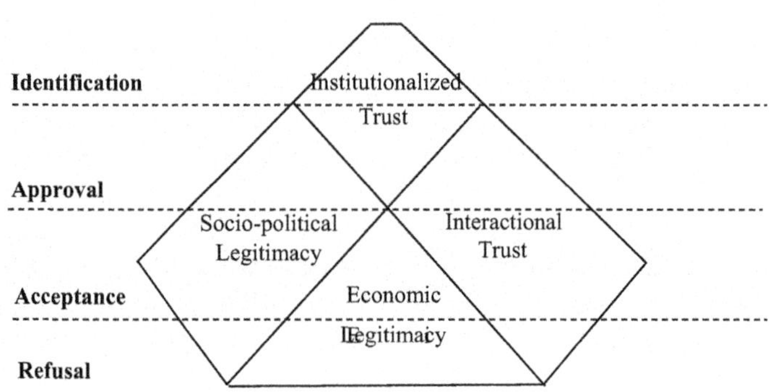


**Fig. 2** Pyramid model by Boutilier and Thomson. *Source* Adapted from Boutilier and Thomson (2011)

**Table 3** Social acceptance survey measures

| SLO variables | Topics of the questionnaire |
|---|---|
| Impacts on social infrastructure | 1. Housing availability<br>2. Housing affordability<br>3. Access to medical and health facilities<br>4. Access to community facilities |
| Contact quantity | 1. Contact frequency in formal situations<br>2. Contact frequency in informal situations |
| Contact quality | 1. How pleasant with personnel from the company<br>2. How positive with personnel from the company |
| Procedural fairness | 1. Whether participate in the decision-making process<br>2. The company listens to us<br>3. The company concerns our interest |
| Trust | 1. I trust the company to act responsibly<br>2. I have goodwill/confidence/trust toward the company |
| Acceptance and Approval | 1. I accept the company<br>2. I approve the company |

*Source* Moffat and Zhang (2014)

one year apart, to determine the project acceptance level. The survey covered the following topics:

1. Impacts on social infrastructure (e.g., medical, health, housing)
2. Contact quantity
3. Contact quality (i.e., pleasantness)
4. Procedural fairness (i.e., whether the company listens, allows participation in the decision)
5. Trust
6. Acceptance and approval.

Each pillar includes several subitems in agree/disagree format using a 5-point rating scale from "strongly disagree" to "strongly agree." A total of 123 residents who lived in areas affected by an Australian coal seam gas (CSG) operation and were not employed in the CSG industry were included in the survey. Participants were recruited using a stakeholder database provided by a CSG company to the researchers for this study (Table 3).

They used path analysis[1] to check the relationship between variables. In their hypothesis, the model specified impact on social infrastructure, contact quantity, contact quality, and procedural fairness as exogenous predictors of trust. Trust, in turn,

[1] Path analysis is a form of multiple regression statistical analysis used to evaluate causal models by examining the relationships between a dependent variable and two or more independent variables. This method can estimate the magnitude and significance of causal connections between variables. Path analysis can be conducted with statistical programs, including SPSS and Stata. The method is also known as causal modeling, analysis of covariance structures, and latent variable models.

was specified as a predictor of Acceptance. In addition, impact on social infrastructure served as an exogenous predictor of Acceptance. They also allowed for correlation between the four exogenous predictors.

Some studies assess the SLO level of a country's mining sector. For instance, Australia is one country that has and implements measures to maintain an SLO. Moffat et al. (2017) examined citizens' attitudes in the mining area based on a social acceptance survey in 2014 and 2017. Overall, they surveyed 8020 Australians chosen from 11 different regions about their attitude toward the mining sector. The survey consisted of three subsections covering the benefits of mining, the negative impacts, fairness, confidence in governance, and trust. Each section included several items measured on a "strongly disagree" to "strongly agree" scale. For instance, the benefit of mining is assessed by ten criteria scaled from 1 (strongly disagree) to 7 (strongly agree). The survey results were compared by mining and nonmining regions and metropolitan and local areas.

**Social Media**

Social media platforms have become a powerful tool to draw attention to social and environmental problems in the mining sector. Stakeholders have used social media to undermine the mining company's SLO. For example, in Western Australia, the local community has used social media in Port Headland to express their concern about BHP's mining operations. It also differs from traditional media, as anyone can communicate information, is relatively uncensored, and can be shared among individuals, groups, and networks at high speed (Robinson et al., 2020).

Mining companies have started to recognize the impact of the social media revolution on public perception and business. Consequently, mining companies utilize social media to advance community engagement and other socially and ecologically "responsible" activities, as well as providing "transparency" after mine site problems and failures (Kirschke, 2013).

**Protesting and Blockading**

When a community resists business projects and developments by protesting and blockading, it indicates weakening SLO. Therefore, protesting and blockading should be included in an assessment of SLO. Protests are among the most powerful levers that communities can use to express their concerns and signals absence of SLO. For companies, protests are warning signs and opportunities to enhance their SLO. When companies identify community concerns early, their SLO can be enhanced (Robinson et al., 2020; Vanclay & Hanna, 2019).

# 4 Social Acceptance Survey: A Case of Erdenes Silver Resource

This section details the social acceptance survey conducted at the Salkhit silver mine by the Economic Research Institute in August 2021. The survey methodology and further analysis followed Boutilier and Thomson (2011) and Moffat and Zhang (2014).

## *4.1 Salkhit Project Overview*

The Salkhit silver mine is located in the Gurvansaikhan soum of Dundgovi Province. China's JPF LLC originally owned the license for the Salkhit silver mine. In 2018, the ownership shares of JPF LLC changed hands several times. However, these changes were not registered with the relevant tax authority. Therefore, the license issued to JPF LLC was revoked and taken over by Mongolia's government.

Following the nationalization of the Salkhit silver mine, its license was granted to Erdenes Silver Resource LLC, a subsidiary of Erdenes Mongol LLC (a state-owned holding company), in July 2019. As of 2020, the company has 108 full-time employees and 307 subcontractors. The exploration license covers an area of 28.8 thousand hectares. The open-pit deposits in total contain an estimated 574 tons of silver and 755 kg of gold (Erdenes Silver Resource, 2020).

In 2020, the Government of Mongolia obtained a loan from the Bank of Mongolia collateralizing the government's expected return from the Salkhit silver mine. Using this loan, the Government of Mongolia rewarded pensioners with one-time cancellation of pension-backed loans in January 2020. Within this scope, 194.1 thousand pensioners without pension-backed loans were disbursed MNT 194 billion, and 43.9 thousand elders with less than MNT 1 million in loans were disbursed MNT 21.4 billion (Montsame, 2021). Thus, this project is responsible for repaying 1.2 trillion MNT in pension loans over five years.

The company built a silver refinery in 2016 with a processing capacity of 300 thousand tons of ore per year. Between 2020 and 2021, the plant processed 196.9 thousand tons of ore and produced 2.8 thousand tons of concentrate. Furthermore, a concentrator with a capacity of 600 thousand tons of ore was planned to be commissioned in July 2021. However, it was not completed due to equipment delivery delays, customs and freight issues caused by the COVID-19 pandemic. Due to these setbacks, there is little chance to repay the debt of MNT 1.2 billion by 2024.

## 4.2 Conducting Social Acceptance Survey

In our survey, 211 in-person interviews were conducted. The sample of individuals was randomly selected from all 672 registered households in Gurvansaikhan Soum. The survey employed a 34-item questionnaire adapted from Moffat and Zhang (2014) and conducted in-depth interviews with representatives of local civil societies, the local government, and local businesses. The questionnaire consists of two parts. The first part provides general information about participants. The second part assesses the respondent's perceptions about the impact of mining on social infrastructure, contact quality and quantity with personnel from the mining company, procedural fairness, trust, and overall acceptance.

**Impact on social infrastructure** was measured with six items asking about the extent to which participants experienced impacts from the mining-related activities relative to their expectations. Five areas of impact were assessed: access to medical and health facilities, access to school and kindergarten, electricity supply, and water supply (1 = much worse than expected 3 = not changed at all, 5 = much better than expected). Participants' scores were reversed and averaged, such that higher scores indicated a worse-than-expected impact.

**Contact quantity** was measured with two items. Participants were asked to rate how many contacts they had with people from Erdenes Silver Resource at formal community meetings and informal meetings before the outbreak of the COVID-19 pandemic (1 = none, 5 = a great deal). Scores from the two items were averaged, with the overall score indicating the frequency of contact with personnel from the Erdenes Silver Resource.

**Contact quality** was measured with two items. Participants were asked to rate how pleasant and positive their contact with the personnel from Erdenes Silver resource was. Scores from the two items were averaged, such that higher scores indicated a high quality of contact with personnel from Erdenes Silver Resource.

**Procedural fairness** was measured with three items. Participants were asked to rate the extent to which they agreed with the given statements. For example, "People in your community have the opportunity to participate in the decisions made by Erdenes Silver Resource," "Erdenes Silver Resource listens to and respects your opinions," and "Erdenes Silver Resource is prepared to change its practices in response to community sentiment". Scores from these three items were averaged such that higher scores indicated high perceived procedural fairness.

**Trust** was measured with four items. Participants were asked to rate the extent to which they trust. For example, "Trust Erdenes Silver Resource to act responsibly," "Trust Erdenes Silver Resource to do what is right," "Trust Erdenes Silver Resource to act in the best interest of society," "Trust Erdenes Silver Resource generally"." Scores from these four items were averaged, such that higher scores indicated more significant levels of trust.

**Acceptance** was measured with two items. Participants were asked to rate how much they accepted and approved of Erdenes Silver Resource's operations in the region (1 = not at all, 5 = very much). Scores on these two items were averaged such that higher scores indicated more significant levels of acceptance and approval.

**Data Analysis and Integrative Model**

The research team calculated the bivariate correlation between variables to assess whether they were correlated. Subsequently, a path analysis approach (a specific multiple regression) was employed to examine the independent relationships between the variables. On the other hand, we tested whether the following hypotheses were true:

- A negative impact on social infrastructure will negatively affect trust in the company and the acceptance of the mining operation.
- Contact quantity and procedural fairness will enhance trust in the company.
- Trust in the company will have a positive relationship with the acceptance and approval of the mining company.

Following Moffat and Zhang (2014), the goodness of fit of the model was assessed using the chi-square test, the comparative fit index (CFI), normed fit index (NFI), and root mean square error of approximation (RMSEA). A satisfactory fit is indicated by a non-significant chi-square test, CFI $\geq$ 0.95, NFI $\geq$ 0.95, and RMSEA $\leq$ 0.06.

## 4.3 *Survey Result*

**Participants' Profile**

Of the 211 participants, 118 (55.9%) were male, and 93 (44.1%) were female. The participants were representative of all broad age groups, with an average age of 47.3 (male—46.4, female—48.4). Regarding education, 22.8% had primary or no education, 57.8% had secondary education, and 19.4% had technical, vocational, and higher education. In terms of employment, 87.2% of the respondents were employed, and 12.8% were unemployed. The majority, or 76.8%, of the total employed were herders. There was no significant difference in employment by gender (Fig. 3).

**Awareness**

We rated the respondents' knowledge of Erdenes Silver Resources on a scale of 1–5, and 64% of the respondents rated themselves as unaware or very unaware (Fig. 4). This indicates that the company did not establish any relationship with local people or provide information. However, it is worth noting that its operations started at the beginning of the COVID-19 pandemic. Therefore, it may have led to a lack of opportunities to communicate with the local community. However, the awareness of the residents of the Chuluut subdistrict where the company is located is higher than the average (Fig. 5).

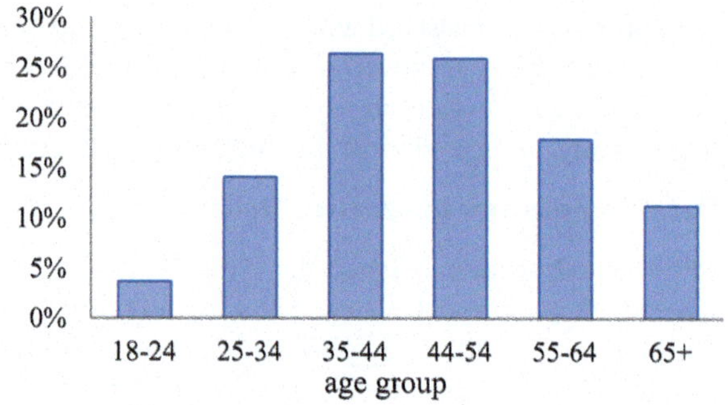


**Fig. 3** Participants by age

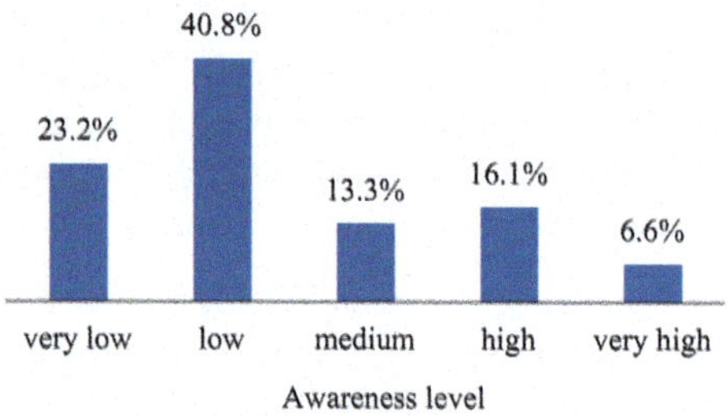


**Fig. 4** Participant's share by awareness level

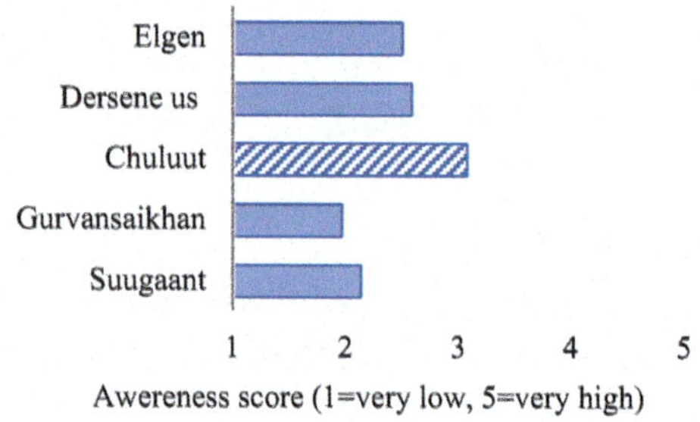


**Fig. 5** Mean awareness score by subdistrict

## Contact Quantity and Quality

Respondents rated the frequency of contact with Erdenes Silver Resources an average of 1.2 points, and most respondents answered that they had never met with the company's employees or representatives (Fig. 6). As the residents do not have any relationship with the company, most respondents could not determine how pleasant or positive their contact was (Fig. 7). Therefore, it was impossible to include contact quality in the assessment model due to the missing value of contact quality.

## Impact on Social Infrastructure

We assessed the impact on social infrastructure with six items. Most respondents rated the impact on each social infrastructure item 3 points (not changed at all). The average score of the combined index of these items was 2.95 points. This indicates

Fig. 6 Frequency of contact with the company

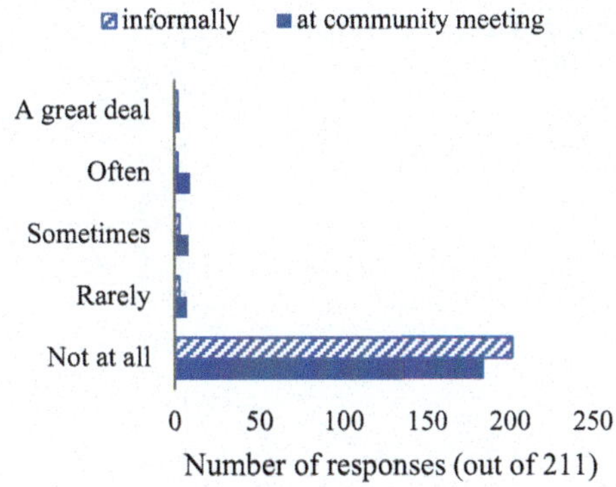


Fig. 7 Contact quality of the company

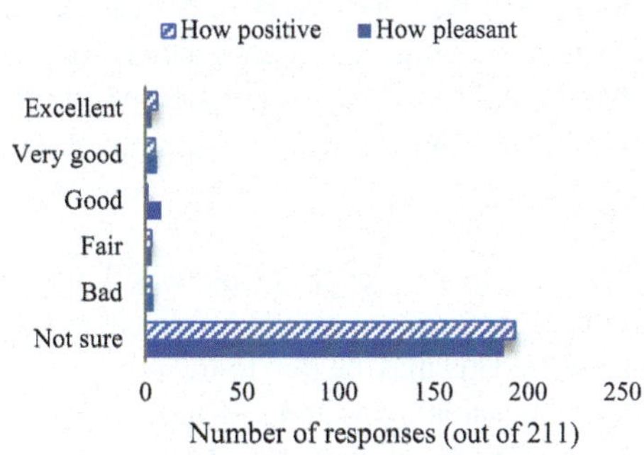


that Erdenes Silver Resource had no significant impact on the social infrastructure of Gurvansaikhan Soum.

When conducting the sample survey, it was noticed that the impact on social infrastructure differed greatly depending on local circumstances and who the respondent was. As mentioned before, five types of social infrastructure were assessed, including access to medical and health facilities, access to school and kindergarten, electricity supply, and water supply. For instance, rural herder households are not connected to the electricity grid, making it impossible to access whether the mining company's operations impacted electricity supply. This highlights the need to adjust questions based on local circumstances.

**Procedural Fairness**

Participants rated Erdenes Silver Resources with a score of 3.23 on whether they are respected and are included in the company's decision-making process. However, the participants' scores on the items only focused on the perceived procedural fairness of the company. For example, the statement "People in your community have the opportunity to participate in the decisions made by Erdenes Silver Resource" was rated at 3.9 points, and the statement "Erdenes Silver Resource listens to and respects your opinions" was rated at 2.6 points. The statement "Erdenet Silver Resource is prepared to change its practices in response to community sentiment" was rated at 2.5

Fig. 8 Procedural fairness by three items

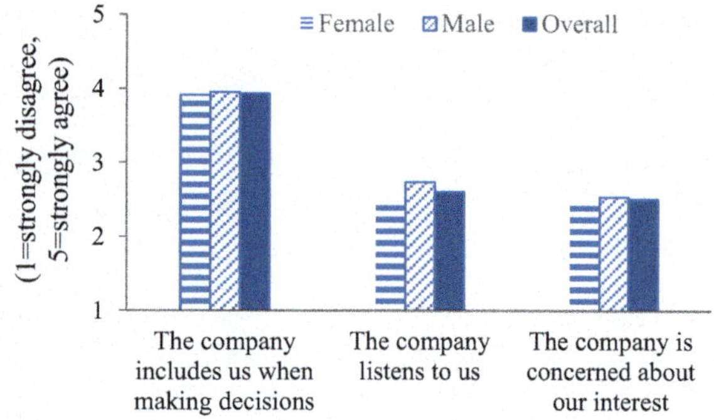


points (Fig. 8). These responses were not significantly different by the gender of the participant. Thus, although residents did not participate in the company's decision-making process, they valued the items highly because they believe that it is possible to influence the company's decisions if they try to participate.

### Trust

The participants' level of trust was 3.5 points. Although the company does not hold public meetings or provide information on its activities, the level of trust was above average. This may be due to the company's relation to the government's decision to cancel pension loans and distribute money to the elderly who do not have loans. This assumption is supported by the fact that trust varies by age group, with the level of trust among the elderly being higher than average (Fig. 9).

### Acceptance and Approval

The participants rated their acceptance and approval of Erdenes Silver Resource 3.5 points (Fig. 10). As with trust, this finding was also above average. These responses were also not significantly different by the gender of the participant. However, it is worth noting that the acceptance level of the district center and the subdistrict where the company is located was lower than that of the other subdistricts (Fig. 11).

Fig. 9 Average trust score by age group

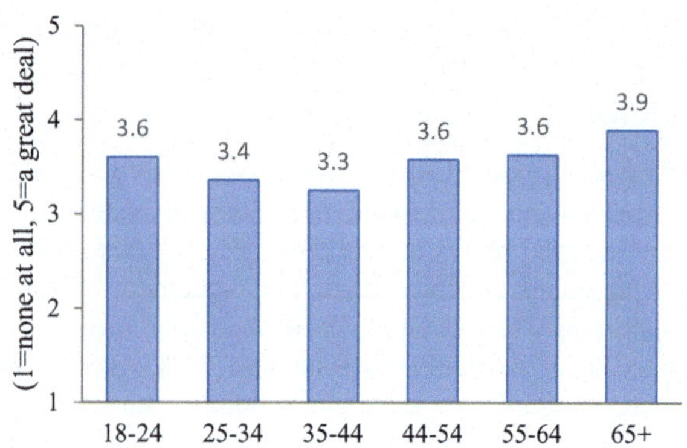

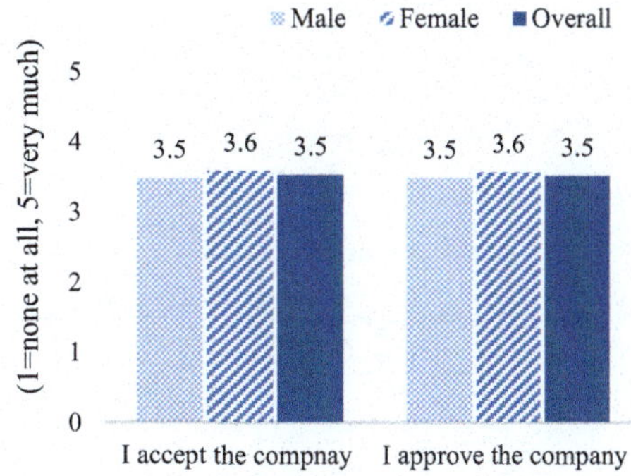


**Fig. 10** Acceptance and approval

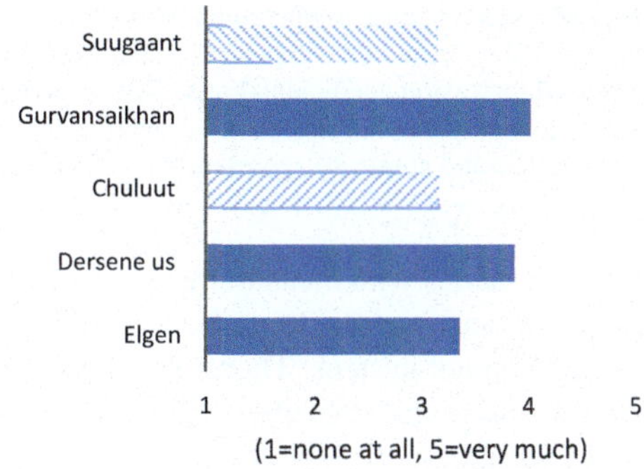


**Fig. 11** Acceptance and approval by sun-district

In Table 4, the bivariate correlation between each variable was calculated. According to the correlation matrix, trust and acceptance are significantly correlated to all factors. However, there is no significant relationship between the other factors.

Based on the bivariate analysis and similar hypotheses of Moffat and Zhang (2014), we performed a path analysis of how mining activity impacts SLO factors and how SLO factors affect each other. We used structural equation modeling, a set of statistical techniques, to measure and analyze the relationships of observed and

**Table 4** Descriptive statistics and bivariate correlation of social acceptance measures

| | SLO factors | Mean (St.D) | 1 | 2 | 3 | 4 | 5 |
|---|---|---|---|---|---|---|---|
| 1 | Social infrastructure impact | 3.05 (0.38) | 1 | | | | |
| 2 | Contact quantity | 1.20 (0.61) | −0.08 | 1 | | | |
| 3 | Procedural fairness | 3.24 (1.14) | −0.23 | 0.07 | 1 | | |
| 4 | Trust | 3.51 (1.17) | −0.25*** | 0.16*** | 0.45*** | 1 | |
| 5 | Acceptance | 3.54 (1.34) | −0.20*** | 0.14*** | 0.37*** | 0.75*** | 1 |

*Note* ***, **, * are significant at the levels of 1, 5, and 10%

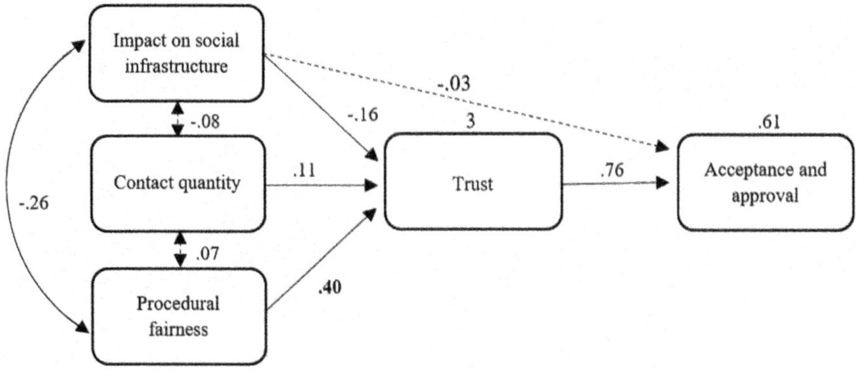


**Fig. 12** Social license to operate path model-1. *Note* Solid lines represent statistically significant relationships, dashed lines represent statistically non-significant relationships. Beta weights (standardized regression coefficients) represent the strength of the relationship between variables, with positive numbers indicating positive relationships and vice versa. The values above "trust" and "acceptance and approval" represent the variance

latent variables with measurement error. Structural equation models may have many different outcomes or dependent variables, affecting other dependent variables in a more complex system. Therefore, these models are more suitable for modeling a causal system and considering both direct and indirect effects.

In our first model shown in Fig. 12, participants who experienced an impact on social infrastructure reported lower levels of trust ($\beta = -0.16$, $\rho = 0.013$). However, this experience did not directly predict their acceptance of the company ($\beta = -0.03$, $\rho = 0.469$). Participants who had a high frequency of meetings with company personnel reported higher levels of trust ($\beta = 0.11$, $\rho = 0.07$). Furthermore, participants who perceived that the company was procedurally fair in dealing with local communities reported higher levels of trust ($\beta = 0.40$, $\rho = 0.00$). Last, trust was a strong and significant predictor of acceptance and approval of the company and mining project ($\beta = 0.76$, $\rho = 0.00$).[2]

We included the age of the participants in the model to test how stable the model was. The older the participant was, the greater they trusted the company. Therefore, we tried to validate this relationship. The model with age did not differ much from the previous model. The age variable has a significant positive effect on trust, indicating that older people trust Erdenes Silver Resources more. The other variables are almost identical to the results of the previous model (Fig. 13).

Our study results demonstrate broad support for the SLO model proposed by Moffat and Zhang (2014). Frequency of contact with company personnel, procedural fairness, and perceived impact on social infrastructure affect community acceptance

[2] This model provided an excellent fit for the data with a non-significant chi-square value (chi(2) = 0.608, p = 0.738), indicating that the hypothesized covariance matrix did not differ from the actual covariance matrix. Other fit indices corroborated this evaluation of the model: CFI = 1.000, NFI = 1.022, RMSEA = 0.000.

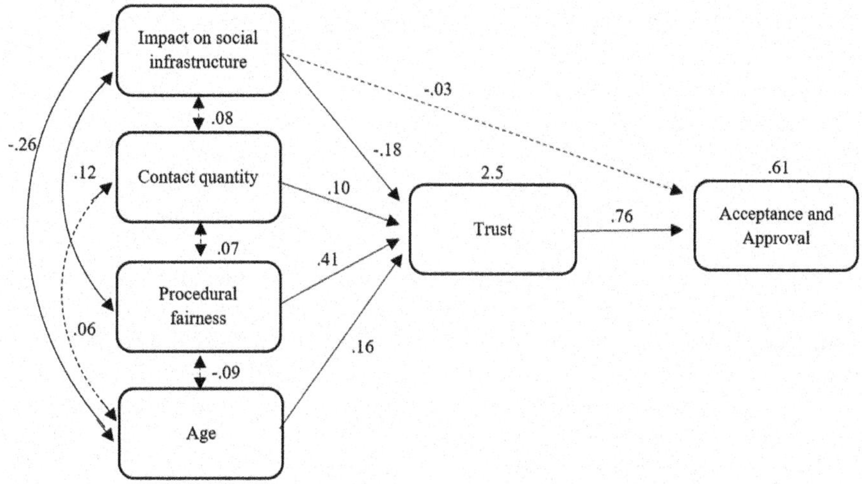


**Fig. 13** Social license to operate path model-2

and approval by increasing or decreasing trust in the company. Procedural fairness was the strongest predictor, impact on social infrastructure was the second strongest predictor, and contact quantity was the weakest predictor. However, contact quantity and impact on social infrastructure were not significantly different in terms of the power exerted on trust.

Consistent with previous international studies, we confirmed trust as a strong and significant predictor of acceptance and approval of the company and mining project ($\beta = 0.76$, $\rho = 0.00$). Likewise, procedural fairness had the highest positive effect on trust, in line with Moffat and Zhang (2014) and Cruz et al. (2020).

Contact quantity, which explains the importance of trust, differs from the results of Moffat and Zhang (2014). This may be due to the exclusion of contact quality in our model. In particular, the results of Moffat and Zhang (2014) showed that contact quality and contact quantity were reasonably correlated ($r = 0.37$) and that most of the trust variations were explained by contact quality. Therefore, contact quantity did not predict community members' trust directly. However, our model did not include contact quality due to missing values. As a result, contact quantity significantly affected community members' trust.

## 5 Conclusions and Recommendations

Although obtaining an SLO is a relatively new concept, the premise of community engagement and approval has always existed in some form. Unlike legal and regulatory licenses, an SLO is not tangible. Additionally, even if an SLO is granted at one point in time, it does not mean that the license will remain valid indefinitely, as the conditions under which the SLO was granted may change due to the ever-changing political, economic and social climate. Based on the practices observed in other mining-dependent countries, the way to maintain an SLO is to continuously assess the community's attitudes toward the mining project and other influencing factors. Then, based on this assessment, a mining company's strategic plans and objectives should include actions to address the community's grievances. There needs to be transparency and an open communication channel in addressing the complaints or issues.

Due to the former socialist regime of the country, obtaining an SLO is an especially new notion in Mongolia. Moreover, Mongolia experienced massive environmental problems due to lax environmental requirements and weak enforcement of existing laws and regulations. The detrimental social and environmental impacts generated community grievances against mining operations. Pushed by local community demand, the government is trying to ensure that SLO addresses relevant issues with necessary amendments to laws and regulations.

Although many mining companies operate in Mongolia, few implement measures to obtain an SLO. On the other hand, companies that have failed to obtain SLO are experiencing public opposition. This is mainly caused by insufficient efforts to provide enough information about their operations to local communities.

Mining companies in Mongolia do not have a good understanding of SLO. Despite the increasing number of mining projects in Mongolia, a social acceptance survey has never been conducted before. We conducted this type of survey for the Erdenes Silver Resources project. We examined how the impacts on social infrastructure, contact quantity, and trust affect the acceptance of the mining company and its operations. From the results, frequency of contact with company personnel, procedural fairness, and perceived impact on social infrastructure affect community acceptance and approval by increasing or decreasing trust in the company. Furthermore, we confirmed trust as a strong and significant predictor of acceptance and approval of the company and mining project. Our findings are similar to those of other international studies.

Based on the research findings, the research team has developed the following recommendations:

- It is essential to strengthen the understanding of SLO to stakeholders, improve transparency and strengthen the enforcement of laws in the mining sector to achieve long-term policy goals.
- To avoid the risk of public opposition, the decision to grant mineral licenses should be based on social acceptance research. Conducting a social acceptance survey from mining-affected communities, including herders, farmers, and local businesses, is an efficient tool to assess the public's perception of ongoing and upcoming mining projects. It is also important to monitor the local community's attitudes in various phases of the mining project and macroeconomic situations.
- It is essential to provide mining-affected communities with transparent and accurate information regarding feasibility studies, including the economic, environmental, and social impacts of mining operations and the environmental and social

responsibilities of the mining company. The GoM has already initiated and operationalized transparent information platforms such as the EITI, www.iltodgeree.mn, Environmental Information Center website (www.eic.mn). However, the information provided through the platforms is insufficient and not well publicized. Thus, the quality of information and the accessibility of the platforms mentioned above should be improved.

- Increasing public participation in decisions and decision-making processes is crucial to improving SLO in the mining sector. As the GoM has already set a goal to establish a Policy Council including representatives from government agencies, investors, professional associations, and civil society organizations, the GoM should implement the steps necessary to achieve this goal.
- It is important to provide transparency and follow-through of complaints and issues raised by local communities. Within this scope, mining companies should implement an action plan for addressing these grievances, be it through specialized actions or short-, medium-, and long-term strategic plans.
- Small- and medium-scale mining companies do not provide transparent information to the general public. Thus, information transparency requirements should be incorporated into relevant laws and regulations to ensure effective communication between mining companies and the general public.
- Mining companies should learn from good practices. To promote good social licensing practices, the Ministry of Mining and Heavy Industry and sectoral associations should provide an opportunity for mining companies to share their experiences as well as provide guidelines for social licensing and communication with local communities.
- The path analysis shows the importance of gaining community trust to garner community approval and acceptance for a project. In turn, trust in a mining company and its project is mainly dependent on the perceived procedural fairness of the mining company's decisions. In other words, mining companies should focus on including the local community in their decision-making process and considering their opinions.
- Mining companies focus significant resources on improving local infrastructure, such as roads, and mitigating the adverse effects of their operations by supporting local employment and other social investments. However, according to the results of our study, procedural fairness plays a more prominent role in determining local community trust than the impact of social infrastructure. This suggests that while improving local infrastructure is essential, particularly in Mongolia, it is unwise for mining companies to allocate all their resources to improving social infrastructure.

## References


Allen, W. (2019). *Learning for sustainability*. Retrieved October 10, 2019, from https://learningforsustainability.net/social-license/

Asia Mining. (2019, July 10). Retrieved 11, 2019, from www.asiamining.mn: http://www.asiamining.mn/view/15

Bauer, A., & Namhaijantsan, D. (2019). *Wild growth an assessment of Erdenes Mongol*. NRGI.

*Bayan-Khundii project*. (2019). Retrieved from Erdene Resouce Development: https://www.erdene.com/en/projects/bayan-khundii/

Boutilier, R. G., & Thomson, I. (2011). Modelling and measuring the social license to operate: Fruits of a dialogue between theory and practice.

Byambajav, D. (2015). *The river movements*. Social Movement Studies.

Centre for Policy Research, Population Training and Research Centre. (2009). *Oyu Tolgoi project socio-economic impact assessment*. Oyu Tolgoi.

Cruz, T. L., Matlabe, V. J., Mota, J. A., & Santos, F. d. (2020). Measuring the social license to operate of the mining industry in an Amazonian town: A case study of Canaa dos Carajas, Brazil. *Resources Policy*.

EITI Mongolia. (2018). *Annual report*. Extractive Industries Transparency Initiative of Mongolia.

EPCRC. (2015). Retrieved from http://aimagindex.mn: http://aimagindex.mn/statistics

EPCRC. (2019). Retrieved from http://aimagindex.mn/: http://aimagindex.mn/competitiveness

Erdenes Silver Resource. (2020). *Financial and operational report*. Erdenes Silver Resource.

ERI. (2017). *Mining impact on local livelihood: A case of Mongolia*. ERI.

ERI. (2019a). *Sustainable mining development*.

ERI. (2019b). *FDI inflow in Mongolia: Dispute resolutions*. ERI.

ERI. (2020). *Suistainable mining development*. ERI.

Ernst & Young. (2021). *Top 10 business risks and opportunities for mining and metals in 2022*. Ernst & Young.

Harvey, B., & Bice, S. (2014). Social impact assessment, social development programmes and social license to operate: Tensions and contradictions in intent and practice in the extractive sector. *Impact Assessment and Project Appraisal, 32*(4), 327–335.

IFC. (2021). *A strategic approach to early stakeholder engagement*. International Finance Corporation and The World Bank.

Kirschke, J. (2013). Mining sector CSR in the age of social media. *Engineering and Mining Journal, 34*.

Lkhagvaa, A. (2017, February 7). *New developments in Mongolian Arbitration Law*. Retrieved from Lehman Law Mongolia LLP: https://lehmanlaw.mn/blog/new-developments-in-mongolian-arbitration-law/

Lassonde, P. (2003). How to earn your social license. *Mining Review*, 7–13.

Moffat, K., & Zhang, A. (2014). The paths to social license to operate: An integrative model explaining community acceptance of mining. *Resources Policy*, 61–70.

Moffat, K., Mccrea, R., Boughen, N., Pert, P., Rodriguez, M., & Lacey, J. (2017). *Australian attitudes toward mining: Citizen survey—2017 results*. CSIRO.

Mongolian Mining Journal. (2019, 06 13). Retrieved from www.mongolianminingjournal.com; http://www.mongolianminingjournal.com/a/70616

Montsame. (2021, May 11). *It is ready to compensate people who do not have pension loans*. Retrieved from Montsame: https://www.montsame.mn/en/read/263486 (in Mongolian)

PoM. (2011, December 23). *Budget Law*. Retrieved from Integrated System of Legal Information: https://www.legalinfo.mn/law/details/12254

Prno, J., & Slocombe, D. (2012). Exploring the origins of 'social license to operate' in the mining sector: Perspectives from governance and sustainability theories. *Resources Policy*, 346–357.

Robinson, L. M., Fardin, J., & Boschetti, F. (2020). Clarifying the current role of a social license in its legal and political context: An examination of mining in Western Australia. *Resources Policy*.

Supreme court of Mongolia. (2019, December 9). Retrieved from www.supremecourt.mn: http://www.supremecourt.mn/news/487

Sustainability East Asia. (2016). *Social impact assessment report Gatsuurt Gold Mine project.* Centerra Gold.

UNICEF Mongolia. (2017). *Mining-related in-migration and the impact on children in Mongolia.* UNICEF Mongolia.

Vanclay, F., & Hanna, P. (2019). Conceptualizing company response to community protest: Principles to achieve a SLO. *Land, 88*(101), 1–31.

**Tuvshintugs Batdelger** is the director of the Economic Research Institute (ERI) and an associate professor of economics at the National University of Mongolia. He has a bachelor's degree in economics from the National University of Mongolia; a master's degree in economics from the University of Manchester, UK; and a Ph.D. in economics from Boston University, USA. He has experience working at the Bank of Mongolia and was the head of the Economics Department of the National University of Mongolia from 2014 to 2017. He has been a member of the Economic Policy Council under the prime minister of Mongolia since 2012 and was a member of the Monetary Policy Committee from 2011 to 2016. He has been actively involved in policy discussions in the country through the establishment and operation of ERI since 2010, one of the longest-running think tanks in the country. Through ERI, he successfully contributed to policy discussions on wide-ranging economic and social issues by coordinating and implementing many projects by international organizations, such as the World Bank, Asian Development Bank, and JICA. In particular, he successfully led research teams conducting an economic assessment of big mining and industrial projects on the country's economy and society in general. He has successfully conducted and published policy research studies in international peer-reviewed journals and publications such as *Applied Economics*, *Resources Policy*, and *East Asia Forum* and has authored chapters on the Mongolian economy in numerous books. His current research interests are the role of mining in the economy and society, the role of monetary policy in regulating the Mongolian economy, and the impact of economic development on income distribution and the country's middle class.

**Dulguun Tuvshintugs** is a researcher at the Economic Research Institute (ERI). She received her bachelor's degree from Bentley University in the United States, where she majored in finance with a concentration in corporate finance and a minor in law. Her research interests include monetary policy, capital markets, and financial modeling.

**Enkhsaikhan Usny-Ekh** is a researcher at the Economic Research Institute (ERI). He obtained his bachelor's degree in Economics from the National University of Mongolia. His research interests include Econometrics and Macroeconomics. Lately, he has been focusing on CGE and GAMS modeling.

**Khorol-Erdene Bayartsogt** is a researcher at the Economic Research Institute (ERI). She received her bachelor's degree from New York University in the USA and completed a double major in economics and political science. She also has an undergraduate law degree from the National University of Mongolia. Her research interests include governance and political economy.

**Manlaibaatar Zagdbazar** is a project manager and senior researcher at the Economic Research Institute (ERI) of Mongolia. He has a bachelor's degree in applied mathematics from the Khan-Uul Institute, Mongolia; a master's degree in economic policy from the Central European University, Hungary; and is currently a Ph.D. candidate in economics at the National University of

Mongolia. He has abundant teaching and research experience, working as a lecturer at Khan-Uul Institute, Mongolia, and the National University of Mongolia. Previously, he worked as a researcher at the Development Strategy and System Research Centre in Mongolia; an assistant researcher at the Research Department of the Central Bank of Hungary; and a consultant at the Independent Research Institute of Mongolia. He has published in international and domestic peer-reviewed journals such as *Resources Policy* and *Sociology* and coauthored several economic textbooks in Mongolian.

**Oyuntugs Davaakhuu** is a researcher at the Economic Research Institute (ERI). She received her bachelor's degree in economics from the National University of Mongolia and is currently completing her master's degree at the University of Finance, and Economics in Mongolia. Her research interests include macroeconomics and development economics.

**Oyunzul Tserendorj** is a researcher at the Economic Research Institute (ERI). She received her bachelor's degree in economics from the National University of Mongolia and is currently pursuing her master's from the same institution. Her research area of focus includes macroeconomics, development economics, and CGE modeling.

**Unurjargal Davaa** is a researcher at the Economic Research Institute (ERI). She received her bachelor's degree in economics from the National University of Mongolia and is currently pursuing her master's from the same institution. Her research area of focus includes CGE modeling and institutional economics.

# Appendix
# Other Survey Statistics

See Tables A.1, A.2, A.3, A.4, A.5, A.6, A.7, A.8 and A.9 and Figs. A.1, A.2, A.3, A.4, A.5, A.6. A.7, A.8 and A.9.

**Table A.1** Demographic information by subdistrict

| | Average age | Average household size | Selected sample | Male | Female |
|---|---|---|---|---|---|
| Elgen | 47.6 | 3.7 | 38 | 26 | 12 |
| Dersene us | 48.9 | 3.2 | 57 | 26 | 31 |
| Chuluut | 47.8 | 3.7 | 43 | 26 | 17 |
| Gurvansaikhan | 43.6 | 3.6 | 39 | 23 | 16 |
| Suugaant | 48.0 | 3.6 | 34 | 14 | 20 |
| Total | 47.3 | 3.5 | 211 | 115 | 96 |

**Table A.2** Frequency of employment status by age group

| | Employed | Unemployed |
|---|---|---|
| 18–24 | 5 | 3 |
| 35–34 | 27 | 3 |
| 35–44 | 54 | 2 |
| 44–54 | 54 | 1 |
| 55–64 | 30 | 8 |
| 65+ | 14 | 10 |



Y. Hosoi et al. (eds.), *Economic Dependence of Mongolia on Minerals*, Contributions to Economics, https://doi.org/10.1007/978-981-19-5515-0

**Table A.3** Reason for not doing a job

| | Frequency | Percent (%) |
|---|---|---|
| Student | 2 | 7 |
| Too old | 17 | 63 |
| Homework, caring for child | 4 | 15 |
| Cannot find a suitable job | 3 | 11 |
| Sick/cares of the sick person | 0 | 0 |
| Disabled | 0 | 0 |
| Other | 1 | 4 |

**Table A.4** Impacts on social infrastructure by subdistrict

| | Elgen | Dersene us | Chuluut | Gurvansaikhan | Suugaand |
|---|---|---|---|---|---|
| Access to medical | 2.97 | 3.12 | 3.09 | 3.00 | 2.91 |
| Access to school | 2.89 | 3.02 | 3.12 | 3.05 | 2.94 |
| Local roads | 2.71 | 2.86 | 2.84 | 2.89 | 2.79 |
| Energy supply | 2.94 | 3.09 | 3.12 | 2.97 | 2.85 |
| Water resource | 2.78 | 2.91 | 2.91 | 2.76 | 2.73 |
| Total impact | 2.84 | 3.07 | 3.00 | 2.95 | 2.94 |

**Table A.5** Contact quantity descriptive statistics

| | Mean | Median | Std. dev. | Skewness | Kurtosis |
|---|---|---|---|---|---|
| Contact quantity in informal situations | 1.29 | 1.00 | 0.84 | 2.92 | 10.53 |
| Contact quantity in formal situations | 1.11 | 1.00 | 0.55 | 5.53 | 34.49 |
| Contact quantity | 1.20 | 1.00 | 0.61 | 3.84 | 19.71 |

**Table A.6** Procedural fairness descriptive statistics

| | Mean | Median | Std. dev. | Skewness | Kurtosis |
|---|---|---|---|---|---|
| The company includes us when making decisions | 3.94 | 4 | 1.24 | −1.21 | 3.44 |
| The company listens to us | 2.61 | 2 | 1.43 | 0.11 | 1.42 |
| The company is concerned about our interest | 2.51 | 2 | 1.34 | 0.22 | 1.63 |
| Procedural fairness | 3.23 | 3.3 | 1.29 | −0.31 | 2.32 |

**Table A.7** Procedural fairness items correlations

| | | 1 | 2 | 3 |
|---|---|---|---|---|
| 1 | The company includes us when making decisions | 1.00 | | |
| 2 | The company listens to us | 0.26 | 1.00 | |
| 3 | The company is concerned about our interest | 0.25 | 0.82 | 1.00 |

**Table A.8** Trust items correlations

| | | 1 | 2 | 3 | 4 |
|---|---|---|---|---|---|
| 1 | Trust the company to act responsibly | 1.00 | | | |
| 2 | Trust the company to do what is right | 0.86 | 1.00 | | |
| 3 | Trust the company to act in the best of interest | 0.79 | 0.81 | 1.00 | |
| 4 | Trust the company generally | 0.86 | 0.89 | 0.86 | 1.00 |

**Table A.9** Acceptance and approval items correlations

| | | 1 | 2 |
|---|---|---|---|
| 1 | I accept the company | 1.00 | |
| 2 | I approve of the company | 0.92 | 1.00 |

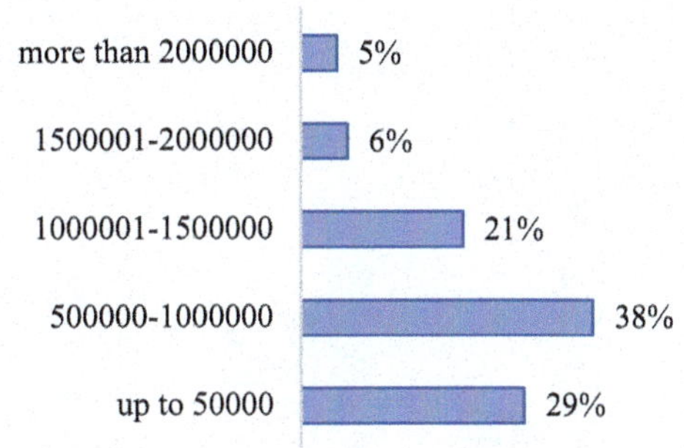


**Fig. A.1** Household share of monthly income groups, MNT

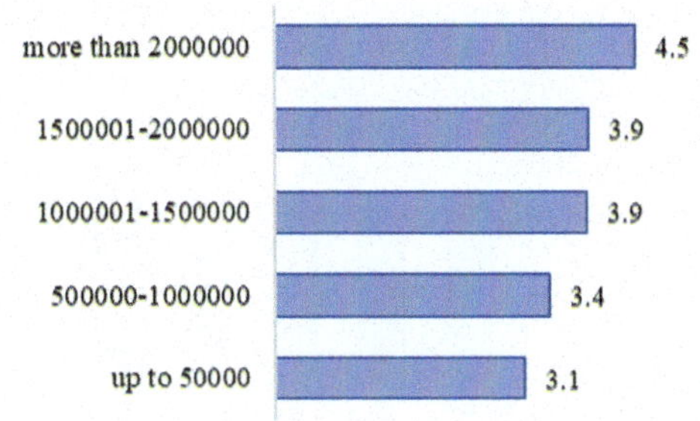


**Fig. A.2** Average household size by income group

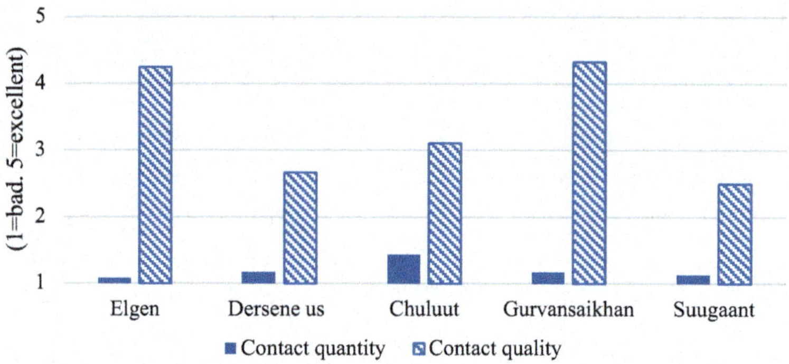


**Fig. A.3** Contact quality and quantity by subdistrict

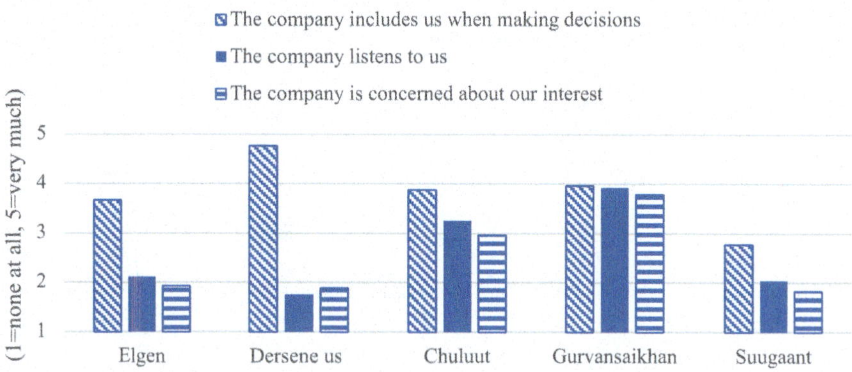


**Fig. A.4** Procedural fairness by subdistrict

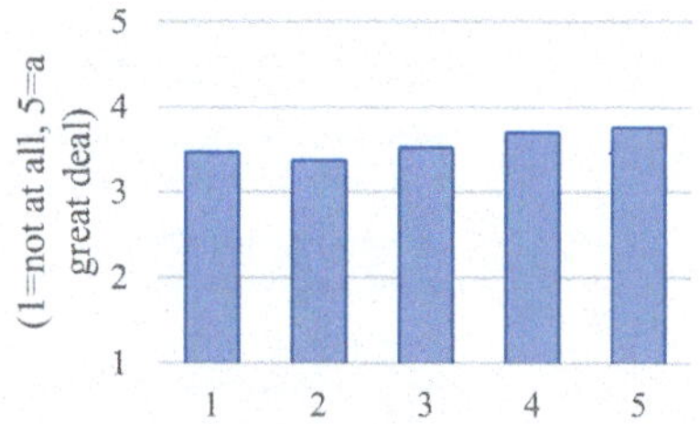


**Fig. A.5** Level of trust by awareness score

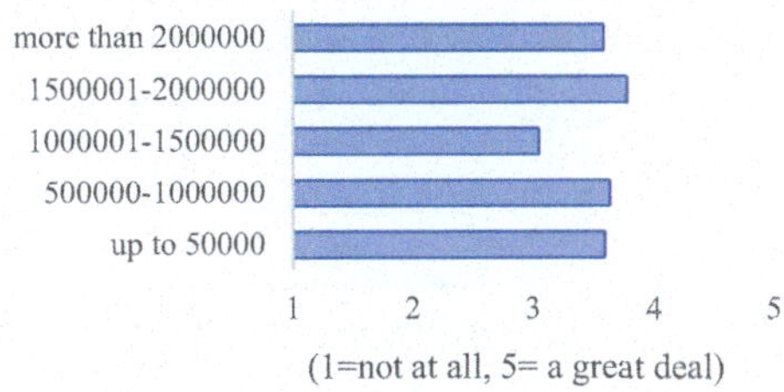


**Fig. A.6** Level of trust by household monthly income, MNT

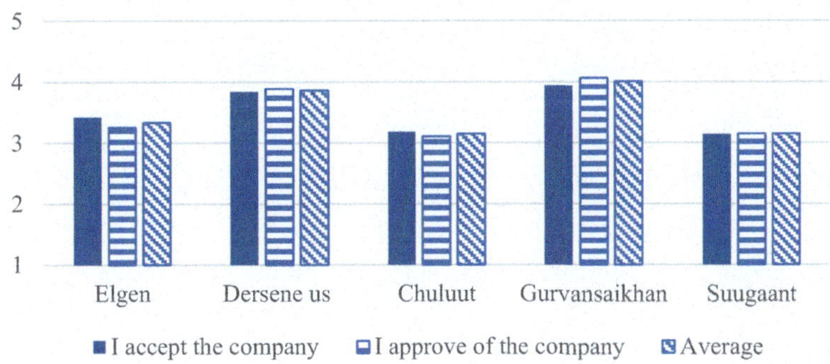


**Fig. A.7** Acceptance and approval by bagh

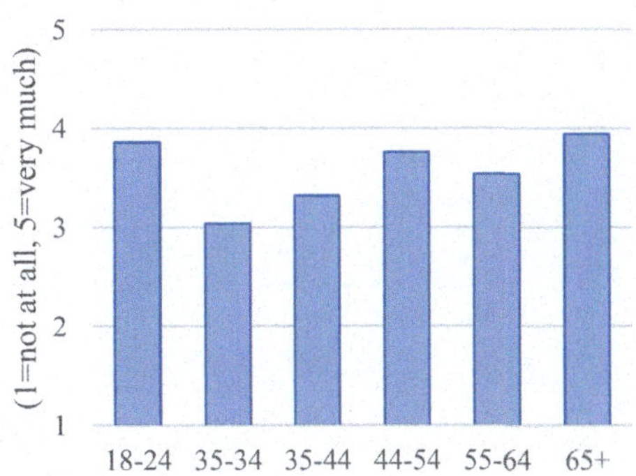


**Fig. A.8** Acceptance and approval by age group

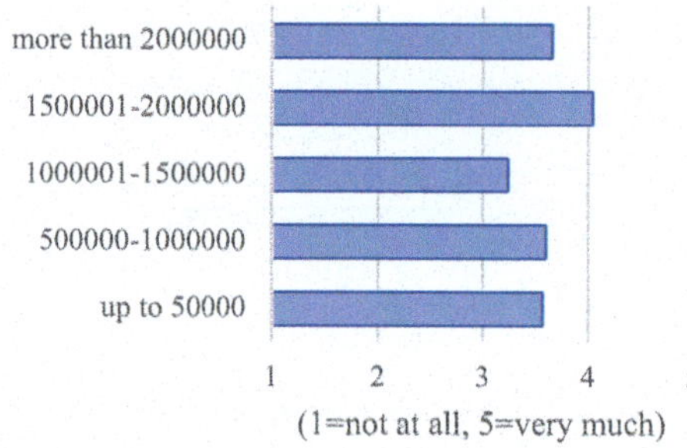


**Fig. A.9** Acceptance and approval by income

The manufacturer's authorised representative in the EU is Springer Nature Customer Service Centre GmbH, Europaplatz 3, 69115 Heidelberg, Germany. If you have any concerns regarding our products, please contact ProductSafety@springernature.com

Printed and bound by CPI Group (UK) Ltd, Croydon, CR0 4YY
30/09/2026
02225266-0003